A HIGHER DUTY

A Higher Duty

Desertion

among Georgia Troops

during the Civil War

MARK A. WEITZ

University of Nebraska Press

Lincoln and London

∞

Library of Congress Cataloging-in-Publication Data
Weitz, Mark A., 1957–
A higher duty: desertion among Georgia troops
during the Civil War / Mark A. Weitz.
p.   cm.
Includes bibliographical references (p.   ) and index.
ISBN 0-8032-4791-5 (cl: alk. paper)
1. Georgia—History—Civil War, 1861–1865—Desertions.
2. United States—History—Civil War, 1861–1865—Desertions.
3. Georgia—History—Civil War, 1861–1865—Social aspects.
4. United States—History—Civil War, 1861–1865—Social aspects.
5. Desertion, Military—Georgia—History—19th century.
6. Desertion, Military—United States—History—19th century.
I. Title.
E559.W45 2000
973.7′8—dc21
99-043003

Contents

Illustrations

Tables

Acknowledgments

Few projects of this size are the result solely of one's own efforts. This project is certainly no exception. First I want to thank Brooks D. Simpson. The successful completion of this work owes much to his efforts and guidance. From his initial marching orders that I would write a book, not a dissertation, to his insistence near the end that still I failed to understand just how important some of my own conclusions were, he maintained a close and constant vigilance over my work. His knowledge of the American Civil War is matched by few and exceeded by none, and his knowledge of the world of academic publishing and his insistence that I devote my time and effort to publishing have proved instrumental in my development as a professional. Roger Adelson spent long hours making the manuscript more readable, and he has asked questions that forced me to more clearly articulate my arguments, not only for this book but in all my work as a historian. I want to thank Philip Vander-Meer for his many contributions to this effort as well as to my training as a historian. He taught me that numbers could be my friends, and he introduced me to the amazing world of community history, without which this work would not have been possible. I would also like to thank Dale Couch and the staff at the Georgia Department of Archives and History in Atlanta. The personal interest he took in my project and the overwhelming support I received from everyone there made it possible for me to tell this story. I owe a special debt of gratitude to Dr. Kenneth Noe for his insightful comments, and I can never repay the efforts of Dr. David Williams, who threw himself into the work and provided important suggestions and material, including much of his own work, to help me better understand Georgia.

I owe a debt to an archivist at the Ft. Worth, Texas, branch of the National Archives who identified herself only as Barbara. She succeeded in locating the Union Register of Confederate Deserters when no one else seemed to know how to find the old record. I want to thank my family. Without the constant support and encouragement of my wife, Patricia, none of this would have been possible. My mother, Ruth Weitz, worked with me for months creating a database from which to tell Georgia's desertion story. Her contribution to this project proved invaluable. Finally, I would like to thank the 3,368 Georgia soldiers who answered the call of a higher duty and the wives, sisters, and daughters who brought them home.

Introduction

It was July 1862. Pvt. Joseph Hodges of the Eighth Georgia Infantry sat down to write his sister Mollie. He poured out his feelings about the commitment he had made without fully understanding what would be required. "We will never get to Georgia until peace is declared," he told his sister. Hodges believed the war might drag on for ten more years, but he felt sure the Eighth was already near its end. The regiment had dwindled to fewer than two hundred men, with some companies barely mustering eight for dress parade. Hodges added, "If I had known there was so many in the army I never would have come back to it, and I want to get out now the first opportunity. No wonder I am so sick, disgusted too, of the war. I am almost tempted to desert." Hodges never had this "opportunity" because he died at Gettysburg on July 2, 1863. For his Georgia comrades who were fortunate enough to survive him, the temptation to desert would prove overwhelming, and from late 1863 through 1864 many did.[1] Their actions and motives form the desertion story of Georgia's Confederate soldiers.

As surely as battlefield casualties, desertion saps an army's strength by diminishing its total numbers and weakening the resolve of those who continue to fight. All too often Civil War desertion is summarily dismissed as a "natural" consequence of war. With their lives constantly endangered by combat, disease, exposure to the elements, and malnutrition, it seems logical that soldiers would eventually forsake their military duty. Civil War desertion, however, was much more complex than a simple reaction to wartime conditions. As the experience of Georgia soldiers shows, desertion was as much a response to the home front as to the battlefield. Desertion measures morale like a barometer gauges weather patterns. Rising incidents of desertion reflect a decline in an army's morale. However, to assume that diminished morale is attributable solely, or even primarily, to conditions on the battlefield is to ignore the unique nature of the Civil War and the importance of the home front throughout the conflict.

Only two major studies have been done on desertion in the Civil War, and both are over sixty years old. Ella Lonn's *Desertion during the Civil War* appeared in 1928, and Bessie Martin published *Desertion of Alabama Troops from the Confederate Army* in 1932.[2] Although dated, these works provide a foundation for any serious study of Civil War desertion.

Lonn addressed desertion broadly in the Confederate and Union armies during the entire war. Although she devoted some attention to the role of the home front in desertion, she focused on where soldiers were when they deserted. She provided aggregate desertion numbers and explained how men deserted, where they hid to avoid capture, and how Confederate desertion benefited the Northern war effort. She also described the means by which Confederate state governments attempted to prevent desertion. Her numbers came primarily from the *Official Records* and from earlier statistical studies.[3] Lonn argued that most desertions occurred in the final eight months of the war. Although causation is only a small part of Lonn's study, the reasons she offered for desertion continue to be cited. These include (1) the backwardness among privates that blinded them to the unlimited duration of their service and contributed to their view of the Confederate cause as a war for a privileged way of life; (2) the lack of necessary food, clothing, pay, and equipment; (3) homesickness and mental anxiety over the well-being of their families; (4) the inequities of a draft that seemed to exempt wealthier men from service; and (5) the eventual reorganization of military units that destroyed the community character of many regiments as they were initially formed locally.[4]

Dr. Martin limited her study to desertion of Alabama soldiers. Using 1860 census records, she identified political, military, social, and economic causes and concluded that poverty provoked desertion. Soldiers feared for the well-being of their families and returned home. The north mountains and southeast corner of Alabama, the state's poorest regions, were home to most deserters.

Martin argued that letters from home to soldiers in the field moved them to desert. As pressure from families increased, the belief that the war was a "rich man's war but a poor man's fight" encouraged poor soldiers to go home. Laws that favored the wealthy, such as the twenty-slave rule and purchasing substitutes, enabled slaveholders to avoid service, but nonslaveholding poorer farmers in Alabama had to go to war when the South instituted conscription in 1862. The Confederate Conscription Act contained exemptions for national and state officials, those engaged in transportation and communications, ministers, miners, doctors, druggists, nurses, printers, educators, and certain manufacturers. While the exemptions made practical sense, they were abused. Martin pointed to vigilante bands, the loss of the male workforce, and crop failure in the southeast portion of Alabama as additional reasons for desertion. She used information from the *Official Records* and statistics concerning absent soldiers contained in a record of Alabama units compiled by a Colonel Fowler. However, some of her estimates of total deserters were based on the statements of company and regimental commanders in Fowler's work who concluded that absentees must have departed permanently.[5] Martin identified three significant waves of desertion in Alabama: from February 1862 to February 1863, from June 1863 to April 1864, and from August 1864 to April 1865.

In this study, I challenge Lonn's analysis of overall Confederate desertion and Martin's periodization of heavy desertion among Alabama soldiers. I also question whether Georgia's soldiers were a significant part of the 1865 desertion wave, and I reassess the notion that desertion occurred mainly among poor soldiers.[6] Many of Georgia's deserters were from the Upcountry and upper Piedmont regions of northern Georgia, where families enjoyed basic comfort, if not affluence, before the war. Northern Georgians lived in communities that were largely unaffected by the national market systems of the day. Their families resembled the economic units of early colonial America more closely than the families prevalent throughout America who were employed in manufacturing and large-scale agriculture. In most of north Georgia, the prosperity of a family depended on the active participation of both husband and wife. In this predominantly small farm, grain-based region, the husband's absence for an extended period eventually destroyed the economic basis of the family and reduced these communities to destitution. This delicate balance was upset by modern warfare that required large professional armies to be committed to the conflict for the duration of the war.

Using both Lonn's and Martin's works as a foundation, I add to each by examining traditional explanations for desertion in specific regions of Georgia. I look at the home front as well as the battlefield. In the case of Georgia soldiers who surrendered to the enemy, swore the oath of allegiance, and went home, there was a correlation between desertion and Sherman's invasion of the state. I selected Georgia because it provided the clearest relationship between Union occupation and Confederate desertion. Moreover, Georgia enjoyed almost total freedom from Union invasion and occupation before Sherman's Atlanta campaign in 1864. The bloody two-day battle of Chickamauga Creek in northwest Georgia drove the Union out in September 1863. A two-month siege of the Union army trapped at Chattanooga, Tennessee, further delayed the invasion of Georgia until 1864. In late February 1864, Gen. John Palmer led a forced reconnaissance of 25,000 men into Dalton, Georgia, and the Union army remained in Georgia until December.[7]

I also chose Georgia because it has never been the subject of a comprehensive desertion study. Aside from Martin's analysis of Alabama, most studies of desertion concern North Carolina. Although the Tarheel state has never been the subject of a large desertion study encompassing all of its soldiers, it has provided fertile ground for smaller historical studies. Two recent studies have added to the body of scholarship on North Carolina. One quantitative study attributes North Carolina's desertion to political beliefs that were unique to certain regions of the state. Another looks at two North Carolina regiments and the impact of changing leadership structures on desertion within each unit.[8] Unlike the North Carolina histories, my study examines Georgia desertion county by county. It is based on a statistical record compiled by the Union as well as the wartime correspondence of Georgia's soldiers and civilians. Georgia desertion has been tracked by the deserter's county of residence, the time when that county fell under Union occupation, and the date on which a deserter took the oath of allegiance and returned home. These sources, particularly the Union records, provide verification of desertion numbers previously unavailable.

The main primary source I used makes it possible to investigate desertion among Georgia's Confederate troops as never before. The Register of Confederate Deserters provides a detailed list of Confederate soldiers who deserted, took the oath of allegiance, and were allowed to return home. These deserters were no different than those who went directly home, except they had to evade neither the Confederate authorities nor the Union army.[9] Finally, those men who are listed in the register have left no doubt that they deserted.

Both Lonn and Martin calculated desertion by using estimates based on the daily rolls of men reporting and absent from duty as listed in the *Official Records*. According to most wartime estimates, over one hundred thousand soldiers deserted the Confederate army over the course of the war.[10] These numbers are speculative and may reflect improper conduct but not desertion. Civil War legal codes defined desertion as leaving the military service without authorization and intending to remain absent. Despite the legal definition, skulkers, stragglers, men absent without leave, members of one unit fighting in another, and anyone who could not otherwise be accounted for were included as deserters in the *Official Records*. Given the vast size of many Civil War battles, as well as the large number of dead and wounded who never were found, the desertion estimates include men who did not desert but whose absence could not otherwise be explained. Survivors who were captured, taken to an enemy hospital, or wounded and left untreated in some remote corner of the battlefield, for example, may have been mistakenly reported as deserters.

Besides various causes of separation, intent was a second key issue. Just because a man left his unit without permission did not necessarily mean that he never intended to return.[11] Some, such as Pvt. Asa Lewis, only wanted a brief

4

respite to visit a needy family member. In December 1862, Lewis was shot for repeatedly leaving his unit to visit his mother in Kentucky long enough to plant a new crop. Admittedly AWOL (absent without leave), Lewis intended to return even though he believed his twelve-month enlistment had expired.[12] The line between unauthorized absence and desertion remained clouded throughout the Civil War, contributing to the difficulty in accurately identifying the extent of desertion.

The register eliminates any debate as to whether the men listed were actually deserters or merely visiting their families before returning to war. By deserting to the enemy, a soldier clearly left the Confederate army without permission. By taking the oath of allegiance, the soldier not only deserted the Confederate army but also renounced the Confederacy and the cause for which it stood. The U.S. oath went as follows and left no room for divided loyalty:

> I do solemnly swear (or affirm) that I will support, protect and defend the constitution and government of the United States against all enemies, whether domestic or foreign, and that I will bear true faith, allegiance and loyalty to the same, any ordinance, resolution, or law of any State, convention or legislature to the contrary notwithstanding; and further, that I do this with a full determination, pledge and purpose, without any mental reservation or evasion whatsoever: So help me God.[13]

The register enables this study to go beyond the older evidence of large-scale desertion, such as daily reports and newspaper accounts.. The register provides the precise information on when soldiers swore the oath of allegiance to secure their release and the precise place where these men were released from Union custody. Unlike newspaper notices or daily muster rolls, which assumed desertion based on the absence of any other valid explanation of a soldier's whereabouts, the register demonstrates both physical separation from the Confederate army and the intent never to return.

The lack of primary sources presented an obstacle to studying desertion motives. Local newspapers, the largest primary source in Martin's work, provided statements of how civilians in Alabama perceived desertion and its causes. Advertisements and notices calling for the return of deserters led Martin to conclude that desertion increased during particular periods. In contrast, this study questions the validity of some of these same sources in Georgia by comparing them with records that reflect the actual desertion numbers within specific periods. Finally, the letters to and from soldiers and their families as well as the letters written to the governor, Joseph E. Brown, provide further insight into the causes of desertion. Because the register provides primary source material on specific soldiers, desertion can cease to be a purely statistical abstract analysis and relate to human experience. Seemingly faceless men have names, home counties, regiment designations, and specific military rank; some are even described down to their height, hair color, complexion, and eye color. Using 1860 manuscript census data, these men can be linked to their families and communities to discover whether they were married, whether they had children, how much property and how many slaves they owned, and what they did to earn a living before the war. While Martin's study tied destitution to particular sections of Alabama, this study matches deserters to their families and economic circumstances in specific Georgia counties.

Most general studies of the Civil War devote only small sections to desertion as one of the causes of Confederate defeat or associate desertion with discipline problems in Civil War armies. Recent scholarship contends that Southern soldiers endured more hardships than their Northern counterparts, and that despite these hardships, they remained committed to the cause. Some scholars insist that desertion has been exaggerated, and they view it as only an extended absence because the majority of men returned. However, there is little support for these conclusions, because Confederate desertion is extremely difficult to identify accurately.[14]

I agree that Confederate soldiers and civilians persisted despite severe hardships. Because desertion served as a barometer of morale for both Georgia's soldiers and civilians, it is argued that war's hardships eventually undermined individual will. From late 1863 through 1864, the will of Georgia's soldiers to continue fighting gave way to a higher duty to home, particularly those from the Upcountry and upper Piedmont regions of northern Georgia. This study addresses the timeless question of why the South lost the war by asking whether desertion acted as a primary cause of Confederate defeat or as a symptom that the Confederacy had already lost its spirit. Historians point to a variety of political, social, economic, and cultural reasons for the South's defeat, but some blame Southern disunity for undermining the Confederacy's ability to wage war successfully. Other historians argue that the South's military heritage and tactics unnecessarily depleted its army.[15] Some recent works, refuting the notions of internal strife, see strength in the Confederacy's national will. They argue that the South lost because nonslaveholding whites and slaves undermined the effort. The notion of the South's shortcomings has given way to the view that strong Union military and civilian leadership enabled the North to wear the South down.[16] The South never suffered from a lack of will—only from a gradual loss of will, following reversals on the battlefield.

Georgia's desertion story provides an opportunity to test notions of

Southern disunity, economic problems, and social differences that may have undermined the South's war effort. If desertion did undermine the war effort, what part did the Union war effort play in Southern desertion? Beyond these historiographical questions about the defeat, this study raises the possibility that much disunity existed within individual Confederate states and not simply between these states.

Because Confederate desertion occurred during a war, this study addresses the broader military problem that desertion always poses in maintaining an army. Vegitius, the Roman military historian of the fourth century C.E., believed that "to debauch the enemy's soldiers and encourage them when sincere in surrendering themselves is of especial service, for an adversary is more hurt by desertion than by slaughter."[17] Organizing and maintaining armies posed serious problems for commanders. After Gettysburg, Gen. Robert E. Lee wrote to James Seddon, the Confederate secretary of war, and later his successor, John C. Breckenridge, to complain about desertion. By the spring of 1864, Lee believed desertion had depleted almost 8 percent of his army, and he expressed particular displeasure with the government's willingness to grant pardons and forgive those who had deserted, claiming such measures cost more lives than they saved.[18] If traditional desertion estimates are correct, the loss of one hundred thousand to desertion during the war clearly damaged the Confederacy. Gen. Ulysses S. Grant thought so when he observed the Confederate army in 1864. "Not a day passes but men come into our lines, and men, too, who have been fighting for the South for more than three years. Not infrequently a commissioned officer comes with them."[19] Grant was impressed by the quantity of soldiers who left the Confederate army as well as the quality of these men, who were hardened veterans, steeled in the ways of war but no longer able to sustain the Confederate war effort. Grant even encouraged Confederate desertion. The South's desertion to the enemy was promoted by a powerful inducement offered by the Union to Confederate deserters: the opportunity to go safely home.

Home as an inducement

The fact that many Southern soldiers fought relatively close to home also influenced desertion. Civil War scholarship has given increased attention to the social aspects of the war. Some significant works have probed the role that civilian community played in wartime.[20] While most social history deals with the Northern soldier, some recent works have explored the South's home front. Some of the most important of these works on the South have dealt with gender, particularly Southern women's disenchantment with the conflict and how this affected the Southern war effort.[21]

This study recognizes the importance of community and family in affecting the military events of 1863 through 1865, and argues that Georgia desertion grew out of a call from community and family that was caused by conditions at home and intensified by Sherman's invasion. Sherman's advance heightened fears for the safety of home and family and created a safe haven for Georgia deserters where they would not be hunted down by the Confederate army or the civilian authorities. When the Confederate Army of Tennessee returned to Georgia in late 1863, the closeness of home made the pull from upcountry Georgia irresistible to many soldiers.

The invasion of Georgia and the corresponding dates of desertion in the register indicate a correlation between the two, but it is the letters and diaries of the Georgia soldiers and their families that reveal the daily lives of the soldiers and the hardships at home that actually led so many Georgians to abandon the Confederate cause and return home. This study gives careful attention to the writings of Georgia's women. The "higher calling" or plea from home almost always came from the women in a soldier's life. "Home" generally meant the place where a soldier's wife, mother, or sisters lived. Some historians have argued that once Southern women abandoned the Confederate cause, their pleas reached the battlefields, destroying the will to fight and causing wholesale desertion.[22] Women thus raised the conflict between duty to the Confederacy and a higher duty to the home.

The writings of women reveal another important aspect of desertion. In antebellum America, honor occupied a prominent place in a man's sense of self-worth.[23] Many Southern men saw fighting as a way of fulfilling their duty. In a letter written in December 1863 to his aunt, Thomas Bigbie, a soldier in Company G of the Thirty-third Alabama Infantry, explained, "Brigade gave way and that broke our line and we all had to leave. I intend that if we are ever run over and subjected it shall never be because I did not do my duty."[24] When duty required such devotion to military service, desertion challenged a soldier's sense of honor. Initially, most units were formed out of the communities where the soldier lived, so he fought with those who had known him his entire life and who could bear witness to his acts of bravery or dereliction of duty once survivors returned home. A good example is Pvt. James K. Newton, Fourteenth Wisconsin, who described the conduct of a junior officer at Shiloh: "Lawton's being so brave was all a hoax." Lawton claimed to have fought bravely, but during the battle he was seen heading toward the Tennessee River, away from the action, allegedly to "draw rations."[25] Desertion carried a black mark of cowardice regardless of the circumstances under which it occurred. Despite the importance attached to honor, this study demonstrates that honor eventually gave way to the duty soldiers felt for their wives and families. Whether a soldier deserted also depended on the ideas of honor held by the women in his life.

Because of the risks that desertion involved, including execution if captured, this study emphasizes the great significance of the Union invading

Georgia. While many historians recognize the human suffering and hardships that were caused by Sherman's Atlanta campaign and his subsequent March to the Sea, this study emphasizes the total effect of Sherman's invasion upon desertion in Georgia. As the Union moved into Georgia and the Confederate army withdrew, the regions behind Sherman's advance were freed from Confederate military control. The Union presence decreased the likelihood that a deserter would be captured and executed. Many needed little or no inducement from the North other than the promise that they could return home safely. The Union's lenient desertion policy gave it a tool for simultaneously weakening the Confederate military and reconstructing the South. Many men predisposed to desert might have stayed in the army, still faced with the threat of execution, without the presence of the Union army.[26]

This study treats desertion not as an act of cowardice but as human agency in the face of declining morale among Georgia's soldiers and citizens. So many soldiers lost their lives that some areas of Georgia were virtually depleted of their male populations. Their families had nothing left to give, and they were unable to sustain themselves in the absence of the men. Many of those who deserted had for years suffered the loneliness of separation from their families and the dangers of camp life where disease and malnutrition killed many even before they saw combat. In deserting, Georgia's soldiers responded to their families and communities, which proved more important than defending the Confederacy.

CHAPTER ONE

Seeds of Desertion

Several weeks after Gen. Robert E. Lee drove Gen. George McClellan away from Richmond, Confederate Lt. Charles C. Jones Jr. wrote his father, a retired Presbyterian clergyman in Liberty County, Georgia. Jones recounted his recent trip to north Georgia where he had recruited soldiers and spoken with men from both Kentucky and Tennessee. Jones painted a picture of growing Southern unity. Kentucky and Tennessee as far east as Nashville had fallen under Union control early in 1862, and the impact on civilians had been evident to the lieutenant. "The mask has been torn from their faces, and the cloud lifted from their eyes. They now see clearly the unhappy results of their own indecision, and the almost fatal consequences of their self-deception, and are prepared with united effort to throw off the galling yoke of the oppressor."[1] While the men Jones met may have expressed a belief in the Confederate cause, the united effort Jones spoke of seems unlikely. Kentucky had made its decision to remain within the Union in 1861. Gen. Braxton Bragg's invasion of Kentucky in 1862 had demonstrated the unwillingness of the civilian population to embrace the Confederate cause. Tennessee had come into the war a divided state and remained split in 1862. The pro-Confederate western portion faced continuous Union occupation, while the eastern half of the state, still under Confederate control, had a strong Unionist civilian population.

Jones did not describe the sentiments of the upper Georgia men, so he may not have spoken at length with them. However, in believing that an occupied and already divided Tennessee and Kentucky might unite with Georgia, Jones presumed that Georgia stood united and ready to welcome the return of two states that had ignored the warnings of their Southern neighbors and finally realized the error of their ways. Kentucky had refused to secede, and Tennessee, although a Confederate state, had failed to show the concerted commitment to the Confederacy that Jones believed to exist in the Deep South. However, Georgians were far from being united in their support of

10

the Confederate cause. Lt. Jones projected Georgian unity from his own loyalties developed as a child growing up in Liberty County.

The Jones family lived, worked, and socialized within the rice belt plantations along Georgia's Atlantic seaboard. They belonged to a culture that was dominated by the planter class and infused with the belief that slavery benefited all white people, whether they owned slaves or not. Because slavery served all whites, it seemed logical to the planters that all white Southerners would resist any attempt to undermine or destroy the institution. However, the planter class did not speak for all Georgians. As the secession crisis intensified, many people would not blindly follow the entreaties of some who believed that "the South should, in an unbroken body, unite as one man."[2]

To comprehend Georgia's desertion story, one must understand both Georgia's importance to the Confederacy and the economic and cultural diversity that made it a divided people. On the eve of the Civil War, geographical, political, and cultural issues split the state into at least three distinct regions: the plantation belt, the Upcountry/upper Piedmont, and the Wiregrass/Pine Barrens. Several cities within these regions tied Georgia's agricultural producers to the rest of the South, the industrial North, and the textile centers of Europe. During the secession crisis, political conflict in Georgia eventually gave way to a temporary compromise that obscured the economic and cultural differences within the state. On the surface, Georgia entered the war a unified state, but these differences reappeared as the war's hardships shaped the different ways Georgia's soldiers and civilians perceived the Confederacy.

Part of the cultural and economic diversity within Georgia arose from the way the different regions of the state developed following the American Revolution. While some communities became industrialized and urbanized as they were integrated into national and, to a lesser degree, world economies, there remained regions where change came at a much slower pace. Such places remained semi-subsistence economies where the family operated as an economic unit. The labor of men and women remained essential to the survival of the household. Certain areas of the state changed more than others, which affected the desertion patterns of its soldiers during the Civil War.

Georgia's importance to the Confederacy in 1860 is evident: it boasted more people, voters, slaves, and slaveholders than any other state in the lower South. Georgia's secession proved crucial to the founding of the Confederacy. Its absence would have all but destroyed the hopes of the new slave nation. In 1850 Alexander Stephens, Robert Toombs, and Howell Cobb spearheaded a Unionist campaign that virtually doomed any hope held by South Carolina's secessionists that Georgia would join their effort to form a slave nation. A similar outcome in 1860 would have geographically split the Confederacy and deprived the South of precious human and material resources. In sheer size, only Virginia was larger than Georgia. Although the eight states in the upper South (Kentucky, Tennessee, Virginia, North Carolina, Maryland, Missouri, Arkansas, and Delaware) had only 41 percent of the total slave population, they represented 67 percent of the South's white population. Only half of the upper South states seceded, which made Georgia's white population all the more crucial to the war effort. Without the lower South there would have been no Confederacy; without Georgia, there would have been no united lower South.[3]

For Georgia to join the Confederacy, its nonslaveholding white majority had to believe that slavery and its institutions justified disunion. Over 60 percent of Georgia's voters did not own slaves, although many did live in counties with high slave populations. About 30 percent of Georgia's registered voters lived in the two areas of Georgia that were virtually devoid of planters: the mountainous areas of north Georgia and the Wiregrass/Pine Barrens area in the southeastern part of the state. Between these two regions lay the plantation belt, which was home to Georgia's small but powerful planter class. Dominated by the fertile Savannah River valley, the plantation belt ran southwest across the center of the state, separating the two large nonslaveholding regions (see map 1).

The rise in staple cotton production produced a shift in Georgia's population center during the antebellum years. By 1860 two-thirds of Georgia's 1,057,286 inhabitants lived in the center of the state, mostly within a ninety-mile radius of the state capital at Milledgeville. Aside from the plantation belt, the only other large slaveholding area was on the Atlantic coast. A narrow strip of heavy slaveholding counties ran 126 miles south from Savannah in Chatham County to Camden County on the Georgia-Florida border, which made up the tidewater region, the major rice-producing area of the state.[4]

Georgia's slaveholders feared that most nonslaveholders lacked sufficient identification with the Southern slaveholding culture to support secession. Their fears were well founded. In 1860, when their social and economic interests were under attack by Lincoln and the North, most slaveholders gained little support from nonslaveholders. A similar political conflict between slaveholder and nonslaveholder affected the rest of the South. A South Carolinian remarked that he mistrusted his own people more than abolitionists; if the issue came to a head, he doubted that 360,000 slaveholders would dictate the future of 3 million nonslaveholders. The South had 11 million

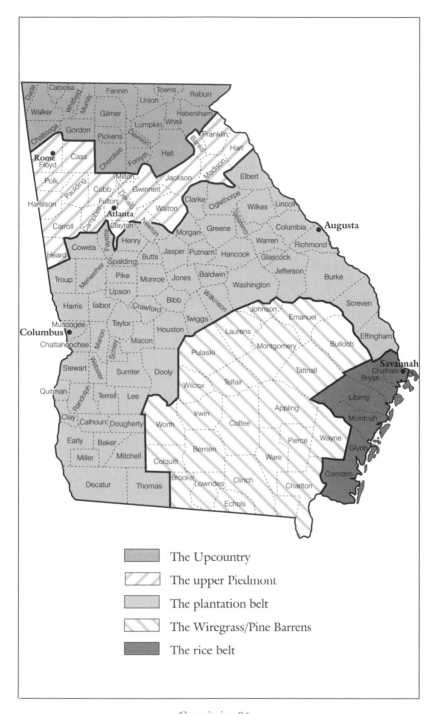

The Upcountry

The upper Piedmont

The plantation belt

The Wiregrass/Pine Barrens

The rice belt

Georgia in 1860

people in 1860, of which 4.5 million were slaves. Of the whites, 75 percent owned no slaves. Moreover, among slaveholders, 73 percent owned fewer than ten slaves.[5]

The South's white population consisted of five classes. At the top of the social and economic ladder stood the planter class, men who owned in excess of twenty slaves but seldom more than fifty. Although planters comprised only 2.5 percent of the total population, they held most of the wealth. Wealthy slaveholding farmers, merchants, and other urban professionals made up the class just below planters. Wealthy farmers owned anywhere from five to nineteen slaves and enjoyed a comfortable if not wealthy lifestyle. This class, although larger than the planters, nevertheless represented a small portion of the white population. In the Chattahoochee River valley of southwest Georgia, for example, this affluent class immediately below the planters accounted for only 10 percent of the white population. Yeoman farmers constituted the largest segment of the South's white population. This class included both slaveholders and nonslaveholders. Slaveholding yeomen generally owned fewer than five slaves. Although the slave labor enhanced their ability to provide for their families, it did not generate sufficient wealth to allow for an overseer. Most slaveholding yeomen worked in the fields and supervised their slaves themselves. Slaves allowed yeomen to grow cotton in addition to subsistence crops. Below the slaveholding yeomen were the nonslaveholders who owned their own land and devoted all their efforts to subsistence farming. In slaveholding areas, like Georgia's lower Chattahoochee River valley, most yeomen were slaveholders. In north Georgia and the southeast Wiregrass region, where cotton did not dominate agriculture, most yeomen owned no slaves. At the bottom of the social and economic chain stood the poor whites. Usually landless, they worked as fieldhands or tenant farmers or found meager employment in cities.[6]

Georgia seceded not because of a great shift of rural nonslaveholders to the secessionist cause but rather because enough town merchants and elites in nonslaveholding areas supported the slaveholding minority to push secession through at the convention in January 1861. Had the issue been decided by the January 2, 1861, popular vote, Georgia might not have seceded. The vote was never made public, and the two best estimates indicate either a very narrow secessionist victory or an equally narrow defeat. One estimate was 44,152 to 41,632 for secession; the other was 42,744 to 41,717 against secession. Voters in nonslaveholding counties opposed secession, confirming the plantation belt's fear. In the extreme northern mountains and the south central Pine Barrens, up to 75 percent of voters opposed secession. Over 5,000 men in nonslaveholding areas who voted for John C. Breckenridge in the November 1860 election voted against secession. Although poor whites in

[handwritten margin note: Strong Unionism]

the plantation belt also opposed secession, their opposition took the form of abstinence. For example, only about half the plain folk in many of Georgia's southwest counties even bothered to vote. Thus, in counties in which at least a third of the population owned slaves, those counties voted for secession. In traditionally Whig counties, secessionists triumphed by a bare majority; in Democratic counties, the margin was more than two to one. The popular vote underscored the divisions within Georgia but did not prevent the state from seceding. In December 1860, each county had chosen two sets of delegates to the secession convention in Milledgeville. The January 1861 election determined which set of delegates would go to the convention from each county. The convention did not reflect the divisions within Georgia between slaveholder and nonslaveholder. The delegates to the Georgia convention voted 166-130 to follow South Carolina, Florida, Louisiana, and Mississippi into the Confederacy.[7]

Despite the closeness of the vote and the resistance of the rural non-slaveholder to the secessionist movement, with but a few exceptions the non-slaveholding regions supported secession once the convention had voted. While antislavery sentiments never disappeared, the open expression against secession dissipated. Dade County, located in the extreme northwestern corner of Georgia, sent two delegates to the convention who voted against secession, but popular folklore claims that once the "die was cast," Dade County went with "her own Southern people." Uncle Bob Tatum, a delegate and legendary figure from Dade, led a movement that promised Dade's secession from Georgia if the state failed to secede from the Union once the vote of the convention confirmed the people's will.[8] Although divisions between slaveholders and nonslaveholders continued after secession, these differences had not prevented Georgia from joining the Confederacy.

★ ★ ★

After the outbreak of war, earlier divisions based on economic and cultural differences continued to shape Georgia's reaction to the war itself. The economies and cultures that developed from the different physical environments of Georgia enabled some regions to cope with the hardships of war, while others lacked the resources necessary to withstand the deprivations caused by the conflict. When combined with adversities at home, the cultural and economic differences within Georgia destroyed the political consensus that had existed at the outset of the war and weakened support for secession and the slaveholding South.

The rich clay and sand soil of the rolling hills of the lower and middle Piedmont provided the foundation for large cotton plantations and the slave populations who worked them. The plantation system produced cotton that Georgia shipped to the North and on to Europe. A transportation network developed that was marked by a dramatic increase in railroad construction to link the cotton plantations with the Atlantic coast. As cotton production soared, so did the slave population. In 1840 the lower and middle Piedmont region claimed black slave majorities in most eastern counties. By 1860 these same counties formed one end of a belt that stretched south and west to the Alabama border.[9]

In a sense Georgia's geography dictated its political beliefs. The strongest support for secession came from the plantation belt. The region had begun small, but as soil became depleted and the cotton gin revolutionized the refinement process, the slave belt expanded, and cotton fields and slavery spread. The counties in the eastern Piedmont region enjoyed the first cotton boom around 1790. By 1850 these older areas had lost some their population, and the southwest portions of the state had become the biggest cotton-producing region, with a heavy increase in both the white and slave populations.[10] The planter class called this entire region the black belt, with its plantations and large slave populations developing a culture unique to the region. Georgians here experienced the war differently from their neighbors to the north.

The plantation culture gave rise to a clearly defined code of honor. White men ruled. Women's responsibilities on the plantation left them isolated and without constant male companionship long before the war began.[11] The development of women's roles defined the kinds of problems they experienced with the long-term absence of their men during the war and their reactions to such hardship. It also influenced men's responses to these wartime problems at home and their families' pleas for help.

Emily Burke, a Georgia woman who lived in the 1850s, described the typical plantation. In the main house lived the father of the family and all the white females. A separate building housed the sons of the master and the overseers. Each plantation also had separate buildings for the washroom, kitchen, schoolhouse, stables, poultry pens, corn mill, and smokehouse. At some distance from the main house and its attendant buildings could be found the slave quarters, which were still within sight of the master. Burke's plantation produced sufficient resources that it could survive without the luxury items purchased from the North or Europe. The plantation had its own mills, tailor shops, barbers, looms, and spindles. This self-contained economic unit with its slave labor force produced all life's necessities except coffee, tea, and spices. One Georgia woman called the plantation a community and business in one.[12]

Plantation life isolated women in a world of slaves and domesticity. When the master absented himself from the plantation, the mistress had to direct it.

As early as 1796, one planter wrote to his wife, "In respect to our private affairs, I need say nothin—you will do for the best, and to your discretion I leave the management of everything." Even when the men were present, slaves provided the actual physical labor under the daily direction of women who were responsible for producing food and distributing key staples and necessities for the entire plantation. Georgia's plantation women, having exercised control over a full range of plantation activities for much of their adult lives, grew accustomed to the burdens of plantation life long before the war broke out. A planter's absence did not create any form of immediate interruption in the economic machinery that drove the plantation. During the Civil War, plantation women actually reveled in the opportunity to do business publicly that they had done for so long behind the scenes: write letters to newspaper editors, make decisions, and assert themselves.[13] With both parties accustomed to the rigors of the plantation, a woman's wartime entreaties may have appeared no different to the steeled sentiments of her husband than her prewar complaints, at least until Sherman's troops arrived late in 1864.

In addition to creating this feminine role, plantation life gave rise to a special role for men. At the center of the planter culture stood each man's reputation. Few things took precedence over a man's personal honor among his peers. Any affronts to honor required immediate rectification by a withdrawal or an apology or through some form of satisfaction. Dispute resolution commonly involved dueling. Georgia outlawed dueling in 1809, but the law was routinely ignored and dueling continued for decades. Most duels involved strictly masculine disputes, and single gentleman felt compelled to defend their honor. One exception to this code of honor was that a family man could decline such a challenge owing to his familial responsibilities, but to honorably decline single combat did not mean that family men attached less importance to their honor.[14]

Honor extended beyond everyday life into obligations of military duty. As the South answered the call for troops in 1861, one Georgian remarked, "I would be disgraced if I stayed home, and unworthy of my revolutionary ancestors." L. H. Ansley of Macon, Georgia, recalled how a young girl tried to persuade him to desert and stay with her. "I don't think she understood what she asked me to do, to desert my army and renounce my honor."[15] An anonymous Georgia woman understood honor in war: "He who would stand by and quietly do nothing, waiting for his neighbors to do all the fighting, undergo all the hardship, is not worthy of the esteem of any." For most men and many women, the Civil War became a test of manhood. Reinforced by community values and family responsibilities, honor was more than a man's self-image; it was his reputation bestowed upon him by others. During the war, comrades from his civilian community judged his valor. A soldier often measured his actions against his family's heritage.[16] A planter's personal reputation followed him onto the battlefield once a man had joined the army. As the war progressed, men from the planter class grappled with their sense of duty and the obligations they owed to those at home differently than did the yeomen, particularly those of the upper Piedmont and Upcountry regions.

Georgia's plantation belt was the most densely populated region in the state, and slaves accounted for over half its population. In some counties, as much as 70 percent of the population was black. Slaveholders represented only a small part of Georgia's white population. The most prevalent class in Georgia was the yeoman farmer.

In the less populated Wiregrass/Pine Barrens region, south of the plantation belt, lived a portion of Georgia's yeoman farmer population. Both large plantations and farm tenancy, where people worked the land but did not own it, were virtually nonexistent south of the plantation belt. To the north of the plantation belt lay the upper Piedmont, a region of yeoman farmers with few planters. To the north of the upper Piedmont was Georgia's Upcountry mountain region, an area with the state's smallest slaveholding population and lowest per capita income during the 1850s. No clear line divides the upper Piedmont from the Upcountry, but the upper Piedmont region marks the beginning of north Georgia's yeoman-dominated farm economies. In such upper Piedmont counties as Paulding, slightly northeast of Atlanta, only a few plantations existed. The two regions north of the plantation belt extended all the way to the Tennessee border and played a significant role in Georgia's desertion patterns.

The boundaries of upcountry Georgia have varied over time. This study defines the Upcountry in 1860 as the north mountainous counties, most of which were formed after 1832 (see map 1). These counties represented Georgia's last frontier, and a culture developed that was similar to that of the upper Piedmont, yet more independent and locally oriented. Beginning with Dade County in far northwest Georgia, the northern boundary of upcountry Georgia runs east along the Georgia-Tennessee border to Rabun County in the extreme northeast corner of the state; from Dade in the northwest Upcountry, Georgia runs south along the Alabama border to the border between Floyd and Polk Counties. From Rabun in the northeast the Upcountry runs south to Habersham County on the South Carolina border and then begins a southwestward line that takes it through part of Hall, Forsyth, Cherokee, the northern part of Cass (later Bartow) County to northern edge of Floyd County in the west.

The upper Piedmont begins in the south with Heard County on the Ala-

bama border. Its southern border forms a line running east through Campbell, Fayette, Clayton, Walton, Jackson, Madison, and Hart Counties. Its
northern border is the Upcountry (see map 1).

Although the mountain areas of America's Appalachian frontier began to
develop in the 1700s and early 1800s, not all of these mountain regions developed at the same pace. By 1860, mountain areas of Virginia, North Carolina,
and Tennessee had begun to break from their early patterns of isolation and
take a small but growing role in their region's economies. North Georgia,
particularly its mountain areas, lagged behind the rest of Appalachia and in
1860 remained more isolated and less a part of the state's economy than Appalachian regions in other parts of the South. Part of this difference in development is attributable to the time of settlement, while some of the isolation
characteristic of 1860s upcountry Georgia was a matter of choice.[17]

Upcountry Georgia existed only as the Cherokee Indian Nation until
1832. After Andrew Jackson defied the U.S. Supreme Court's ruling in *Cherokee Nation vs. Georgia*, the native American population involuntarily mi-
grated to areas west of the Mississippi River. In 1831 the Georgia legislature
organized the entire region into Cherokee County, which in turn split to
form Murray County; by 1860 the Georgia legislature had carved Walker,
Whitfield, Catoosa, Gordon, Dade, and Chattooga Counties and part of
Cass (Bartow) County out of Murray. That same year Lumpkin County was
formed from the other part of Cherokee, and by the start of the Civil War
Gilmer, Floyd, Fannin, Rabun, Towns, and the remaining northern Georgia
counties had been formed. At first the promise of gold brought a rapid influx
of settlers to upcountry Georgia. Small villages sprang up and gave the appearance that more development was only a matter of time. However, these
towns proved to be only gold mining boom towns, and most people who in-
habited them during the gold rush years were there for the promise of quick
wealth. When the gold played out, most of these people went on to the next
strike. Those who stayed or arrived after the gold strike would call the Upcountry home and make their living as farmers, not goldminers.[18]

Upcountry counties were small. The mountains isolated people from one
another; with inadequate roads and dense wilderness, few people traveled far
to court and other community functions. Parts of the Upcountry were isolated from Georgia itself. The mountains so severely restricted Dade County
in Georgia's northwest corner that to reach it via Georgia was extremely difficult. The most passable roads came from Alabama and Tennessee. For almost
a century Dade interacted more with Tennessee than with Georgia. Lumpkin
County, the site of a gold strike in 1829 and a federal mint from 1835 to
1860, had no railroad connection until after the war.[19] The Upcountry was

Isolation

Georgia's last frontier, a region very different from the plantation belt and the yeoman farms of southeast Georgia.

The north Georgia farmers of the upper Piedmont and Upcountry enjoyed fertile land and adequate waterways that meandered through their counties, but terrain and climate discouraged cotton farming. Farms rested in hilly, mountainous, and broken terrain, with a cooler climate and shorter growing season that made grain products, not cotton, the staple agricultural product. The 1850 U.S. Census indicated grain crops comprised 90 percent of Upcountry crop land and almost 80 percent of the region's agricultural crop value. Small farms, with an overwhelmingly white population, dominated the northern Georgia counties. The percentage of slaves equaled or exceeded 20 percent of the population in only two Upcountry counties. Slaves represented less than 10 percent of the population in nine Upcountry counties. In the upper Piedmont the percentage of slaves to the total population was slightly higher. Only in Walton County did slaves represent as much as 40 percent of the residents.[20] The racial composition of the upper Piedmont and Upcountry was overwhelmingly white, and by 1850 slaves constituted less than 25 percent of the upper Piedmont and Upcountry population.

The dominance of the white population throughout northern Georgia remained stable during the 1850s, while the plantation belt counties with high white population figures slowly gave way to increased slave populations. The 1860 census showed that the upper Piedmont region had 192,940 residents; 74.2 percent were white. The total population figure is higher than the number for the upper Piedmont in this study because of a broader definition of the upper Piedmont used by the 1860 census, which includes counties that this study places within the plantation belt or the Upcountry. The mountain areas of the Upcountry showed an even higher proportion of whites to the total population. Of the counties in that region, only Murray (20 percent), Gordon (21 percent), and Chattooga (29 percent) show slave populations in excess of 20 percent of the total population. At least half of the mountain counties have black populations that do not exceed 10 percent, and some were as low as 2 and 3 percent. The culture that developed in this region during the antebellum period resembled that of colonial America because, unlike the plantation belt, northern Georgia experienced none of the urban, industrial, and transportation revolutions that occurred elsewhere. Aside from the Atlantic and Western line that connected Chattanooga to Atlanta, and a small feeder line to Rome in Floyd County, the Upcountry counties from Atlanta to the Tennessee border had no railways. Despite a willingness of some residents to become more integrated into the rest of Georgia's economy, on the eve of the Civil War, upcountry Georgia, even some of its more southern regions, remained physically isolated. The journey between Atlanta and

Dahlonega, the largest town in Lumpkin County and site of a federal mint, required days and sometimes weeks. By 1860, with gold long since played out, Dahlonega remained a frontier town of about 1,000 residents. Although a small segment of the population had begged the Georgia legislature for a rail line, such entreaties fell on deaf ears, and the area waited until 1879 for a railroad.[21] The delay hardly bothered the majority of the region's residents, who saw the railroad and what came with it as an intrusion on their way of life.

The geographic and climatic differences between north Georgia and the lower Piedmont determined the agricultural economies and diverse subcultures of each region. Rooted in their differences was the strength or weakness of one's convictions on slavery and therefore of one's commitment to the Confederacy. As the war dragged on into its third year, the loyalty of the people from north Georgia to the Confederate cause snapped under severe pressure. They saw the Confederacy and their state government demonstrate that neither could protect their soldiers' homes and families. Salt and food shortages, the presence of vigilantes and irregular bands of men who preyed on the region, and eventually Sherman's invasion affected soldiers from north Georgia differently than those from the plantation belt. North Georgia's men came from a culture less tied to slavery, a world separate and apart from the planters, wealthy farmers, and even the slaveholding yeomen of the plantation region. North Georgians could not endure the rigors of war and the long-term absence of their male population from the farms upon which their survival depended.

Several factors unique to the Upcountry region and the upper Piedmont transition belt produced north Georgia culture. While the Upcountry and the upper Piedmont region differed in some respects, they were more similar in most. Thus, while some upper Piedmont counties displayed slavery and some aspects of a plantation culture that did not exist in Upcountry counties, the lives of the small farmers/common soldiers were in many ways identical. Although the plantation belt and the regions north and south boasted large yeoman farmer populations, in some cases the similarities were purely economic. The yeomen in north Georgia and yeomen in the rest of the state lived in different worlds.[22]

Subsistence agriculture in northern Georgia required continuous physical labor, with the crop cycle setting the patterns of life and all else being secondary. In Gilmer County, school opened in mid-July and closed in mid-September, the period between the laying of the corn crop and fodder pulling. Neighborhood activities centered around shared work.[23]

This survival economy remained local; if something could not be grown or taken from the forest, most people did without it. Large families dominated the region. The only source of cash came from selling nuts, excess dairy products, and bark from certain trees used in the tanning process.[24] With so little cash, barter served as the most common form of exchange. Most clothing came from the family's home loom. Most men and boys wore long-legged trousers and home-dyed cotton shirts but no shoes.[25] This rugged culture prevailed from the mountainous regions of upcountry Georgia, down through the upper Piedmont as far south as Heard and Carroll Counties, west of Atlanta on the Alabama-Georgia border.

Life in Carroll County before the war was described in the memoirs of Pvt. Jim Kugler of the Fifty-sixth Georgia Infantry. Carroll County lay south of the Upcountry in the southwest corner of the upper Piedmont. Kugler's father purchased a hundred-acre farm for six hundred dollars in 1857 and built a simple log cabin. Kugler's mother clothed the family in homespun and made everything else except shoes. The Kuglers grew or made all their food except sugar, coffee, and syrup. The children went to school only after the crop was planted.[26]

Paulding County, north of Carroll County on the northern edge of Georgia's upper Piedmont, had an identical economy and culture. It contained mostly small freehold farms with a small planter population at the top and an even smaller, very poor population at the bottom. Men in leather breeches cleared their own land, cut timber for their homes, and raised all their own provisions. The ax and the rifle were the main tools. Although some education and religion existed in these counties, the average citizen was illiterate and had little interest in religion. After 1852, when most of the good land in and around the creek bottoms had been claimed, the county presented few practical opportunities for plantation farming.

Although Paulding's population shifted significantly during the antebellum period as new settlers arrived from South Carolina, east Georgia, and North Carolina, its culture changed little. Large families predominated, and most farmers in Paulding County did not own slaves. The census indicates that in 1860 only 563 slaves lived among the county's 6,478 whites, a mere 8 percent of the county's population. The slaves probably belonged to the few plantations in the county. Couples married early, and the wife became an integral part of the economic unit. Divorce rarely occurred and was considered a social taboo. Like Georgia's Upcountry, the social life of Paulding County was simple. Such work-related ventures as turkey shoots, corn huskings, and log rollings combined with dances, militia calls, and house-raising and formed the basis of neighborly interaction. Male social activities generally involved alcohol, and most grocery stores sold and served liquor on the premises.[27]

Despite the newness of settlement in the Upcountry and portions of the upper Piedmont and the isolated nature of life, the families that occupied the region and the culture they developed reflected a clear, if rudimentary, community structure. Community depends both on some shared physical location and on common or similar beliefs, ideas, and institutions. North Georgia possessed both.

Although terrain isolated North Georgians from one another, the smaller size of the mountain counties made physical contact among residents possible. In addition to the leisure and work-sharing activities, certain institutions, although basic and often inadequate, nevertheless existed. North Georgia communities had both churches and schools, each a fundamental attribute of community life. The prevalence of the semi-subsistence yeoman farm required certain essentials that could not be produced at home, most notably farming equipment. Small stores and groceries found appreciative customers for such items and served not only as a source of essential goods but as places of social interaction, particularly for men. Most groceries had provision shops in the front and a bar or "doggery" in the back, with the two areas separated by wooden screens to obscure the identity of the back room occupants. In addition to stores and groceries, north Georgians also depended on local mills to grind their grain. The importance of these institutions to the community became apparent during the war in petitions sent to the governor pleading for the return of the local miller and signed by residents from across the county.[28]

Carroll County retained its frontier character through most of the antebellum period. Nevertheless, even before the war Carroll possessed some of the same community institutions found in other portions of the upper Piedmont and the Upcountry. By 1850, twenty-eight churches dotted the countryside. Not only did the county have schools for its children, but by 1857 a small log-constructed college existed in the Bowden district. In addition to the small stores, groceries, and taverns characteristic of the region, Carroll County boasted a gold mining operation that added to its work-related community institutions. Gold mining also existed in the Upcountry. Union County had a mine in Coosa, and Lumpkin County's gold strike not only provided a source of employment for the region but proved so large that the U.S. government established a mint in Dahlonega. Although most miners left for California and the gold rush of 1849, the mine and mint still served as an important nonagricultural community institution.[29]

Community in north Georgia also existed through a set of common beliefs that served as a mudsill to fill the gaps caused by isolation and rudimentary physical institutions. North Georgia's small slave population and resistance to secession reflected more than an environment ill suited for cotton plantations. By 1860 "north Georgia" described a location as well as a particular kind of people. Independence was most important to Georgia's upper Piedmont and Upcountry population. Freedom from government, creditors, and any other form of outside interference had more value than monetary wealth. Common ideas often make communities cohesive units despite few well-developed institutions or the presence of other differences. Few notions were more fundamental than a man's relationship to his neighbors and the outside world. North Georgians' voting patterns on secession and their resistance to changes in their way of life reflect group activity, not the disjointed actions of individuals loosely bound by similar culture.

Community provides a sense of protection and belonging for its members and at the same time restricts their actions. Nowhere is this more apparent than in the notion of reputation and honor. Honor was an important aspect of community life. Unlike the rituals of gentlemen settling disputes by dueling, Upcountry disagreements were usually resolved outside the law in a more haphazard manner. Formal laws existed but were rarely used. Fights in the Upcountry seldom involved dueling, but participants often disregarded the 1787 laws forbidding gouging and biting. Such differences in the resolution of affronts to honor reflect more significant differences between yeomen and gentlemen. Plantation gentlemen lived in a culture where misstatements or dishonorable acts gave rise to conflict among elite members of the community or men of lesser social standing not otherwise totally dependent on one another for survival. The resolution of such disputes did not affect the community at large. The disputes among the elite remained private, confined to their social circles. A planter's life might remain stable within his plantation even if social conflict rendered him at odds with certain other members of his class. However, outside this landed aristocracy, stability meant community stability. The plain folks in the Upcountry lived in a world where community constituted a vital support network. If individuals took conflict too far, the stability of the entire community would be threatened. Work and leisure required that the community remain socially stable. Upcountry society allowed for conflict until it disrupted community harmony. Thus, both the sense of honor and the methods of dealing with affronts to honor differed between the plantation belt and north Georgia.[30]

Honor among Georgia's plain folks had another limitation. The South faced the same problem the colonies had encountered during the American Revolution: the inability of the common citizen to recognize a duty higher than family and community. Confederate patriotism found its basis within a duty to local peoples and places. Abstract notions of democracy involving states' rights lost their relevance if taken beyond the immediate context of family and community.[31] One key to honor is that the community acts as a mirror in which the individual sees himself reflected, with the perceptions of others being crucial to reputation. When conduct receives community approval, it ceases to be dishonorable. As the war continued, the realities of the home front across Georgia altered notions of honor in north Georgia more than in the plantation belt. In the belief that the individual must yield to community and family, north Georgia eventually disallowed military duty adversely affecting the home front.

These specific examples of Upcountry life and different notions of honor help to distinguish antebellum society in north Georgia from that of the plantation belt. This difference does not suggest that other yeomen families, particularly nonslaveholding yeomen in the plantation belt and the Wiregrass, did not suffer during the war. It simply demonstrates how economic and geographical differences had created distinct cultures. The beliefs held by north Georgians of duty to family and community above everything else found little if any competing notions of loyalty that might exist in regions where communities were a mix of planters, wealthy farmers, slaveholding yeomen, and nonslaveholders. Even north Georgia farmers who did not own their own farms and had to work as tenants followed the family economic structure of the landed nonslaveholding yeomen. The upper Piedmont and upcountry Georgia economy focused on the household, not some broader notion. Like some northern farm communities in colonial America, economic productivity depended more on family and kinship than on the marketplace. At the core of this stood the family unit, which prized its own independence above all else.[32]

The success of the family economic unit lay in a clear division of labor that was defined by both sex and age. Husbands took charge of the fields, supported by sons after they reached early adolescence, to clear, plow, and plant the farm. Women helped harvest, but for most of the year they worked in and around the house. Virtually every home had its own loom, even if crude, and from this home spinning device came most of the family's clothes. In a familial economic unit that depended on each person to perform his or her essential functions, the family survived only if everyone contributed.

Most farmers in the region produced foodstuffs: wheat, oats, potatoes, sweet potatoes, and especially corn. Some farmers planted small areas with cotton or tobacco for their own use and to barter, trade, or sell to raise a little cash. Such nonconsumable goods were sold through small country merchants or to a nearby plantation owner, if one existed. North Georgia's farmers participated in a local market governed by community customs, in contrast with the national, or at least regional, market system of Georgia's plantation economy.[33]

Although not wealthy, upper Piedmont and Upcountry people lived within a culture so comfortable in its simplicity that they feared whatever threatened to alter their way of life. The advent of the railroad before the Civil War demonstrated the overwhelming preference for the old customary ties and values. Farmers feared the loss of land from railroad right of ways, the destruction of crops as sparks from engines flew out, and the noise that shattered the calm of their surroundings, frightening both livestock and children. Upcountry merchants tied to the wagon trade and local craftsmen dependent on the steady patronage of area farmers also saw the railroad and the national economy as unwanted evils. The farmers, merchants, and craftsmen in north Georgia, living within a culture of familial relationships and kinship ties, were content with a level of existence that provided enough to feed and clothe their families without threatening to destroy their independence.

The upper Piedmont and Upcountry people existed in a world where the "whole" was greater than the sum of the parts. Not only did each family member have to contribute to the household economy, but local millers, merchants, and craftsmen provided the essential services or goods that the family could not produce with its own labor. The upper Piedmont and Upcountry functioned like a handmade timepiece, with each component carefully crafted to perform a specific role, with the slightest disruption causing it to cease. This society of agricultural households tied to the local economy constantly struggled internally to maintain its equilibrium. This precarious balance was upset as the demands of a war removed half of its labor force, depleted vital nonagricultural support, and left women without companionship and stripped of an essential economic component. As the war progressed, the Upcountry/upper Piedmont economic and family structure would face the challenge of surviving without the male workforce.

On the eve of the Civil War, the upper Piedmont and Upcountry were not the only regions to reject slavery and the plantation economic system. The Wiregrass and Pine Barrens of southeast Georgia possessed many similar characteristics of little wealth, a white population, and a subsistence economy. In addition, unlike Georgia's Chattahoochee River valley and other areas of the plantation belt, nonslaveholding yeomen farmers formed a significant portion of the population. Although less numerous, nonslaveholding yeomen also lived within the plantation belt. They served the same labor function in their households as men from the Upcountry or the Pine Barrens of Georgia. Did they view the war and their own sense of honor like the men from north Georgia, or was theirs a perspective based on social ties that transcended the differences in economic status between themselves and their planter neighbors?

Geographic location provides a clue as to how yeomen outside north Georgia reacted to the war, particularly the hardships placed on their families and the calls for soldiers to return. One's residence within the plantation belt may have dictated the social circles in which a man functioned and the code of honor that governed his conduct among his peers. Men who owned few if any slaves and shared in the great wealth of the plantation economy only indirectly, might nevertheless have embraced the slaveholders' cause with more fervor than the men of upcountry Georgia. It is also possible that, as the war continued, nonslaveholders from central and south Georgia emotionally abandoned the Confederate cause, but because of where they lived, they were in no position to physically abandon a cause that they did not believe in.

While the yeoman farmer in Georgia's plantation belt resembled his Upcountry counterpart in terms of how he farmed and made a living, he differed in what he farmed. The geographical proximity to the planter culture led many yeomen to plant cotton, although they still relied to some degree on subsistence farming. The realities of a cotton-based staple agriculture in turn forced yeomen to depend on the planter class for necessities that Upcountry farmers either produced on their own or acquired locally. Few yeomen living in the planter regions could afford cotton gins, so they looked to planters to both gin and market their cotton for a small fee or used marketing houses or merchants run by planters. Because cotton agriculture sometimes left yeomen with temporary food shortages, they relied on their wealthier planter neighbors for essential supplies. In contrast, an Upcountry farmer made crop choices based on a local economy and the desire to be self-sufficient. When shortages occurred, these yeomen looked to their neighbors. With its customary recognition of common use of private lands for such things as hunting and fishing vital to a subsistence-based economy, the Upcountry bonded the north Georgia yeomen to the poorer white classes rather than to any wealthier persons.[34]

The economic ties between yeoman and planter in the plantation belt may have led to closer social relations and engendered closer cultural mores and notions of honor, ideas that influenced how cotton yeomen viewed their world. Scholars have examined how this relationship affected support by yeomen for secession. Yet, if the relationship carried over into the war and a man's conduct as a soldier, it helps explain Georgia's desertion patterns. The shared notions of a white man's place in society, as defined by the existence of black slaves, united the Southern planters and the yeomen in the plantation region during the secession crisis. It may have extended the planter's sense of honor to his yeomen neighbors. This social tie also may have allowed women in yeomen families to rely upon the planter's family for essential supplies just as they had before the war.

Even if yeoman and planters shared certain economic and cultural similarities that bound them to similar notions of honor and obligation to military duty, this would not explain the low incidence of desertion among plantation belt denizens whose lives mirrored those living in the Upcountry and Wiregrass regions. Despite the prevalence of slaves, plantations, and large yeoman farms throughout Georgia's black belt, smaller farms and plain folk also lived in the plantation belt. Without social or economic connections to their wealthier neighbors, their families suffered from the lack of bare necessities as the war moved into its third year. However, the desertion patterns found in the register indicate that very little of the desertion came from this region. Perhaps the answer lies not so much in the lack of a desire or need to desert but in the lack of opportunity. Desertion, whether to the enemy or by going straight home, required both opportunity and the chance of remaining free once one had left. For many soldiers of the plantation belt, their circumstances provided neither the opportunity nor a safe haven.

The homes of central and south Georgia soldiers lay in areas that remained under Confederate control for most of the war. Unlike many Upcountry soldiers, most central and south Georgians fought in Lee's Army of Northern Virginia, duty that took them far from home. Thus, if social and cultural reasons do not explain the lack of desertion among plantation belt soldiers, the answers lie in the course of the war itself. The presence of the Union army throughout north Georgia encouraged desertion, but the plantation belt experienced no significant Union occupation. Those counties through which General Sherman passed en route to Savannah felt the effects of his army's presence, but the Union did not occupy those areas long enough to secure them from Confederate authorities.

Before the war, the region of southeast Georgia, situated between the rice belt on the Georgia Atlantic coast and the plantation belt of the lower Piedmont (map 1), possessed many qualities of upcountry Georgia. Not all counties in this region had low slave populations, but these southeastern yeomen had significantly less wealth than the planters or the slaveholding yeomen to the north. The Pine Barrens and Wiregrass regions show some of the same slaveholding patterns as the Upcountry, while the rice belt counties like Chatham and those surrounding Savannah show higher slave populations, between 45 and 80 percent of the county population. Although there is a large river system in southeast Georgia, dominated by the Ocmulgee and Altamaha Rivers, that cuts the region in two from east to west, the rail systems tend to run around the area leading out of the plantation belt to Columbus, Atlanta, Savannah, Athens, Augusta, and Macon and through Milledgeville. Only a branch from Savannah running southwest goes through the area.[35]

If the Wiregrass desertion patterns mirror those of the Upcountry, similar cultural and socioeconomic systems may have been the cause. Many of the same family and community attributes found in the Upcountry and upper Piedmont existed in the Wiregrass regions of southeast Georgia. These same qualities brought similar hardships to this region as the war dragged on.[36] Although Georgians in the Wiregrass region shared far more similarities than differences with the common folk in northern Georgia, conceivably some of the differences between the yeomen in these counties and those in north Georgia may have accounted for the desertion patterns. For example, some Wiregrass counties lay along the rail routes between the plantations and the markets. Soldiers from some of these counties who shared the same economic world with plantation belt planters and slaveholding yeomen may have embraced some of the cultural aspects common among such men. Their ideas of honor and commitment to family and community may not have been as strong as their northern Georgia counterparts. The more likely explanation, however, is that if soldiers from these southeastern counties accounted for little or no desertion, the region's location in the extreme south of Georgia, and not its culture, defined the boundaries of desertion.

The Georgia desertion patterns reflect a clear correlation between desertion and county location. Some of the factors that made desertion among north Georgia's soldiers possible may have contributed to the lack of desertion in the southeastern areas. The distance from the encampments of military units to home, the absence of any concerted Union presence, the continued maintenance of Confederate civil authority, and police activity during the war may offer better reasons for the lack of desertion in these counties of southeastern Georgia.

This analysis of the diversity of Georgia before the war explains the state's wartime desertion patterns. Despite the distinct social, economic, and cultural differences existing in Georgia in April 1861, every county in Georgia answered the Confederacy's first call to arms and sent a company of volunteers. The register documents 102 Georgia counties that sent soldiers to the war and had at least one soldier who deserted and took the oath of allegiance. Only thirty counties did not report any deserters: Appling, Baker, Brooks, Bryan, Bullock, Calhoun, Colquitt, Early, Echol, Emanuel, Glascock, Glynn, Irwin, Johnson, Lee, Lowndes, McIntosh, Mitchell, Morgan, Pulaski, Putnam, Quitman, Schley, Screvin, Taylor, Terrell, Ware, Wayne, Wilcox, and Wilkes. Georgians fought in two main armies: the Army of Northern Virginia and the Army of Tennessee. For the most part, the Army of Northern Virginia rarely left Virginia, and with the exception of the men under Gen. James Longstreet, they never fought in Georgia. The Army of Tennessee fought in Kentucky, Tennessee, and eventually north Georgia throughout the Atlanta campaign. It was this army which returned to Georgia in November 1863.[37]

Total enlistment figures for Georgians are difficult to calculate. For example, the Army of Tennessee formed from two smaller armies, Kirby Smith's Army of Kentucky and Bragg's Army of Mississippi, which were consolidated in November 1862. The Army of Tennessee fought its first major engagement at Stones River with 38,000 men and claimed 54,500 "present for duty" and 43,887 "effectives" in April 1864. By October 1864, the Army of Tennessee still had 40,000 soldiers as it made its way north out of Georgia. The Army of Northern Virginia was larger, but its numbers do not reveal the total enlistment of Georgia soldiers. It claimed 69,391 excluding cavalry in December 1862. By April 1864, despite great losses, its strength remained at 63,998. Not only are total enlistment figures for any one period difficult to determine, but it is virtually impossible to know how many Georgians remained in the Army of Tennessee and the Army of Northern Virginia at any one time.[38]

Georgia contributed 797 infantry companies to 66 infantry regiments between April 1861 and the end of the war. Georgia also sent 67 cavalry units to the war varying in strength from regiments of ten companies to battalions with as few as five. Unlike infantry records, the most reliable data on cavalry units do not reveal where these units formed and do not allow for an analysis of enlistment in the cavalry by county. The register identifies cavalry deserters by county, but there is no proof that the county of the deserter was also the county where the unit formed without the ability to cross-reference those units with some type of muster roll. The infantry figures do not include soldiers from counties that joined one of Gov. Joseph Brown's Georgia State units or militia units between 1862 and 1864. However, despite these shortcomings, most soldiers were in the infantry, and therefore some conclusions can be drawn without matching cavalry units to their county of origin or precisely identifying total numbers for Georgia cavalry.[39] Of Georgia's 132 counties, only 14 contributed ten or more infantry companies to the war effort. Georgia's twenty Upcountry counties sent 114 companies, or 14 percent of the total.[40] The twenty-one upper Piedmont counties[41] provided 173 companies. The twenty-three Pine Barrens/Wiregrass counties sent 68 companies,[42] and the six counties in the narrow rice belt sent 38,[43] with all but 14 from Chatham County. The remaining sixty-three counties forming the plantation belt contributed slightly over 50 percent of the volunteer infantry companies (see table 1).

Georgia's counties contributed volunteer infantry in percentages of their white male populations almost identical to the proportion of their white

TABLE I. DISTRIBUTION OF INFANTRY COMPANIES BY REGION

Region	Number of companies	Percentage of total no.	Percentage of population
Plantation belt	404	50.7	47.0
Upper Piedmont	173	21.7	22.1
Upcountry	114	14.3	17.2
Wiregrass/Pine Barrens	68	8.6	9.5
Rice belt	38	4.7	4.2
Total	797	100.0	100.0

Note: The figures in column 3 (percentage of population) were arrived at by using the total white population of each county as set out in Smith, *Slavery and Rice Culture in Low Country Georgia*, 33. The data there provides total population and percentage of slaves. By subtracting the slave population from the total, what remained was a total white population for each county. For purposes of this table, Floyd and Cass (Bartow) Counties are included in the upper Piedmont populations, even though the two counties form the boundary between the Upcountry and upper Piedmont. Laurens and Pulaski Counties are included within the Pine Barrens and Wiregrass region. Based on these calculations, Georgia's total white population was 588,928 distributed as follows: Plantation belt: 276,621; Upcountry: 101,419; upper Piedmont: 130,274; rice belt: 24,510; Wiregrass/Pine Barrens: 56,104.

populations to Georgia's total white population. Fulton, Chatham, Richmond, and Muscogee—the home counties, respectively, for Atlanta, Savannah, Augusta, and Columbus—had large enlistments consistent with large urban areas. Chatham County sent more than twenty companies to the Confederate army, and Richmond sent more than fifteen. Fulton County sent thirty-two, more than any other Georgia county. Muscogee County sent twenty-three companies, all but one of which went to war before the end of March 1862. Several unidentified citizens of Muscogee County asked Gov. Joe Brown if he had noticed how many men the county contributed. Muscogee County formed four companies for service in March 1862, and its citizens complained that it had "given more men than any other county had or would give."[44] The Upcountry and upper Piedmont did not contribute most of the soldiers, yet those regions have most of the deserters because the seeds of desertion, planted long before the war, grew as the conflict continued.

Studies of armies before and during the American Revolution point to their seasonal nature. Winter soldiers and springtime farmers, men who could only be spared for a brief period, made up colonial America's provincial armies. When war jeopardized the delicate balance of these pre-Revolutionary societies by threatening to remove the men for unacceptable periods, armies dissolved as war was subordinated to family and community. Colonial soldiers lived in an economy that could only temporarily spare its men for military service.[45] As the United States grew from a rudimentary agricultural nation into a country tied together by regional, national, and international trade and industry, the character of the country's soldiers changed. By the early 1800s the United States had a military academy at West Point, New York, that trained professional officers. Upon graduation these officers led a small standing army. By the mid-1800s those areas in market economies had men who could serve for extended periods.[46] A community's ability to supply men for war depended on whether it still functioned as a semi-subsistence unit or had been part of a market economy.

The plantation belt represented the South's version of a modern market society. It functioned as an integral cog in a national and international commercial agricultural economy. Its labor force remained constant and could function regardless of whether the plantation owner remained at home or went to war. Although some Georgians feared that slaves would rebel once the war began, others expressed such fears only after the Union army moved into Georgia.[47] Slaves themselves helped sustain the continuity of the plantation economic unit, even during long periods of planter and overseer absence. Blacks constituted more than just a dependable workforce for the white population; slaves developed complex and enduring community and family networks within these plantations. Fleeing, rebelling, or other actions that served to dissolve the relationship between the slave and the plantation also severed or altered the nature of slave family and community. Despite a few isolated instances of attempted rebellion and a wide variety of nonviolent resistance, the slave labor network remained intact for reasons other than fear of the planter or Southern white authority. Slaves stayed within the system out of a desire to preserve their own community's integrity and value system.[48]

In contrast to the plantation belt economy, the removal of men from the north Georgia Piedmont and Upcountry communities struck at the very core of the family economy. Unlike the plantation regions where the underlying labor force remained intact, albeit more difficult to manage, the departure of the father and his adult sons stripped the region of its labor force. Even yeomen families within the plantation belt who owned as few as two or three slaves were better off than families with no male workforce. While women clearly demonstrated the ability to perform many physical chores crucial to the success of the family economy, there were some tasks they could not perform. Men cleared, plowed, and planted. Without them there could be no crop, and without the crop the family unit broke down. No one could foresee that destitution might follow on the heels of mass military enlistment even under ideal circumstances. If weather, embargo, fire, or other acts of God intervened, the situation might quickly become unlivable. Furthermore, the removal of men who provided essential services to the community further crippled the region. Letters from north Georgia's women not only implored the government to release their husbands but begged it to return millers and certain essential craftsmen. Like their colonial forefathers, these men left a household economy where they were essential. The crisis for these communities came with the reality of modern war that required men to enlist for years and ultimately for the duration of the war.

On the eve of war, Georgia's leaders preached cohesion, not disunity. In direct reference to the Upcountry counties, Governor Brown stated, "They [the yeomen] know that the Government of our state protects their lives, their families, and their property . . . Every dollar the wealthy slaveholder has made may be taken by the Government of the State, if need be, to protect the rights and liberties of all." Brown's comments held the key to the difference between Upcountry yeomen and their plantation belt counterparts. Lacking the bonds created by social and economic closeness, or the tenuous connection created by the ownership of even a handful of slaves that made the black belt yeomen embrace the planters' fight, Upcountry loyalty rested on the government-citizen relationship that saw the individual relinquish his right to govern himself in exchange for the government's obligation to protect his life, liberty, and property. Brown boasted: "When it becomes necessary to defend our rights against so foul a domination . . . I would call upon the mountain boys as well as the people of the lowlands, and they would come down like an avalanche and swarm around the flag of Georgia."[49]

Brown's commitment to protect the soldiers' families went to the core of Georgia's desertion pattern. How well did the government protect the lives, families, and property of the "mountain boys"? Did they receive any of that "planter money" when they could not provide for their loved ones? Did the people of the lowlands contribute in kind to the sacrifice of blood to the cause? If so, did it exhaust either their human or material resources? Questions that Brown did not even consider also arose. Did law and order prevail uniformly throughout Georgia during the war? Given the different notions of honor and allegiance to the Confederate cause, did the local communities alter their definition of honorable conduct as the war placed disproportionate burdens upon the various regions of the state? Concerning World War I,

Woodrow Wilson once said, "It is not an army that we must train for war: it is a nation."[50] As Georgia's men answered the Confederacy's call to arms, their absence would soon demonstrate how prepared the state was for war. In the end, some parts of Georgia were better prepared than others for the war that lay ahead.

CHAPTER TWO

Preparing for the Prodigal Son

With winter rapidly approaching in December 1863, Pvt. Samuel M. Bird of the Thirty-ninth Georgia Infantry unceremoniously swore the oath of allegiance to the United States, gathered up his few remaining possessions, and began the short journey from Nashville, Tennessee, to his home in Walker County, Georgia.[1] It had been almost two years since the thirty-one-year-old Bird had left his wife and five young children to fend for themselves as he went off to war. He was from Tennessee, and his wife, Susan, had been born in Georgia. Together they farmed the land, made their home in Georgia's mountainous Upcountry, and raised three daughters and two sons, all under the age of ten when he and the rest of Walker County's men answered the Confederacy's call.

Private Bird deserted his unit and made his way directly into the Union lines, where he took advantage of the Union desertion policy, which allowed him to swear his loyalty to the Union, secure his release, and return to his family. Bird was one of more than 30,000 Confederate soldiers, almost 3,400 of whom came from Georgia, who deserted in this manner. He was among the first Walker County soldiers to desert to the Union and become a reconstructed citizen. Bird and the others redefined desertion by leaving no doubt they intended to desert the Confederate army and to abandon the cause for which it fought.[2]

Historically, desertion has served as a barometer of an army's morale. High desertion rates indicate that an army has lost its will to fight. Desertion reveals much about a unit's determination to continue fighting, but it seldom indicates that an army or its soldiers have embraced the enemy's cause. Desertion simply means a voluntary, illegal departure from service with the intent never to return. During the American Civil War, desertion took on a deeper meaning. Unlike European wars of the eighteenth and nineteenth centuries, where disputed territory and other issues rested on the outcome of a war, the outcome of the Civil War decided the fate of the new Confederate nation. By abandoning one's military duty, a soldier essentially abandoned the Confederacy. This became clearer when the Union began offering deserters the opportunity to swear an oath of allegiance to the federal government in exchange for their release to return home. When this program became a reality late in the summer of 1863, Confederate deserters abandoned more than the army. They became the first rebels to return to the Union. Like the biblical prodigal son who left his father's house, squandered his resources, and then returned, these Confederate deserters reaffirmed their loyalty. Some Confederate soldiers remained in the North until the war ended; others braved the rigors of the journey home, which was made easier as the Union occupied more of the South and rid those areas of Confederate civilian and military authorities. Some became "galvanized Confederates," joining Union army units sent to the frontier.[3]

President Abraham Lincoln issued his Proclamation of Amnesty and Reconstruction on December 8, 1863. The executive order offered a full pardon and restoration of all rights to persons within the Confederacy who reaffirmed their allegiance by taking an oath of future loyalty. The program represented Lincoln's first attempt at comprehensive reconstruction designed to bring the rebellious South back into the Union by giving its civilian population the opportunity to come home voluntarily. Lincoln's proclamation also provided a way to shorten the war by undermining civilian enthusiasm and support in areas occupied by the Union army and to prepare the South for the emancipation of slaves. Known as the Ten Percent Plan, Lincoln's executive order allowed any state whose loyal members, equaling at least 10 percent of the 1860 registered voters, to form a new state government that would be entitled to federal representation in Washington.[4]

Lincoln's vision for reuniting the nation excluded those Confederates generally deemed unworthy of amnesty, allowed Congress to establish its own qualifications for readmitting members, and provided an acceptable loyalty oath. Those who took the oath also accepted administration policy on emancipation and congressional legislation on it. By taking the oath, slaveholders could lose their slaves. Although commonly acclaimed as the first Reconstruction program, Lincoln's plan did not represent the first attempt at reuniting the country.[5] Lincoln's proclamation came nearly three months after the War Department finalized a policy for releasing Confederate prisoners of war and deserters in August 1863. Like Lincoln's Ten Percent Plan, this military "reconstruction" policy provided Confederate soldiers with an opportunity to reestablish their loyalty to the Union. The program preceding Lincoln's Proclamation of Amnesty and Reconstruction served a military purpose of shortening the war by undermining the South's military strength. In the process, it demonstrated that desertion had a wider significance than merely committing a military crime.

For many historians, the Civil War and Reconstruction represented a second American Revolution. The war transformed the United States from a nation divided by slavery to a more united country and destroyed the slaveholding aristocracy of the South. An essential part of the revolution required the North to bring the rebellious Southerners back into the United States without the institution of slavery. The key to reintegrating the South lay in successful reconstruction. Despite all of the historical attention focused on Lincoln's Ten Percent Plan as the genesis of Reconstruction, the first "prodigal sons" to return to their "father's house" were not Southern civilians but Confederate soldiers. The most recognized preludes to Reconstruction occurred in Louisiana and the South Carolina sea islands, which experienced Union efforts to reintegrate blacks and civilian white populations. Historical preoccupation with wartime reconstruction ignores the military effort that began late in 1861, and continued throughout the war, to reconstruct the South by destroying its ability to wage war.[6] While there were some isolated attempts at reconstruction, the North's policy for deserters and prisoners of war was one of the first comprehensive attempts to bring Confederates back into the Union.

As with so many aspects of the Civil War, neither side anticipated the administrative and logistical demands arising from large numbers of prisoners and deserters. Union authorities simply invented rules and modified them as they went along. Using the oath of allegiance to release Southern soldiers began as an informal process and significantly changed over time. The early policy amounted to ad hoc determinations of field commanders who constantly sought guidance from their superiors and the U.S. War Department, which was unsure how to proceed, before a system with clearly defined procedures evolved by the end of 1863. In 1862 and 1863, a release process emerged that distinguished between prisoners of war and deserters. It was based on the recognition that winning the war required destroying the Confederate army. Important policy considerations affected the distinct treatment of prisoners of war and deserters. The differences reflected war aims that had to balance the intent to undermine the enemy's war-making capacity with the responsibility to the Union soldiers held in Confederate prisons. Eventually, humanitarian considerations that stressed prisoner exchange over all other means of release yielded to the need to crush the South. By 1864 concerns over released prisoners returning to duty in the Confederate army left desertion as the only means to swear allegiance and go home.

Instead of passively allowing desertion to deplete its smaller army, the

Confederacy took steps to counteract the Northern efforts that encouraged desertion. The Confederacy tried to mend the divisions in Southern unity evidenced in civilian disobedience and in state laws that subordinated the needs of the Confederacy to those of local and regional interests. Southern efforts to fight desertion proved unable to combat Union policies that invited desertion and created safe havens for those who were willing to desert. Akin to the first federal witness protection program, the North combined a generous release policy with its military occupation of the South, which created an environment more conducive to desertion. In the process, the Union produced the unique statistical record upon which this study is based.

The swearing of oaths started almost immediately after the war began. In the autumn of 1861, the Union and Confederates both showed a willingness to release any enemy soldiers who swore allegiance to the other side or who agreed not to take up arms against its side. The assistant adjutant general of the United States Army, Lt. Col. Edward D. Townsend, issued Special Orders No. 170 on the release of prisoners of war on October 12, 1861. He indicated that fifty-seven Union prisoners of war (POWs) held in Richmond had taken an oath to the Confederacy and were then released. The Confederate POWs then held in Washington and New York would be allowed to do the same. Townsend's order provided two forms of the oath: the standard oath of allegiance and the "Oath of Obligation Not to Bear Arms," which stated, "I do solemnly swear (or affirm) that I will not take up arms against the United States or serve in any military capacity whatever against them until regularly discharged according to the usages of war from this obligation." This alternative proved inadequate to ensure loyalty and did not last the war.[7] Although small in number, the early releases of Confederate prisoners revealed a problem that continued for most of the war: Where would a deserter go after renouncing his duties as a soldier and a citizen? In 1861 Confederate POWs taking the oath traveled to Fort Monroe, Virginia, where under a flag of truce they passed south through the Union lines. For those Confederates who took the oath and renounced the Confederacy or at least refused to fight against the Union, the return through rebel lines accomplished little, for they returned to the custody and control of the government they had renounced. Solving this problem proved no easy task.

The influx of prisoners of war and deserters stopped in late 1861 and early 1862, when there was little if any fighting and few opportunities to take prisoners or to desert. In February 1862, Gen. Ulysses S. Grant began his offensive into Tennessee and seized Forts Donelson and Henry. David Farragut sailed up the Mississippi, bypassing Fort Jackson and taking New Orleans. The two sides collided at Shiloh in April in what proved to be the bloodiest encounter yet and foreshadowed what was to come. Union Gen. George McClellan finally attacked the Virginia Peninsula and began a period of almost continuous campaigning that lasted until the end of December 1862. The increased fighting added to the numbers of POWs and began the desertion problem.

In June 1862, the first signs of a weakened Southern resolve created the need for a coherent Union policy to release soldiers who were unwilling to fight for the Confederacy. In letters to the commandants of two Union prison camps, the assistant secretary of war, C. P. Wolcott, offered general assurances to those officials holding Confederate soldiers who were willing to renounce the Confederacy. Both commanders indicated that some prisoners under their control wished to remain in prison rather than be released and sent back through the Confederate lines. The commandant at Fort Columbus, Governor's Island, New York, even provided signatures of the rebel soldiers who refused to return to the Confederate army. Wolcott assured both commanders that after the establishment of a general system of exchange, no POW who took the oath of allegiance and of "whose future loyalty there is no question" would be sent back through the lines to the rebel army.[8]

In the summer of 1862, Wolcott could not foresee the eventual magnitude of the problem. His statements reveal how little consideration the Union had given to desertion and the potential for widespread abandonment of the Confederate cause by its soldiers. Although Wolcott said POWs would not be returned to the rebel authorities, he did not address the greater problem of what to do with them. Only those prisoners whose loyalty was beyond question could take the oath and avoid exchange. Their release depended on loyalty, so Wolcott's letters raised questions no one had yet answered: How did one verify loyalty? To whom did that responsibility fall? What happened if loyalty could not be verified?

By July 1862, the confusion surrounding desertion grew as the magnitude of the problem became clearer. The situation got worse. Gen. Henry Halleck issued a directive to Gen. George Thomas that added to Wolcott's earlier statements but failed to clarify them. Halleck believed anyone within U.S. lines corresponding with the enemy was a spy and should be tried and punished. Yet Southern deserters could be released after taking the oath of allegiance and giving parole. Halleck ignored the question of POWs who were unwilling to return to the rebels, but he ordered that any who wanted to return to the Confederacy should be delivered to the enemy when captured if they agreed not to serve in the army again until regularly exchanged.[9] Thomas then received a letter from William Hoffman, a colonel in the Third United

States Infantry, that asked the question Halleck had avoided. Hoffman began the war as a prisoner when the federal installations in Texas surrendered in 1861. Formally exchanged in August 1862, Hoffman served as commissary general of prisoners throughout the war and assumed a major role in the development of Union desertion policy. Hoffman told Thomas that POWs and their friends wanted to know if everyone had to accept the exchange and go south in the case of a general exchange of prisoners? Many Confederate soldiers wanted their release, but did not want to return to the Confederate army. Could these men be singled out, allowed to join the U.S. army and take the oath of allegiance? The commissioner's request was one of many. In late July, General Thomas also received an inquiry from the commander at Fort Warren, Massachusetts, along with a list of prisoners professing their loyalty and "urgently requesting" that they be allowed to take the oath of allegiance and remain in the North.[10]

The release requests from both Union officials and POWs themselves continued, which resulted in many efforts to create a uniform policy supported by various arguments in favor of release. Andrew Johnson, who succeeded Lincoln as president, served as the military governor of Tennessee until 1864. In the summer of 1862, he wrote to Lincoln about a forthcoming prisoner exchange. Johnson suggested that POWs who refused to take the oath should be exchanged first. Johnson hoped that any Confederate soldier unwilling to return to the army could swear loyalty to the Union and be released immediately to go home. As for any rebel POWs who wanted to return to the Confederate army, Johnson urged, "Let them go." The "expense of maintaining such men, still in a state of rebellion, should be borne by the rebels themselves."[11]

Johnson's letter revealed how logistics and expense might dictate Union policy. He reasoned that men still committed to the South should be fed, clothed, and housed by the South and exchanged as soon as possible in return for Union soldiers. Although Johnson did not say so, he implied that deserters belonged in a different category. Deserters from the Confederacy benefited the North in three ways. First, their safe return might encourage others to desert. Second, they could return and provide for themselves and their families. Third, the Union would not have to feed and house them or spend valuable military resources guarding them. Johnson spoke as both a loyal Unionist and a Tennessean who wanted his state restored to the Union and returned to political normalcy as quickly as possible. Understanding Tennessee's importance to the war effort and its strong Union sentiment in the eastern part of the state, Johnson believed the release of Tennessee soldiers willing to swear allegiance to the North and their return home would "exert a powerful influence upon the state at this time."[12]

Lincoln understood Tennessee's importance to the war effort, and he knew East Tennessee represented a center of Unionist civilian support. The region offered great promise for an early Union reconstruction government in the upper South. William G. Brownlow, editor of the *Knoxville Whig*, vowed to "fight the Secession leaders till Hell freezes over, and then fight them on ice." However, such patriotic fervor could do little without Northern military support. From the early months of the war, Lincoln pressed his military commanders to invade and occupy East Tennessee, where rugged terrain, poor transportation routes, and inclement weather made military operations difficult.[13] Johnson's suggestion of releasing Tennessee soldiers who swore the oath and allowing them to return home provided the North with an opportunity to occupy the region with a "fifth column" of loyal citizens who could stoke the embers of Unionism until the military could successfully occupy the region.

From military and civilian government officials came requests, pleas, and questions to cope with increased numbers of Confederate prisoners of war and deserters who seemed willing to abandon the Confederate cause. In July 1862, Maj. Gen. John Dix informed Secretary of War Edwin Stanton that some "insurgent" Confederate POWs had refused to go south. Among the soldiers who insisted on staying north was a captain from a family with large property holdings in New Orleans. Although an isolated example, this officer's unwillingness to return south indicated wealth alone was an insufficient inducement to go home. Money would be of little use if a man found himself standing before a firing squad.[14]

The commander of Camp Douglas, Chicago, wrote to Adj. Gen. Lorenzo Thomas and forwarded requests from Confederate prisoners to take the oath and avoid exchange. The commander supported these requests saying the Confederate POWs had "entered the rebel service unwillingly; some through fear of being drafted, some to escape from actual imprisonment and from the impossibility of finding other employment." Many of these prisoners lived within Union lines. They admitted to voluntarily joining the Confederate army, but had grown tired of the rebellion and wanted to return to "their loyalty and their homes." One Union officer, James A. Ekin, asked Stanton point blank what to do with Southerners who refused to be exchanged, indicating somewhere between 1,000 and 1,200 men, mostly from Tennessee, fell into this category.[15]

Such unwilling participants, whether poor or fearing criminal prosecution in the South, seemed to be likely candidates for release. However, the most significant class of men were those "whose homes are now within our lines" and who professed to be tired of war. They had joined willingly, but could not escape their obligation to the Confederacy while its forces held the territory where their homes were located. With Union occupation, release became a realistic and desirable option. The combination of home and safety, critical factors to the Tennessee POWs and deserters, was also vital to Georgia desertion later in the war. However, unlike the deserters, the men who voluntarily joined and claimed to be tired of war might not go home, and their release posed a risk that they would return to the Confederate army.

A prisoner exchange system was in place by May 1862, but the Union still lacked a uniform release policy for deserters and POWs who refused to be exchanged. Ohio's governor wrote the War Department on behalf of the rebel POWs in Ohio who, despite their capture and ongoing military obligations to the Confederacy, refused to be exchanged. The assistant secretary of war replied, repeating the advice he had given to the Union prison commandants in June: no POW taking the oath of allegiance who would "evidently abide by it" would be exchanged. However, without any guidelines for verifying a soldier's intent to abide by his oath, the War Department's statement provided no assistance.[16]

Throughout most of 1862, Union policy did not distinguish between POWs and deserters. As long as they showed a willingness to take the oath of allegiance, they should be released and sent home or allowed to remain in the North. John J. Mudd, a Union major from Illinois, argued that doing otherwise would undermine the Union war effort. Mudd believed that paroled Confederate POWs would "at once disperse to their several homes and few of them will ever again enter the army even when exchanged." On the other hand, if exchanged, they would return to their units and, embittered by confinement, they would fight "more desperately than before, rather than surrender and go into confinement again." Mudd felt obligated to inform President Lincoln of the dangers of a straight exchange and the wisdom of sending loyal men home.

In his letter to the president, Mudd argued that the romance of war had passed away for many Southern soldiers. The inducements held out to them to enter the army, amounting almost to compulsion, were in fact baseless except the necessity of keeping their social status good at home, a goal apparently satisfied by a full year of sacrifice. Most of the soldiers Mudd saw were of the poorer classes and, he believed, represented the more conservative element of Southern society. Paroling prisoners made no sense to Mudd, and he told Lincoln, "Many men will surrender on any pretext if assured they will be paroled, and the rebels are constantly profiting by this knowledge while we reject the teachings of reason." On the other hand, if the Union released these men to civilian life, "Many homes and firesides could be reached . . . which will never be reached by any other course. I know this is not military, but although in the army I am yet a citizen, and when I see what I believe to be a great and alarming error persevered in I would prove false to my obligations as a citizen were I to fail to raise my voice in warning."[17] Mudd wrote from Jackson, Tennessee, so many of his views came from personal observations.

Mudd's reference to "social status at home" referred to the duty of Southern men to serve in the Confederate army. For some, this sense of duty may have been satisfied after a year of fighting and personal sacrifice, but men secure in their honor also needed to know they could safely return home, free from the reach of the Confederacy to which many stilled owed military service. Most of the soldiers Mudd referred to came from Kentucky and Tennessee. Aside from Bragg's ill-fated and short-lived excursion into the Bluegrass state, Kentucky enjoyed complete freedom from Confederate military law throughout the war. Tennessee remained a contested battlefield, yet some regions in the west from Memphis south to Mississippi and from Nashville north to Kentucky were no longer under Confederate control by November 1862. Some of the men Mudd referred to could return home to their families without fear of being recaptured by the Confederate army because the Union army would protect them.

Mudd identified an important military problem inherent in the exchange system. Capture in the early years of the war meant parole, a release based on promising not to fight until formally exchanged. In a contest between two sides of unequal strength, the smaller side invariably benefits more from an equal exchange of prisoners. Both Grant and Lincoln justified eliminating the prisoner exchange system in 1863–64 based, in part, on the arithmetic "teaching of reason."[18] However, the most profound aspect of Mudd's reasoning was his belief that releasing men to return home reached deeper into the South's war effort than casualties on the battlefield. Vegitius's maxim held true in nineteenth-century America: An army is hurt much more by desertion than by slaughter.

Mudd failed to understand that many of the men seeking release to return home were prisoners and not deserters. They had not voluntarily left the Confederate service, and the validity of their oath remained questionable. Their desire to return home did not override a sense of military duty, so their obligation clearly prevented them from being classified as deserters. In August 1862, the head of the Union prison at Springfield, Illinois, told William Hoffman, commissary general of prisoners in Washington, that many had recently signed the rolls to take the oath of allegiance. The Union prison official assured Hoffman that the soldiers had done so voluntarily and that no inducements had been offered them. More would have signed, but felt that they had sworn an oath to fight for the Confederacy, their term had not expired, and they could not conscientiously take the oath. The Union prison official wanted to know what to do with such men while expressing his frustration at keeping a roll of men with data "so limited, conflicting and unreliable."[19] Slowly, Union authorities understood that there was a big difference between deserters and prisoners. The requisite intent to leave the Confederate army voluntarily did not exist in the hearts and minds of many captured soldiers. They would not abandon their military duty, and releasing such men would only increase the ranks of the Confederate army.

E. H. Sutton, a private in the Twenty-fourth Georgia, confirmed the risks inherent in releasing POWs. He spent a part of the war imprisoned at Fort Henry. Sutton recalled a notice, posted soon after his arrival, that offered prisoners the opportunity to swear loyalty to the Union, join the army, and leave prison. Some men took the offer and returned to prison to influence their comrades to do the same. This accounted for the abuse oath takers received. According to Sutton, many men took the oath "just from the teeth out" to keep from starving. He remembered a biblical inscription hastily scribbled under one of the notices that was designed to discourage men from swearing allegiance: "They went out from us for they were not of us that it might be made manifest that they were not all for us." The soldier responsible for this graffiti understood his Scriptures. The passage refers to the deniers of Jesus who still called themselves Christians. It is easy to see the analogy to the deniers of the Confederacy who still called themselves Southerners. Many men believed they had sworn an oath to the Confederacy, so they would not even consider swearing loyalty to the Union until their military service expired. Some men actually took the oath, went into federal service, and were sent to North Carolina. There they deserted the service and rejoined their Confederate units at the risk of being executed if recaptured by the North. Some men who swore the oath and joined federal units were not so fortunate. In 1864, Gen. George Pickett executed twenty-two members of the Second North Carolina Infantry captured at New Bern.[20] Private Sutton confirmed what others had hesitated to believe and most Union prison authorities feared: Unlike deserters, prisoners could not be trusted.

In August 1862, efforts continued to release rebel deserters and POWs despite the problem of verification and the absence of formal guidelines from the War Department. Most of the activity involved Tennessee, but POWs from eastern prisons also lined up for release. Andrew Johnson appointed the ex-governor of Tennessee, William Campbell, as the official commissioner to visit each camp. Campbell's task was to examine and liberate qualified Tennessee POWs who met the conditions he set. Campbell would then report to the War Department those POWs he had paroled and the conditions of their release. The only conditions apparent from the correspondence came directly from Johnson, who indicated that only enlisted men could take the oath. Once Campbell approved a release, the prison camp commander had to send a list of paroled POWs to the military commander of his district and to the War Department.[21]

In the midst of this flurry of activity in Tennessee, the commissary general of prisoners halted the releasing of POWs. At the same time the War Department issued a directive on oath taking. Gen. Henry Halleck officially defined one condition of the oath that most already understood: it had to be voluntary. His order stated that no one could be forced to take the oath of allegiance against his will and that compulsory paroles of honor would also be refused. Oaths taken to avoid arrest, detention, imprisonment, or expulsion were deemed voluntary and those who then violated their oaths would be punished by law and the "usages of war." Halleck's order merely restated the obvious. It did little to clear up the confusion, and did not countermand the commissary general's order, which effectively halted Johnson's efforts to release Tennessee POWs.[22]

While the Union struggled to adopt a uniform policy, a pattern developed among the released POWs. Soldiers from Tennessee and Kentucky when released in the west went home, while many of those released in the east from such places as Fort Delaware chose to remain up north. Going south presented severe transportation problems for many soldiers, most of whom had nothing but their tattered clothing. Northern commanders had no directives detailing what if any necessities the POWs should be given upon release. Men who had been transferred to camps in Illinois and Indiana would find the journey home on foot difficult. Those who could not go home still had to get out of jail once they had taken the oath. For prisoners who remained loyal to the Southern cause, oath taking amounted to desertion. Loyal Confederate prisoners threatened their disloyal comrades with bodily injury and death.[23] Rebel officers openly condoned the harsh treatment of those who had abandoned the Confederacy. By 1864 the situation had grown so bad in some prisons that commanders had to confine those who had taken oaths to separate facilities within the same prison.[24] This helps explain why, before 1864, some men had chosen to stay north after they were released. Men from areas still under Confederate civilian and military control, such as Georgia, risked capture and execution or reenlistment in the Confederate army if they returned home. Since remaining in prison threatened their lives, most deserters had to seek refuge in the North.

Administrative problems and not a change in policy delayed the releases of

POWs and deserters. In August 1862, when the release process resumed, there was a triplicate form that had to be completed by the releasing officer, with one copy for the POW, a second copy for the commander releasing him, and the third one for the commissary general of prisoners. Hoffman asked that duplicate rolls be kept, one for him and one for the secretary of war in Washington. Upon release, each man had to get home as best he could because the Union supplied no transportation.[25] Modification of the release system provided the released soldier with documented evidence of his renewed loyalty to the Union that enabled him to avoid being harassed by Northern authorities who suspected him of being a spy or enemy soldier. If that same scrap of paper were found on his person by Confederate authorities, they had evidence of his desertion. Many men remained unwilling to return through Southern lines to their homes in communities that were still under Confederate control.

In areas under Confederate military control, Southern commanders took steps to discourage desertion. Braxton Bragg, commander of the Army of Tennessee, believed men actually straggled from the ranks in order to fall into Union hands, get paroled, and return home. Bragg issued an order in September 1862 that treated straggling as desertion. Any paroled prisoner who came under his control would be held in the army until formally exchanged and returned to active duty.[26] The Confederate legislature, realizing that desertion could severely damage the war effort, began drafting laws in August 1862 that punished AWOL officers as deserters.[27] Laws treating temporary absence as desertion, regardless of motive or intent, indicated the tenuous hold the Confederacy had on many of its soldiers and the Confederate army's desperate need for manpower. A brief respite from war could easily become a permanent discharge, and the South could ill afford losing its soldiers because of a short unauthorized trip home.

Late in 1862, the release of Confederate POWs stopped. Hoffman sent word to prison authorities and commanders in the field that no releases were to take place without authority from the secretary of war. Because rebel prisoners fell into different classifications, field commanders needed to know whom to release. At Louisville, Kentucky, Capt. Stephen E. Jones classified the various prisoners who came into the Union lines under his command. There were Confederate deserters and conscripts who had been captured but remained unwilling to be exchanged, as well as Kentuckians who had been recruited into the Confederate army after the state had been occupied but who remained in Kentucky once the South had withdrawn. The latter group, according to Jones, had only joined under the threat of conscription. Jones also had to deal with Southern civilians who had aided the Confederate army during Bragg's autumn invasion. Before Hoffman's order came from Washington, Jones would handle each case on its own merits, releasing some, sending others to prison at Camp Morton, or exchanging some at Vicksburg, Mississippi. As the prisoner population exceeded Louisville's facilities, Jones had to know how to bring release cases to the attention of the secretary of war.[28]

As with Jones, other district commanders and prison officials tried to resolve individual cases and establish some uniform policy for releasing Confederate soldiers and civilians. Questions arose as to how much discretion, if any, each commander should have in deciding whom to release or whether to release anyone. Were POWs and deserters to be considered the same? What standards or criteria, if any, were commanders to apply in determining whether a man deserved to take the oath? Field commanders advocated a lenient Union policy based on military reasoning. Capt. H. W. Freedley wrote from Indianapolis adamantly arguing for a "soft" policy in Kentucky because so many Kentuckians had served only a few days or weeks, deserted and returned home, or turned themselves over to the federal army. "All are tired and disgusted with the Rebel service and desirous of returning to their homes, taking the oath of allegiance and becoming loyal citizens." Freedley believed a lenient policy would help secure Kentucky, but if these men were sent back to the South through the exchange system, the state would become a rebel recruiting ground and "add so many more desperate men to fight against the country."[29]

The Union military governor of Kentucky, Gen. Jeremiah T. Boyle, agreed with this reasoning. He argued his position emphatically in a letter to Gen. Horatio G. Wright, the district commander of western Kentucky. Boyle feared that forcing rebel POWs back to Vicksburg for exchange converted Kentucky "into a recruiting field to fill the thinned and decimated ranks of the Rebels." By forcing these Kentucky Confederates into prison, the Union gave these men no choice but to either try to make their way south and join the Confederate army again or form irregular bands within the state, thus preying upon both the civilians and the Union in order to stay out of prison and survive. Boyle believed there were hundreds of rebel soldiers willing to desert if given the opportunity to then return home. He pleaded with Wright: "Shall all inducement to desert be withdrawn? Shall we punish for desertion from the Rebel army? Shall we announce to them that they shall have a felon's cell in our prisons or be sent to Vicksburg to a Rebel gallows?"[30]

The argument for leniency presented compelling reasons not only to free Confederate deserters but to encourage their desertion. Wright endorsed Boyle's reasoning and forwarded his letter to Gen. George Thomas. The promise of freedom eased the strain on the Union prison facilities and damaged the South's military effort. Forcing men to go South against their will virtually guaranteed their impressment back into the Confederate service.

Moreover, reneging on the apparent Union invitation to desert the rebel army could damage the Union war effort. General Rosecrans's order seemed a clear invitation to desert. He required a bond of good conduct that offered not only freedom but also protection as long as deserters faithfully observed the laws of the government and comported themselves as good citizens. Some prison officials resisted holding deserters captive in the belief that such actions held out a false hope for deserters and risked embittering those who had deserted in reliance on the Union release policy.[31]

One way that releasing prisoners and deserters damaged the Southern war effort is clear from the Southern commanders themselves. In mid-December 1862, Gen. Ulysses Grant replied to Confederate Gen. John Pemberton's claim that Grant had withheld information on the actual number and condition of Confederates captured in recent action. Grant told Pemberton that he had taken over 1,000 men, excluding the sick and stragglers, freeing most to go home after they had taken the oath.[32] The fact that Pemberton questioned Grant's numbers suggests Pemberton expected to get some of those men back. Grant's failure to exchange healthy prisoners obviously cut off a valuable source of Confederate replacements.

At the end of 1862, the War Department still had not resolved the POW/deserter problem. Stanton's department crossed a critical threshold with the pronouncement that deserters were not to be considered POWs. While POW requests would go directly to the War Department in Washington, deserters could swear allegiance and return home if the commanders in the field verified each soldier's story and believed his oath was sincere. The Union still feared that deserters might be spies, but the field commanders had to make that determination with each deserter judged individually. The death penalty for violating the oath offered some reassurance to the Union leadership, but only the factual circumstances of each case could verify whether a soldier had genuinely deserted. Therefore, <u>the deserter's story carried great weight, with the suspicion that he was lying enough to hold a man as a prisoner of war</u>. To coordinate the release of deserters in Kentucky, Maj. Gen. Gordon Granger issued General Orders No. 36: those deserters who had already returned to their homes must report to the Union authorities, be properly adjudged a deserter, and swear the oath in order to obtain their official release. Failure to report would leave deserters open to arrest as spies or to be incarcerated as POWs. Even with such efforts as Granger's, Washington's directives fell short of a comprehensive and concise policy.[33]

★ ★ ★

Union policy now distinguished between prisoners and deserters. Soldiers who had been involuntarily captured lacked the same degree of conviction to renounce the Confederate cause as those who had voluntarily left the service to seek sanctuary in the federal lines. While deserters intended to depart permanently, the men going AWOL or merely trying to get home briefly to check on family would go directly home, not surrender to the enemy. Those who never intended to return left no doubt as to their motives. This distinction casts considerable doubt on the official desertion figures. Only those going over to the Union, the men in the register, had actually demonstrated clear intent. Yet many Confederate soldiers who were captured en route to their homes were reimpressed in the service or executed. Thus it is impossible to know for certain that AWOL soldiers never intended to return.

As 1863 began, Union field commanders continued their efforts to bring uniformity to the discharge policy for Confederate deserters and POWs. Both Fredericksburg in mid-December and Stones River on New Year's Eve witnessed large battles. The bitter fighting and harsh winter that followed increased the numbers of prisoners and encouraged desertion. To clarify the confusion surrounding the oath of allegiance and to "secure uniformity of action in these particulars for the future," efforts were stepped up in Kentucky. From the Lexington headquarters, Maj. Gen. Gordon Granger issued General Orders No. 5, which emphasized the distinction between POWs and deserters: Prisoners could not take the oath and would be immediately forwarded to Vicksburg for exchange; officers could not be exchanged or paroled until further orders. Deserters had to report to Granger's headquarters for examination. Granger's new order added an additional requirement to ensure loyalty: the posting of a bond. The amount of the bond required was unclear, but still had to be "a sufficient amount with sufficient sureties" to guarantee obedience to the oath.

Granger's initiative brought uniformity within his command, but his authority extended only over the military district of central Kentucky. The bond requirement severely limited the ability of many soldiers to take the oath. Then, too, Granger's order had stated that the oath and the bond would absolve no deserter of any past offenses, particularly taking up arms against the government or serving in the military of the enemy. Therefore, despite swearing his allegiance, any soldier could be arrested, tried, and convicted for treason. Granger's order lacked the incentive of a similar order issued from Tennessee that promised protection as long as the oath was honored. Granger's order only provided an assurance against immediate arrest as a rebel soldier or spy. While serving an immediate military objective, the order failed to protect those who took the oath. It proved at best a short-term solution.[34]

While the Union grappled with its release policy to protect Confederate deserters, the South struggled to maintain its army. The threat of desertion's crippling effect on the South's war effort brought severe penalties in the field and a renewed effort to provide laws to meet the problem. Punishment in the field, although sometimes falling short of death, bordered on the inhumane. Pvt. L. B. Seymour of the Fiftieth North Carolina received a sentence that called for thirty-nine lashes on his bare back every three months until the end of the war, being branded on the left hand with the letter *D*, and doing hard labor in Richmond with ball and chain for the remainder of the war. At least ten similar sentences were handed down in late 1862 and early 1863. The civilian authorities questioned the legality of these measures. Representative Perkins from Louisiana wanted the secretary of war to explain under which rules and regulations governing the army such a harsh punishment could be meted out. Eventually such sentences were eliminated, but the Confederacy moved to limit desertion by devising other sanctions for both soldiers and civilians. The Confederate legislature passed resolutions specifying punishment for military desertion: flogging became illegal, while imprisonment and execution continued. The Confederacy also strengthened laws prosecuting civilians found guilty of aiding and abetting deserters from the army.[35]

As the South tried to discourage desertion, the overcrowding in the Union prison system elicited pleas from the district and prison commanders for discretionary authority to release prisoners as well as deserters.[36] The absence of a clear directive from the War Department threatened to destroy what little uniformity had been achieved. The commissary general of prisoners had explicitly distinguished between the treatment afforded POWs and deserters. Yet because Union commanders continued to receive contradictory information and inconsistent release policies, commanders discharged POWs who seemed willing to renounce the Confederacy by claiming that there was no specific order prohibiting them from doing so. Gen. Samuel Curtis, the Missouri Department commander, went directly to General Halleck for discretionary authority to continue releasing POWs. Halleck granted Curtis the authority to do so, although Hoffman continued to deny field commanders discretion to release POWs. Hoffman's position consistently stated that POWs were not deserters, that only deserters could be released by the local commander's discretion, and that they were on their own after their release.[37]

Hoffman believed deserters offered a certainty of conviction that POWs did not provide. To him, desertion sufficed as a guarantee that a soldier would not return to the rebel army. While Hoffman believed the release of deserters weakened the enemy, he recognized that POWs had never voluntarily left the Confederate army and might return to duty and thereby strengthen the South. Not even Confederate POWs who had claimed to be from Illinois, having traveled south for work before the war and been drafted, escaped confinement. As captured soldiers they had not voluntarily left the rebel service when the opportunity presented itself and did not provide the level of assurance that they had abandoned the Confederate army and cause. Even desertion did not always convince Hoffman that officers deserved release. He refused to allow commanders the discretion to release a single officer, even those who claimed to be deserters. Officers not only volunteered but were usually prominent leaders of the civilian community and unlikely to desert. Similar to Lincoln's Amnesty Proclamation of December 1863, which excluded Confederates deemed unworthy from taking the oath, Hoffman ordered that, even if an officer's desertion could be established, his case must nevertheless first be reviewed by his office.[38]

During the winter of 1862–63, both sides encouraged the enemy's soldiers to desert. Gen. Horatio G. Wright instructed Brigadier General White, commander of the Eastern District of Kentucky, to treat deserters with "all the leniency compatible with our own safety, it being a well established principle to weaken the enemy as much as possible by encouraging desertion among its ranks." Similarly, Confederate authorities tried to encourage desertion among Union troops and even offered to relocate deserters in Virginia as free laborers. Many of these Union deserters took jobs at the Tredegar Iron Works in Richmond, Virginia.[39]

By the summer of 1863, the Union policy toward POWs and deserters became more consistent. At the same time, Hoffman tried to address the problem that the release of deserters might not be enough. Without a safe haven, many deserters faced great danger in the South, as did POWs if they were confined with loyal Confederate prisoners in Union prisons. In June 1863, Hoffman sent Secretary Stanton a list of POWs who wanted to take the oath and be released. Hoffman indicated how these men's lives had been threatened by "the enmity of other rebel prisoners" and how they might die if they were exchanged. He resurrected an earlier suggestion that Confederates be allowed into the Union army. Such men could be released in Philadelphia if they promised to remain north until the war was over or to enlist in the U.S. army. Stanton approved the idea, and Hoffman put it into practice.

This "protection" program required the prisoner to prove he had been impressed into the Confederate army and now wanted to join the United States Army in good faith. This still amounted to a subjective judgment by the examining officer. Even without giving broad authority to release Confederate POWs, this did allow some Confederate soldiers sanctuary in the United

States Army or in the North until the end of the war. The criterion appeared to be based less on a voluntary departure from the Confederate army than on the involuntary nature of their enlistment. Aside from this program, Hoffman continued to resist efforts to approve the discretionary release of POWs by field commanders. Consistent with the War Department's instructions, Hoffman insisted that without special authorization, no Confederate POW could be released by taking the oath.[40]

Despite the confusion that allowed some department commanders discretion to release POWs, Hoffman and the War Department stayed the course. In an August 1863 letter to the commander at Fort Delaware, Hoffman established several key points. First, he repeated that commanders in the field had no discretion to release POWs who took the oath of allegiance. Second, no POW applications submitted by commanders would be accepted without good reason, which meant it "must be shown to the satisfaction of the examining officer that the applicant was forced into the rebel service against his will, and has taken advantage of the first opportunity to free himself, or it may be granted as a favor to his family or friends." The applicant's family or friends had to be loyal and willing to vouch for him. Even if the applicant had been very young and had been led into the army by someone older, his Union friends still had to guarantee his loyalty. Applications that did not meet this criteria should not be sent to the War Department, and Hoffman returned some requests with his letter. Hoffman sent similar letters to Maj. Gen. John Schofield, commander of the Department of Missouri, and Maj. Gen. William Rosecrans in the Department of the Cumberland, adding that Confederate soldiers impressed into the service could take the oath and enlist in the federal army.[41] Involuntary enlistment, coupled with voluntary departure at the first opportunity, had become the criteria for releasing POWs.

Although Hoffman's communiqués had defined the more stringent criteria for processing and releasing POWs, the overcrowded prisons and the threat posed by bands of Confederate soldiers wandering the countryside still prompted some commanders to release more POWs. Ambrose Burnside, commander of the Department of Ohio, established his own clearinghouse for POW applications. Secretary Stanton negated Burnside's order within a week and said that he would issue a directive on the discharge of POWs. Rosecrans, commander of the Department of the Cumberland, faced with a burgeoning prisoner population and the threat of Confederate deserters who were hiding in the countryside because they were afraid to surrender for fear of being exchanged, wrote Hoffman to request special authority to parole prisoners. Rosecrans unilaterally issued a general order granting his subordinates the discretion to release POWs. While his plan seemed judicious to the War Department, it went too far in its treatment of POWs and was rejected.

However, Rosecrans's concerns over pockets of Confederate deserters had merit. What he identified in Tennessee, Confederate Gen. Jubal Early experienced in Virginia a year later. After the war Early described "very large numbers of deserters from our army who had taken refuge in the mountains between the counties of Loudoun and Farquir, and the Valley, who claimed to belong to Mosby's command whenever questioned by any of our officers."[42]

The debate over POWs ended with War Department General Orders No. 286, on August 17, 1863. This order recognized that "irregularities" had occurred in the discharge of POWs because departmental and other commanders had exercised too much discretion. The order now made it clear:

1. No prisoners of war, after having been reported to the commissary general of prisoners, will be discharged except upon an order from the commissioner of exchange of prisoners, who will act under instructions from this Department.
2. All applications and recommendations for discharge will be forwarded to the commissary general of prisoners, who will indorse on each application such facts bearing on the case as may be a matter of record in his office, when the applications will be submitted for the decision of the Department through the commissioner of exchange of prisoners.
3. In general, the mere desire to be discharged upon taking the oath of allegiance will furnish no sufficient ground for such discharge; but cases where it can be shown that the prisoner was impressed into the rebel service, or which can plead in palliation extreme youth, followed by open and declared repentance, with other reasons, whatever they may be, may be specifically reported.
4. In all cases a descriptive list of those discharged will be furnished by the officer making the discharge for file in the office of the commissary general of prisoners.
5. The oath of allegiance when administered must be taken without qualification, and can in no case carry with it an exemption from any of the duties of a citizen.
   By order of the Secretary of War[43]

Although silent on the issue of deserters, the secretary of war's statement eliminated the confusion in discharging of POWs.

The commissary general of prisoners quickly wrote the secretary of war to request permission to set a uniform policy for deserters, using Rosecrans's

August 16, 1863, letter to bolster his request. Because large numbers of deserters began to come in from the West and Southwest, holding them as POWs could become costly while each case awaited War Department approval. A simple release without the oath of allegiance offered no benefit to the Union, according to Hoffman. Such a release put deserters "in a very doubtful position in which they certainly are not for us and may be against us. They have a decided advantage over their loyal neighbors, in as much as they take no part in defense of the Union and are not called upon to risk their lives in defense of their own homes." Hoffman advised Stanton to formalize the policy then in effect, allowing departmental commanders to investigate deserters and decide if they could take the oath of allegiance and reassume all the responsibilities of a loyal citizen. Hoffman further called for recording the military history of each case with the deserter's name, rank, regiment, company, circumstances of his desertion, release, and physical characteristics to be specified. This list would be forwarded by the commissary general of prisoners to the War Department. Whenever commanders released large groups at one time, the names would be sent in alphabetical order.[44] This is the list that became the register. Besides serving the reconstruction purposes of the Union administration, it provided verification of any Confederate soldier apprehended in violation of his oath.

Stanton approved Hoffman's suggestions. On August 29, 1863, Hoffman set out the policy for releasing Confederate deserters that must be followed by all commanders in all theaters. Every commander had to prepare a descriptive list of each group of released deserters. The list would remain at each departmental headquarters so that violations of an oath or conditions of discharge could be detected. A copy would be sent to the commissary general's office for entry in a comprehensive record for all departments. The purpose of recording the physical characteristics of age, height, eye color, hair color, and complexion was to distinguish men who shared the same last name, which enabled the Union to verify if any man violated his oath. Since General Orders No. 286 dictated POW releases, Hoffman enclosed a copy with his letter. By the end of September 1863, every Union departmental commander had been notified of the desertion release policy.[45]

After over a year of ad hoc administration, a comprehensive policy was finally established that distinguished clearly between prisoners and deserters. This afforded deserters an almost immediate ticket to freedom, to return home, if they chose, and if home was unsafe they could stay in the North. By late 1863, "home" had become increasingly more dangerous in the Confederacy, not only for deserters but for anyone harboring them. Given the Union's policy of requiring each deserter to make his own way home, a deserter could hardly make the journey south on foot without the assistance of Southern civilians. In December 1863, the Confederate Congress passed a law designed to prevent aiding, abetting, or encouraging desertion. Entitled "An Act to Prevent the Procuring, Aiding and Assisting of Persons to Desert from the Army of the Confederate States, and For Other Purposes," the bill stated:

> That every person not subject to the rules and articles of war who shall knowingly procure or entice a soldier, or person, enrolled for service in the army of the Confederate States to desert, or shall aid or assist any deserter from the army, or any person enrolled for service, to evade their proper commander or to prevent their arrest, to be returned to service, or shall conceal or harbour any such deserter, or shall purchase from any soldier or person enrolled for service any portion of his army equipments rations or clothing, or any property belonging to the Confederate States, or of any officer or soldier of the Confederate States, shall upon conviction before the District Court of the Confederate States having jurisdiction of the offence, be fined not exceeding $1,000 and be imprisoned not exceeding two years.[46]

Deserters released in the North who made their way home could expect no help if this law were obeyed. Transporting, feeding, or sheltering deserters was illegal. Although proving procurement of desertion presented almost insurmountable problems, this act made it a crime to encourage soldiers to come home.

As the South grew desperate to maintain the integrity of its army, the laws governing civilian conduct became more stringent. The Confederate Congress removed a legal impediment to proving the crime of aiding and abetting desertion. If the government proved a civilian helped a Confederate soldier who was recognized within the community as a deserter, that was sufficient proof that the soldier in question was a deserter. A mere rumor that Private Jones had deserted was enough to make anyone feeding, clothing, sheltering, or transporting him guilty of harboring a deserter.[47] Because execution was a standard punishment for desertion and harsh war measures were to be taken against civilians who assisted deserters, getting home was extremely difficult. If a deserter were to reach home, the area would have to be under Union occupation, or the deserter would have to be helped by individuals who were willing to break the laws of the Confederacy.

Some deserters chose to bring their wives north rather than risk the journey home. For most of the war, the Union granted passports to Southern civilians that allowed them to travel north. In September 1864, Halleck stopped this practice because so many of the Southerners who took advantage of the passport privilege turned out to be spies. However, the procedure had apparently been widely used by Confederate deserters who could not safely go home. The ability to bring their wives, mothers, and daughters north after they deserted represented an important component of the federal protection policy. One commander wrote Halleck, "With reference to passports for females to come north, I do not understand by your communication that restrictions are placed upon wives of deserters from the rebel army who may wish to join their husbands."[48]

The evolution of the Confederate laws for civilian conduct responded to a problem that worsened the longer the war lasted, just as Union policy concerning the discharge of POWs had grown more stringent. A deserter offered some assurance that he would not return to the Confederate army because he had already voluntarily left it with the intent not to return. His return meant punishment, in many cases death. Prisoners of war, on the other hand, still required officials to surmise their true intentions. The onerous requirements that a POW prove his involuntary enlistment, as vouched for by his loyal friends and neighbors, reflected the belief that POWs could not be trusted. With harsh and unpleasant conditions in most Union prisons, why not lie about one's intentions? The worst that could happen was being refused, so many took the oath and returned to the Confederate army.[49]

Another reason for treating deserters differently than POWs was that deserters could never be exchanged. From mid-1862 to late 1863, Confederate POWs could be exchanged for Union POWs under the tenuous cartel system.[50] The Union's obligation to its own POWs added force to a growing conviction that no POWs should be discharged as long as there were Union POWs waiting to be exchanged. In a letter to a Confederate prisoner who sought to take the oath and secure his release, the office of the judge advocate general explained that Union policy forbade allowing rebel prisoners of war to take the oath of allegiance so long as there were Union soldiers held captive. Securing the release of Yankees in Confederate prisons took first priority, and they could not be freed if the Union set Confederate prisoners free who, under the cartel, "constitute the only available means of effecting exchanges." The judge advocate's office admitted that by releasing rebel prisoners, "soldiers are withdrawn from rebel ranks, but this is not regarded as such a gain to our cause as is the ransom of our own tried troops from Southern prisons. There are in addition considerations of humanity involved which cannot be disregarded."[51]

The obligation to secure the release of their own POWs soon gave way to the exigencies of winning the war. By the autumn of 1864, only deserters were being released. General Grant believed, as many officers had stated, that many Confederate POWs who swore the oath returned to the South to fight her battles, just as did those who had been exchanged. Grant told Secretary Stanton, "It is through our leniency that the South expects to reap great advantage. We ought not make a single exchange or release a prisoner on any pretext until the war closes. . . . We have to fight until the military power of the South is completely exhausted, and if we release or exchange prisoners captured it simply becomes a war of exhaustion."[52] While the Union's military reconstruction policy continued to redeem deserters, it denied POWs any promise of reconstruction until the war had ended.

Grant believed that desertion by the enemy should be both encouraged and rewarded. In August 1864, he issued Circular No. 31, which stated that rebel deserters could not be enrolled, drafted, used as substitutes, or otherwise recruited into the United States Army. As the Petersburg siege continued, Grant rewarded Confederate deserters with freedom, subsistence, and transportation home if they lived within Union lines. He also found work for them in the quartermaster departments. Deserters bringing in arms, mules, horses, or any other property were paid the highest price available in Union currency. Southern civilians who were railroad conductors, engineers, boiler operators, mechanics, or telegraph operators, as well as anyone employed by the Confederate authorities, could come into the Union lines and receive the same benefits as those offered to military deserters.[53] The Union policy not only redeemed former rebels but made them vital parts in the North's war machine.

During the course of the war, the Union policies toward deserters and POWs had moved in different directions. Prisoners of war went from a status of being almost on equal footing with deserters to soldiers who were doomed to confinement until war's end. Desertion at the outset of the war, although seen as a benefit to the Union effort, gradually became another weapon of war. From a policy that left them on their own from the moment of their release, the Union began providing monetary inducements and transportation home in an effort to undermine the Southern war effort. The Union's desertion inducements reached Confederate soldiers through circulars and notices, delivered to their own pickets, that promised indefinite parole and free transportation home.[54] Transportation was an important inducement. It hastened a man's return home and prevented his having to endanger civilians in reaching his destination. In addition, because the Union could only transport a man as far as it had occupied Southern territory, anyone transported home need not fear Confederate military retribution. While the war was going on, the North could "seed" occupied areas in the South with reconstructed soldiers, who might make the transition of its civilian population easier once the war had come to an end.

The opportunity to escape military obligation would prove critical to the Georgia desertion experience. In the later stages of the war, another pull from home came, but it did not include freedom from one's military obligations and could not be accomplished by deserting to the enemy. The disobedience of individuals represented only one aspect of Confederate desertion. Led by Gov. Joseph Brown, Georgia subordinated the Confederate cause to its own needs. On August 13, 1864, Gen. G. W. Smith, commander of the First Georgia Militia, then attached to the Army of Tennessee, wrote Brown challenging his authority to interfere with the Confederate army. Smith discovered Brown had detailed approximately one hundred officers from his division to return to Georgia and organize the most recent militia call. Smith learned that after completing their organizational duties, these men had subsequently been reassigned to return to their home counties permanently and organize local police forces. Smith conceded he had no control over who came into the army, but once there, he insisted that Brown no longer had the power to countermand his orders. With Atlanta threatened, Smith demanded that no one be taken from the city's defenses: "If the domestic, industrial and social interests of the people and society are endangered by continued service of those called out, it is better to return them in a body, than ruin their efficiency by details."[55]

Governor Brown apparently grew bolder the longer the war lasted. Georgia laws passed in 1865 withdrew men from the Confederate army so they could return and defend the state. By March 1865 Confederate authorities declared Georgia to be in a virtual state of insurrection. With the Confederate army in Tennessee, civilian authorities no longer enforced Confederate laws. However, the men answering the state government's call still had to get home on their own; even on the brink of destruction, Southern roads remained unsafe for deserters.[56] With growing Union control of the South, deserters enjoyed the benefits of transportation that reached further and further into the South. Not only were deserters returning home, sworn to uphold and defend the Union, but in some cases they returned to states and communities more disposed toward reconstruction.

To fight the disintegration of the Confederate army, Gen. James Longstreet suggested issuing orders that warned local military authorities not to take Georgians into their ranks at risk of punishment for procuring or harboring deserters. Longstreet, himself a Georgian, had information that civilians and local authorities wrote to Georgia soldiers in his command to recruit them for local units. He blamed the Georgia desertions on these invitations.

Yet, in light of the Union desertion policy, this seems improbable for several reasons. First, the register reveals that most Georgia desertions to the enemy occurred in 1864. Second, return to a local unit meant one still had to fight somewhere in Georgia. Third, the journey home offered little safety because the Confederate army in Virginia continued to patrol the countryside for deserters. Although Longstreet insisted these men went home, he did not know what route they took. The safest route south went through the Union lines after taking the oath, as many Georgians had discovered. Desertion appealed to men who were weary of fighting and anxious to return home safely.[57]

The Union wartime reconstruction policy lacked the ability to reorganize and transform entire states or regions within them, but the significance of the military effort should not be underestimated. The register lists the names of over 35,000 Confederate deserters to the Union. These men represented citizens from every Confederate state. During a period when President Lincoln and the U.S. Congress grappled with the question of Southern reconstruction, the Union desertion program actually brought Southerners back into the fold, and eventually sent many home to lead communities in postwar reconstruction. Although Lincoln's personal beliefs on reconstruction do not appear in this program in the same way as his proclamation of December 8, 1863, it could not have survived and developed without his approval. Lincoln's penchant for delegation and his willingness to allow his various department heads and military officers to operate free of interference from him did not extend to fundamental principles. Early in the war the president did not hesitate to squelch any notion of slave emancipation while the loyalty of the border states remained in question. Both John C. Fremont and David Hunter received polite but swift rebukes for suggesting immediate emancipation of slaves in military districts under their command early in the war.[58] The reconstruction of the South also proved central to Lincoln's overall vision of the war. His proposing a wartime civilian reconstruction plan demonstrated the importance he attached to reconstructing the South in his own way. This military policy that allowed for the return to the Union of Southern deserters fit neatly within Lincoln's subsequent proclamation so as to provide a solid beginning for what he hoped would be an amicable reunification of the entire South after the war.

Pvt. Thaddeus Oliver of the Second Georgia Infantry knew the lonely vigil of picket duty. Serving in General Lee's Army of Northern Virginia, far from his home in Marion County, Georgia, Oliver must have spent countless lonely nights thinking of those he had left behind and questioning his decision to fight. He wrote of his loneliness and familial concerns in a short poem:

> There is only the sound of the lone sentry's tread
> As he tramps from the rock to the fountain
> and thinks of the two in the low trundle bed
> far away in the cot on the mountain
> his musket falls slack—his face dark and grim,
> grows gentle with memories tender
> as he mutters a prayer for his children asleep
> for their mother, may heaven defend her[59]

Oliver was not alone in his thoughts of home as 1863 neared its bloody end. An entire army began to bed down for the winter in northern Georgia. It was an army full of Georgians, many of whom had not seen home for years and whose instincts told them that neither heaven nor the Confederacy would defend the mothers of their children. For these men, the time had come to make a choice, and the openness of the Union lines made the choice much easier for the South's sons. Still, these men did not take desertion lightly. Their choice stemmed from the needs of home and family that grew out of economic and cultural factors peculiar to Georgia. These differences had developed in the decades before the war and made these men susceptible to desertion when their duty to the Confederacy came in conflict with the duty they owed to their home.

CHAPTER THREE

Patterns of Flight

In March 1864, nine men of the Georgia State Line from Lumpkin, Hall, and Marion Counties faced a court-martial on the charge of desertion. They stood accused of leaving their camp at Resaca, Georgia, with the intent to desert to the enemy. In addition to the contents of their haversacks and the admissions they had made to fellow soldiers, the evidence against them included a letter one man, F. E. Franklin, had written to his brother. The letter discussed a plan conceived by Franklin, his brother, and seven others to "slip away" and desert to the Yankees. It is unclear why Franklin would have written to his brother if both were in the same unit; however, the records reflect that some of the men had actually gone home legally, and the letter may have been written while the two men were apart. In the letter, Franklin cautioned his brother against moving too soon and suggested that they wait for Sherman to push the Confederate army back into Georgia. By waiting, argued Franklin, their chance of success improved vastly because the closeness of the two armies would make it easier to slip quietly into the Union lines. Franklin failed to convince his brother or to heed his own advice. Swayed by his brother's zeal or the opinions of the rest of the group, who insisted on going immediately, Franklin joined in the scheme. Not one of the nine men made it to the Union lines. Despite the letter, none were convicted of deserting to the enemy, although all nine were found guilty of unauthorized absence. One of their party, Pvt. Francis C. Tumlin of Hall County, the apparent ringleader, received a sentence dismissing him from his Georgia unit and reassigning him to a unit as far from Georgia and Hall County as possible.[1]

The court-martial of the nine soldiers represents only one example of Georgians who tried to desert to the enemy. This scheme failed, but others succeeded throughout the year. The Register of Confederate Deserters, compiled by the Union army, documents thousands of soldiers who deserted to the Union army. The register demonstrates a clear pattern among Georgia troops from late 1863 to the end of 1864. As the war-weary Confederate army withdrew southward through Georgia and passed an equally distraught civilian population, Georgia soldiers deserted into the Union lines, took the U.S. oath of allegiance, and went home. The newspapers and correspondence of the period reveal incidences of desertion, but Georgia's overall desertion pattern appears only faintly in these contemporary accounts. The Union register reflects a smaller number than traditional desertion claims, but provides a clearer picture of what happened. The register establishes a detailed pattern only hinted at by other sources.

Before describing the pattern of Georgia desertion, an important aspect of the Union record of deserters to the enemy requires explanation and analysis. The register provided a column that identified the date and place a man deserted, but that information actually appears in only a handful of cases. Therefore, it becomes essential to determine whether the releases during 1864 reflected desertions during that same time, men deserting much earlier and turning themselves over to the Union authorities in 1864, or men deserting who quickly reached the Union lines but waited to take the oath. Because the desertion pattern is based on the dates these men took the oath and secured their release, it is important to have some idea of the lag time, the period that elapsed between desertion and oath taking.

For most deserters to the enemy, the lag time cannot be determined with certainty. Some of the earliest deserters from Georgia, those listed in the register as deserting and taking the oath before December 1863, include the date of their desertion in addition to the date of their release. Those entries show the two events occurred within days of one another. However, as Confederate desertion increased, the lag time is harder to define. A longer lag time may have resulted from the volume of deserters requiring more time for the Union departmental commanders to verify a soldier's desertion claim. The evaluation period created a gap between the date of desertion and date of release. The picture becomes clearer when comparing the data in the register with information from several other sources.

The postwar muster rolls for Company D of Lumpkin County, Fifty-second Georgia Volunteer Infantry, show that Pvt. J. H. McBrayer and Pvt. W. E. McBrayer enlisted March 4, 1862, deserted from Dalton, Georgia, on December 16, 1863, took the oath, and secured their release in Chattanooga on March 1, 1864. The register lists J. H. as Jesse H. McBrayer and W. E. as William E. McBrayer from Lumpkin County and confirms their release date of March 1, 1864. If both passed into the Union lines almost immediately after deserting, then three months elapsed between desertion and release. However, it is possible that after deserting they hid from the Confederate authorities and then made their way into the Union lines when they felt safe. If so, their release may have come very soon after they surrendered to Union authorities. While there is no way to be certain, it is clear that the McBrayers deserted in late 1863, and even with a three-month lag time, they fall squarely into the 1864 desertion pattern reflected in the register.

The McBrayers appear as deserters in both the register and the muster rolls. Some men identified by the register as deserters appear in the muster rolls only as absent without leave (AWOL). These soldiers present a problem because some were never tracked after being reported absent. The roll for Company C of the Fifty-second Georgia lists Pvt. Decatur Stansell, of Lumpkin County, as AWOL from October 1, 1863. The register lists a Pvt. Cader Stancell, from Lumpkin County. Despite the difference in spelling, the phonetic pronunciation makes it very likely that this is the same man. According to the register, Stansell (or Stancell) took the oath and secured his release on April 5, 1864. The roll indicates his unit never declared him a deserter. He may actually have returned to his unit after the Battle of Chickamauga in September 1863, with no record having been made of his return, and then chosen to desert sometime after October 1, 1863. Because the muster roll itself was created after the war, based on the data available, it is impossible to know how much time elapsed between Stansell's desertion from the Confederate service, his surrender to the Union authorities, and his release. Robert Hodge, a thirty-year-old private from Catoosa County, appears as AWOL on October 2, 1863, one day after Stansell. The register lists him as taking the oath of allegiance on December 22, 1863. His lag time is one-third of Stansell's.[2] However, like the McBrayers, Stansell and Hodge fall within the late 1863–64 desertion pattern. They left the service in late 1863 and secured their releases between December 1863 and May 1864. At worst, the muster rolls reflect an earlier beginning to the desertion wave, perhaps even immediately after Chickamauga.

Benjamin F. Cain of Company C, Fifty-second Georgia Infantry, presents a different case. Private Cain was taken prisoner by the Union in July 1863, presumably at Vicksburg, paroled on July 8, 1863, and formally exchanged on October 8, 1863. His unit's postwar muster roll claims he took the oath of allegiance to the U.S. government on February 27, 1864, and was released at Chattanooga, Tennessee. The register confirms Cain's name, unit, and release date. The muster roll shows no indication of his being AWOL or having deserted, yet the register shows that he deserted sometime before February 27, 1864. Cain's comrades, William C. Woody and James Grindle, followed the exact same path but did not take the oath until April 4, 1864, and April 13, 1864, respectively. Yet, like Cain, they were exchanged on October 8, 1863, with no subsequent indication that they deserted or went AWOL thereafter. These exchanges may reflect unilateral exchanges by the Confederate army. The cartel system was in the process of total collapse due to the position taken by the Confederate army with regard to black prisoners. The

South's release of prisoners outside the agreed-upon conditions hastened the demise of the cartel system of exchange. Correspondence in November 1863 indicates that Robert Ould, the Confederate agent for the Cartel prisoner exchanges, unilaterally released Confederate prisoners from their paroles. These men may fall into that group. Although improperly released and "put into the field to fight against Federal troops," the Union's belief that they had been improperly returned to the ranks does not alter the fact that as to the South they were nevertheless treated as deserters.[3]

Although Cain, Grindle, and Woody all deserted sometime after their exchange, these men may actually have been at home and refused to return to their units when notified of their exchange. Fearing they would be forced back into service, they deserted and made their way to the Union lines. However, given Braxton Bragg's order in September 1862 requiring paroled prisoners to remain in camp, the more likely case is that, after being formally exchanged, they stepped back into active duty and then deserted. Why they do not appear in the muster rolls as deserters or AWOL remains unclear.

Lag time can be analyzed by looking at men who tried but failed to desert to the Union. The court-martial records of one man attempting to desert to the enemy in March 1864 reveal that after ten days he returned voluntarily. He was tried for desertion and acquitted but found guilty of being AWOL. The records do not reflect why he did not make it to the Union lines. Another soldier's experience revealed that he hid in the hope that the Union would move through the area and he could safely come forth. However, he also failed to make it to the Union lines and was subsequently apprehended by the Confederate authorities.[4]

The presence of Confederate military authority may have shortened the period between desertion and surrender to the Union. Many north Georgia citizens openly criticized the Confederate cause. By the winter of 1862–63, reports indicated that a large number of "Tories," citizens loyal to the Union, lived in north Georgia. These reports also indicated increasing numbers of deserters from the Confederate army running freely in the mountains of north Georgia and the upper Piedmont. The reports do not identify them as Georgia soldiers, just as deserters. It is possible they were from East Tennessee counties or counties in Tennessee bordering Georgia. However, the significance for Georgia lies in Gov. Joseph Brown's wartime effort to organize statewide military units. These units, working in conjunction with Confederate army regulars, spent 1863 sweeping through the north Georgia mountains and upper Piedmont regions searching for pockets of citizen disloyalty and bands of deserters. In all, they arrested 53 citizens and returned about 500 conscription-aged men to the service.[5]

The government's effort to hunt down deserters meant that most men who deserted from camps in Georgia may have moved to the Union lines as quickly as possible. The likelihood that a soldier could escape into the mountains seems good. However, as the military operation of 1862–63 indicates, an escapee could not safely remain there indefinitely. By late 1863, the only safe place for deserters was the Union lines. Until the Union gained control of the region, escape into the mountains offered no guarantee of continued safety. Not only did the Confederate military authorities create a safety risk, but deserters also had to avoid Confederate vigilante groups. These irregulars preyed upon Union sympathizers and did not hesitate to pursue Confederate army deserters. Between the Battle of Chickamauga and Sherman's Atlanta campaign, three such bands roamed Walker, Dade, Chattooga, Floyd, Whitfield, Catoosa, and Murray Counties, in addition to parts of Tennessee and northern Alabama. The most notorious was a band led by a man named Gatewood.[6] These bands made it dangerous to desert or to be presumed a deserter. They also made it difficult to travel openly, requiring more time for those who deserted before May 1864 to travel through Confederate-held territory to the Union lines.

Many citizens in such northern countries as Lumpkin remained loyal to the Confederacy. There were examples of civilians and deserters tried by civilian authorities in 1863 for treason or disloyalty. The bloodiest example occurred in Elijay, Georgia, sixty miles northeast of Dalton, after loyal Confederate civilians captured a group of former Confederate soldiers. Although these ex-soldiers had formed a local unit, the Walker County Guards, to protect their homes, the Confederate loyalists shot or hanged one hundred of them as traitors.[7]

The presence of Confederate military, irregular, and civilian authority sheds some light on the gap between desertion and release. While one could use the mountains as a place of refuge, such respite was short-lived. However, one could not risk the speed of open travel because Confederate authorities remained in place. Therefore, the appearance of lengthy gap periods, some as long as three months, may reflect longer travel time between desertion and reaching Union lines, with release occurring quickly after entering the Union lines. Later in 1864, when the Union lines lay just across the battlefield, the travel time could be minutes. The release dates of men who deserted to the Union after the Atlanta campaign began to reflect gap periods of only a few days. Although the federal release program began months before Sherman's Atlanta campaign, the actual invasion of Georgia decreased the lag time significantly. The journey from Confederate to Union lines was made much shorter without the Confederate authorities slowing a deserter or subsequently apprehending him after he returned home.

One final way to examine lag time is to look at prisoners of war who experienced federal efforts to encourage their desertion. William Sylvester Dillon, a private in the Fourth Tennessee Volunteers, kept a diary while imprisoned from October 23, 1863, to March 9, 1865. He reluctantly placed his name on the roll of those willing to take the oath after receiving news from home that his father had died. He applied to take the oath May 1, 1864, and his diary indicates he received a letter from his brother releasing him from any obligation at home on July 5, 1864. When he removed his name from the application, his file had not been acted upon by the War Department. There is no indication from his diary that the two-month period was inordinately long.[8] Unlike Dillon, James Blackwell, a private in the Fifty-second Georgia, was captured May 20, 1864, and he secured his release from Rock Island, Illinois, on June 20, 1864, by joining the U.S. navy. Only a month elapsed between his capture and release because the circumstances made his intentions clear. By joining the navy, he demonstrated that he never intended to return to the Confederate service.[9] Deserters provided a similar degree of assurance, although obviously not the same as physically remaining in Union custody. However, the Union policy allowing field commanders to authorize releases in the interest of expediency makes one month between desertion and release a good estimate of the lag time. A deserter's wait would be more akin to Blackwell's than Dillon's.

On March 29, 1864, Thomas Sharp, a Walker County boy, was captured while returning to duty from his north Georgia home. His diary entry reveals that his captors immediately offered him the opportunity to take the oath of allegiance and go home. Sharp declined by saying that he had not deserted. The Union soldiers immediately treated him as a prisoner of war and sent him north, where he remained until at least November 17, 1864, when his diary entries stop. Sharp's experience raises the possibility that the lapse between desertion and release may not reflect delay by Union forces but the time needed for deserters to make their way through the mountains and Confederate lines to the enemy. The quickness with which Sharp was offered the opportunity to take the oath indicates that the Union swiftly disposed of any men who could prove they had deserted and who willingly took the oath.[10]

Union
treatment

Before Sherman's Atlanta campaign in 1864, deserters to the enemy may not have had the luxury of going directly into Union lines because their winter camp was inside Georgia and the Union army remained in Tennessee. After Sherman's Atlanta campaign began, a soldier might easily slip several hundred yards across the battlefield after dark and be within the Union positions minutes after deserting the Confederate army. Therefore, even with the un-

TABLE 2. TOTAL DESERTERS TO THE ENEMY BY MONTH, DECEMBER 1863–1864

	Number	*Percentage*
December 1863	96	3.1
January 1864	269	8.9
February 1864	405	13.4
March 1864	349	11.5
April 1864	246	8.1
May 1864	234	7.7
June 1864	294	9.8
July 1864	356	11.8
August 1864	260	8.7
September 1864	220	7.3
October 1864	93	3.0
November 1864	86	2.9
December 1864	106	3.6
Total	3,014	100.0

certainty of the lag time, those shown in the register as taking the oath in 1864 must have actually deserted shortly before their release.

The register identifies 3,368 Georgia soldiers who deserted the Confederate army and sought sanctuary in the Union lines.[11] The Union finalized its procedures for releasing prisoners and deserters, and the first entries in the register show the first Confederate deserters took the oath of allegiance and securing their release in late August and early September 1863.[12] From September through November, only seven Georgia soldiers appear in the record.[13] Beginning in December 1863, the numbers escalate dramatically (see table 2). Of the 3,368 Georgians who took the oath of allegiance and deserted to the enemy, 90.59 percent of them did so between December 1, 1863, and December 31, 1864. This figure is significant: of the 354 men who deserted and took the oath after January 1, 1865, only 161 did so before the end of the war; the remaining 193 swore the oath of allegiance after Lee's surrender on April 9, 1865. Even if deserters to the enemy did not constitute the majority of Georgia's deserters, these numbers alone demonstrate that Georgia desertion did not reflect traditional notions of mass desertion in 1865 around Petersburg fueled by the belief in Lee's eminent defeat. The data also strongly suggest that Georgia desertion did not follow the patterns for Alabama, which occurred in three long waves beginning in 1862 and running through 1864. The figures for Georgians deserting to the enemy reflect a desertion pattern driven by where the Confederate army was situated, Sher-

Nature of pattern

man's unyielding advance to Atlanta, and the needs of soldiers' families growing desperate by 1864. Contrary to Ella Lonn's conclusions, Georgia's desertion escalated after December 1863 and actually began to taper off in the fall of 1864.[14]

What happened in December 1863 that started this yearlong exodus from the Confederate army? On November 28, 1863, Sgt. I. V. Moore of the Thirty-seventh Georgia Infantry, Army of Tennessee, noted in his diary that his unit had made camp at Dalton, Georgia. For almost three months, the Thirty-seventh Georgia lay idle in winter camp, roused only in late February 1864 by a Union reconnaissance into Georgia.[15] By this time most Georgia soldiers, including those in the Army of Tennessee, had been at war almost two years and many had seen neither their home nor their family for nearly three years. In late 1863 Georgia's sons, brothers, and fathers had finally come home, camping just across the Tennessee border on their native soil.

The steady Confederate withdrawal through middle and East Tennessee took place in the summer of 1863 during the Tullahoma campaign. Although briefly interrupted by a victory at Chickamauga Creek in mid-September 1863, Gen. Braxton Bragg's "Fabian"-like retreat came to an end when Grant broke the siege at Chattanooga, forcing the Confederates into Georgia. The regimental history of the Forty-second Georgia, of Hood's and later Stewart's Corps, claims the unit fought in twenty-two battles from Tazzwell to Bentonville, including Vicksburg, the Atlanta campaign, and eventually the Nashville campaign.[16] For those hardened and weary veterans, the lure of home proved overwhelming. Pvt. P. D. Stephenson, Fifth Company, Washington Artillery, described the Army of Tennessee as it arrived in Dalton shortly after Bragg resigned. "Our sufferings were such as we had never known before, for the winter was upon us with all its rigor," wrote Stephenson. The weary soldiers of the Army of Tennessee knew they had suffered a severe blow to "the cause we fought for" and acted "as a body ignominiously." Somehow, though, Stephenson and his comrades knew that defeat had not come from a lack of devotion on their part, and they felt undeserving "of the stigma which the whole country would certainly put on us." Nevertheless, the army was in a state of "reckless despair" when Johnston arrived.[17] Stephenson spoke of the Confederate loss at Missionary Ridge and the army's retreat into Georgia. These men had fought hard but had nothing to show for their efforts. For many of them, December 1863 marked their first opportunity to desert and go home.[18]

Dalton, the site of the Army of Tennessee's winter quarters, lies at the center of Whitfield County. Whitfield is in the very heart of upcountry Georgia and borders Catoosa, Murray, Gordon, Walker, and Chattooga Counties. Together with Dade County in extreme northwest Georgia, these seven counties accounted for 1,105 of the deserters who were listed in the register, or 33 percent of Georgia's deserters to the Union (see map 2). Of that number, over half deserted and took the oath before May 1864. The numbers from Catoosa, Chattooga, Whitfield, and Walker Counties are significant. In these four counties, over 50 percent of the county's total desertion to the enemy occurred during winter camp, before Sherman's invasion. Of the western Upcountry counties, only Gordon County experienced significantly less than 50 percent of its desertion during the months preceding Sherman's invasion. Observations by soldiers confirm the register's numbers. In late January 1864, Sgt. James L. Tucker of the Thirty-seventh Alabama wrote home from his camp at Dalton, Georgia: "They are enforcing the law to the full extent on the deserters and absentees. We have had it published in one address parade the names of several who are to be shot and punishment too tedious to be mentioned."

The desertion pattern described by the register (see table 2) indicates that 1,365 of Georgia's total deserters to the enemy, roughly 39 percent, deserted to the enemy between December 1863 and April 30, 1864. Over 41 percent of the men deserting in this period came from Whitfield County, where the Army of Tennessee camped for the winter, or one of the other six western Upcountry counties. Proximity seems to have provided sufficient inducement for many soldiers to risk the journey from their lines to the Union camps. Although the location of winter quarters by itself does not explain the entire story, it provides clear evidence that being so near home contributed to the yearlong desertion wave.

The register lists the regiments of the deserters, and over two hundred units are represented. Most are either in the Army of Northern Virginia or the Army of Tennessee. In some instances, the deserter identified his unit only by the commander's name or by the local name given to the unit when it initially formed. These units could be traced through a list of field officers, but none were among the list of high desertion units. Of the 3,368 Georgia deserters to the enemy, more than half, 1,709, belong to twenty regiments, all of which were in the Army of Tennessee. Not only did Johnston's army have higher overall desertion numbers than any other Confederate army listed in the register but the individual units with the highest rate of desertion all belonged to the Army of Tennessee.

Regiments were supposed to have 1,000 soldiers. By late 1863 most regiments were fortunate to have five hundred men able to fight. The desertion among regiments from the Army of Tennessee reinforces the importance of proximity. Only twenty-two regiments had more than twenty deserters to the enemy. Of those with over fifty deserters, all but one was from the Army of Tennessee or came from a cavalry unit that, although not officially attached

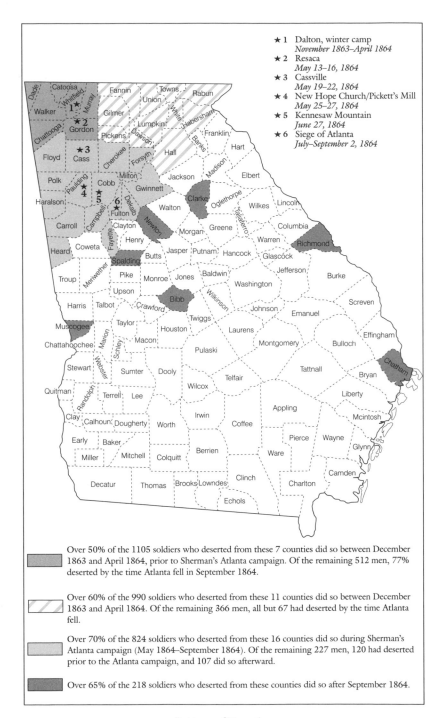

★ 1   Dalton, winter camp
      November 1863–April 1864
★ 2   Resaca
      May 13–16, 1864
★ 3   Cassville
      May 19–22, 1864
★ 4   New Hope Church/Pickett's Mill
      May 25–27, 1864
★ 5   Kennesaw Mountain
      June 27, 1864
★ 6   Siege of Atlanta
      July–September 2, 1864

Over 50% of the 1105 soldiers who deserted from these 7 counties did so between December 1863 and April 1864, prior to Sherman's Atlanta campaign. Of the remaining 512 men, 77% deserted by the time Atlanta fell in September 1864.

Over 60% of the 990 soldiers who deserted from these 11 counties did so between December 1863 and April 1864. Of the remaining 366 men, all but 67 had deserted by the time Atlanta fell.

Over 70% of the 824 soldiers who deserted from these 16 counties did so during Sherman's Atlanta campaign (May 1864–September 1864). Of the remaining 227 men, 120 had deserted prior to the Atlanta campaign, and 107 did so afterward.

Over 65% of the 218 soldiers who deserted from these counties did so after September 1864.

Patterns of Desertion

TABLE 3. HIGH DESERTION UNITS

Unit	Number of deserters	Army/Theater
39th GA Inf.	233	Army of Tennessee
36th GA Inf.	184	Army of Tennessee
1st GA Inf.	163	Army of Tennessee
40th GA Inf.	125	Army of Tennessee
8th GA Batt.	106	Army of Tennessee
4th GA Cav.	105	Tennessee
6th GA Cav.	92	Tennessee
43d GA Inf.	91	Army of Tennessee
52d GA Inf.	86	Army of Tennessee
65th GA Inf.	83	Army of Tennessee
56th GA Inf.	81	Army of Tennessee
3d GA Cav.	64	Tennessee
11th GA Inf.	55	Army of Northern Virginia
34th GA Inf.	53	Army of Tennessee
1st GA Cav.	46	Tennessee
60th GA Inf.	45	Army of Northern Virginia
42d GA Inf.	42	Army of Tennessee
30th GA Inf.	41	Army of Tennessee
41st GA Inf.	40	Army of Tennessee
23d GA Inf.	30	Army of Tennessee
37th GA Inf.	23	Army of Tennessee
63d GA Inf.	21	Army of Tennessee
Total	1,809	

to that army, fought with it in Tennessee. More important, these units comprised soldiers from upcountry Georgia counties. The Thirty-ninth Georgia Infantry had 233 men desert to the enemy. Every company in the regiment was from either Murray, Whitfield, Dade, Walker, or Catoosa Counties, the very heart of the western Upcountry. The Thirty-sixth Georgia Infantry had the second highest number of deserters to the enemy with 184. The twelve companies that made up the Thirty-sixth came from Cherokee, Pickens, and Whitfield Counties in the Upcountry and Bartow, DeKalb, and Gwinnett Counties in the upper Piedmont.[19]

Table 3 is a list of the regiments with twenty or more deserters to the enemy. Only six regiments had more than one hundred deserters and only one had more than two hundred. However, the total number of deserters for each unit reflects deserters from regiments already badly depleted by battlefield losses and disease. The overwhelming number from regiments within the Army of Tennessee, made up of men from north Georgia, reflects the importance of proximity to Georgia's desertion pattern.

Aside from these units, only the Rossville Battery had as many as twenty deserters, but it was not listed in the roster of Georgia Infantry units or the *Official Records*.[20] An exception to the concentration of deserters in the Army of Tennessee was the one hundred deserters to the enemy who came from two units of the Army of Northern Virginia. Despite serving in the east, both units shared the regional similarity of the Georgia units fighting in the West: they were formed predominately from Upcountry counties. The Eleventh Georgia had fifty-five deserters to the enemy. Of the ten companies that made up the Eleventh Georgia, six were from the heart of the Upcountry. Fifteen of the fifty-five deserters from the unit were from Gilmer County and twelve were from Fannin County. Not only were many of its soldiers from the Upcountry but the Eleventh served in General Longstreet's Corps and returned to Georgia in September 1863. Longstreet left Georgia in November 1863, but remained in East Tennessee for part of the winter. By January 1864, East Tennessee was firmly under Union control, providing those Georgians in Longstreet's Corps with the opportunity to slip into the Union lines.[21] Likewise, the Sixtieth had twelve companies, and half were formed from Upcountry counties. Of the other six, two were from Bartow and Paulding, counties in the upper Piedmont.[22] Although these men fought in Virginia, soldiers from north Georgia may have taken advantage of the safe passage that came with deserting to the enemy and taking the oath of allegiance. When the situation at home reached intolerable levels, not even distance kept many of these men from deserting. However, for those units in the Army of Tennessee camped in north Georgia, distance posed no such problem.

The relationship between the Army of Tennessee's return to Georgia and the subsequent desertion of Georgian troops may not have surprised the Confederate high command. Its polices aimed at keeping soldiers away from home may have actually contributed to the desertion rate. For most of the war, the military leadership believed that if Georgians made it home, they might not come back. This connection between being home and desertion can be understood by examining the Confederate furlough policy.

Furloughs were the passes allowing soldiers to return home for a brief stay or to otherwise leave their units with permission. The evolution of the Confederate furlough policy demonstrated a fear among Confederate authorities that a short respite in Georgia might turn into a permanent stay. Furloughs proved increasingly more difficult for Georgia soldiers to obtain. Commanders understood that furloughs served an important purpose, and many had actually been allocated to officers until early 1862. In a letter to Col. Paul J. Semmes, regimental commander of the Tenth Georgia, Maj. Jasper Whiting, assistant adjutant general, outlined a plan for granting furloughs to those who enlisted for a year. He indicated that furloughs would be issued to both privates and officers, with officers receiving fewer because they had already received more than their numbers allowed.[23] The desire to provide Georgians with a much deserved home visit proved secondary to the greater concern of keeping the army intact.

Soldiers wrote home repeatedly to complain that furloughs were impossible to get. A. J. Rees, a private in Phillips Legion, could not get a furlough to go from South Carolina to Georgia. Solomon Harper of the Seventh Georgia wrote his parents suggesting they try to secure a work detail for him because he could get no furlough. Henry Jackson, Third Georgia Infantry, broke the news to his cousins: "I expect to remain here until the war ends if I should live for I think my chances for a furlow is a bad one unless I get wounded or sick in the hospital." His chances of getting home grew worse because "I expect to witness a scene in a few days that I have by no means ever desired that is the shooting of two of our regiment of Co. E."[24] Enlistment bound Confederate soldiers for the duration of the war. Not only could the men not get furloughs but, as Jackson described, the death penalty discouraged desertion.

Even when furloughs became available in 1863, Georgia soldiers seldom got home. Thomas Howard wrote his wife, "I think of you and my little ones at home and wonder if I will ever be permitted to see you. It is time some of the boys are at home on furlough and if we stay here some more may get off but before my time will come they will stop granting them." Howard's fears became reality, as a soldier had to tell his loved one, "If I do not get sick or wounded I will not get home any more until the war ends."[25] Furloughs resumed in 1864 but ended in the spring, when heavy campaigning began. When the practice resumed again in August, only 2 percent of the men could obtain furloughs. For Georgians in Virginia, furloughs were worthless because transportation went only as far south as Petersburg, Virginia.[26]

What had to be most distressing for Georgia soldiers was watching men from Virginia receive leave to go home when they were denied such privileges. In a letter to his wife in October 1862, Samuel J. G. Brewer lamented that "the boys that are doing guard duty here in Danville, Virginia are getting furloughs everyday to visit their friends but they say I live too far to go." He went on: "I have as much right to it as anybody for I cannot help living so far away and home has as much or as many enticements for me as theirs have for them, but I am detained on this very ground."[27]

Evidence that the desertion pattern in the register accurately reflects Georgia's desertion pattern came in December 1864 from Gen. Robert E. Lee. John A. Johnson, a soldier from Coweta County, Georgia, wrote his fiancée in December 1864, in reference to his father's death. Her reply to him has not survived, but she obviously wanted him to come home. Johnson told her, "Lee has ordered no more furloughs for Georgia troops" and "the Georgians here are not well pleased with the way in which Georgia has been treated." Johnson added that had such an order been issued to Virginia troops, it would not have been very well received.[28] Given the large number of desertions recorded in the register during 1864, Lee had little choice.

The Confederate general's order appears to have been a reaction to circumstances. Having observed what had happened in Georgia in 1864, he concluded that his thirty regiments of Georgia infantry could not be allowed near home if he was to keep the Army of Northern Virginia intact. The register shows how few Georgians hesitated to leave once they got close to home. The correspondence between soldiers and their homes further supports Lee's convictions. As early as 1862, one Georgian who had just returned from a furlough wrote his wife that he was ready to "go over the hill" to get home again.[29]

By late 1863, the Upcountry men camped in north Georgia needed no furloughs. With the Union facilitating desertion and the Confederacy trying to prevent it, being camped in Georgia proved devastating to Johnston's army. By December 1864, Lee knew what happened in Georgia. Unable to control matters in the West, he took steps to see that the Georgia experience before, during, and after Sherman's invasion was not repeated in Virginia.

The men in Lee's army, aware that their comrades in the Army of Tennessee were camped in Dalton, Georgia, admitted that they would use such an opportunity to go home. Israel E. Linder wrote his mother in May 1864, "[W]ee will leave in the morning to go to Richmond, Va. I hate to leave hear [Charleston sc] I want them to have the fight before we get the air for I am tired of it. I want the war to close. . . . I hear that wee had to go to Dalton, Ga. And I hoap that wee wold for I could come home." Linder tried to get home even after he was transferred to Petersburg, Virginia. Gone four days before he was captured, he apparently received no disciplinary action. If camped in Dalton, Israel would have made it home.[30] Jesse M. McDonald, a captain in Phillips Legion, Army of Northern Virginia, confirmed Lee's worst fears. McDonald received permission to return home for twenty-four days, and after reaching home safely he informed the officer commanding the company that he "should never return." The wartime diaries and postwar memoirs of Confederate soldiers indicate Lee remained resolute up to the very end. Although a few men received furloughs, usually those who had not been home, most were stopped completely. After the war, A. H. Brantley recalled, "As nearly as I can ascertain the furlough granted to me in March 1865 was the last approved by General Lee. It had been customary to grant two furloughs to the Regiment, but as times grew harder, General Lee disapproved all unless circumstances were most urgent."[31]

For the Georgians in both the Army of Northern Virginia and the Army of Tennessee, being home presented a strong temptation to remain. Without furloughs and the ability to travel the roads legally, Georgians in Virginia faced a long trek home that almost certainly risked capture. However, for the men in Georgia, distance ceased to be a factor, as the risk of capture drastically decreased and Sherman eliminated Confederate military resistance and the provost powers and law that accompanied it. Men already close to home could now more easily desert and return to their homes, as more areas were freed from Confederate control. In her postwar memoirs, Mrs. Thomas J. Lockridge of Bartow County described how easily soldiers slipped out of camp. "You can never know how the wild excitement and joy when one of my big brothers would slip home through enemy lines at night to get a supply of much needed articles of clothing."[32] A man now only had to risk being caught by one army instead of two. The Upcountry and upper Piedmont soldiers continued to desert in the spring and summer of 1864.

Entrenched on the outskirts of Atlanta in July 1864, William Dickey, a company commander in the Georgia State Militia, surveyed the situation. Two and a half months of Sherman's steady, grinding push through Georgia had left the Army of Tennessee dug in at the gates of Atlanta. The city's fall became almost a foregone conclusion, and the morale barometer indicated the situation was getting worse. The virtual storm of desertion that began in late 1863 continued. Writing to his wife, Anna, on July 13, 1864, Dickey admitted, "There is some demoralization in this army no doubt, and more of it than I like to hear of. There are a great many Tennesseans and up Georgians that are leaving the army and say they are going back home." Dickey also understood why these men were leaving. "I tell you it is enough to make any man desert. If the Yankees were to drive our army through our country & we were to pass on by you and the children, I could not say that I would not desert and try to get to you." According to Dickey, the level of despair engendered among the soldiers of Johnston's army as the Confederates retreated had become epidemic. "They know their families are left behind at the mercy of the yankies and it is hard to bear."[33]

Across the trenches in the Union lines, M. B. Gray of the First Ohio Artillery realized the Army of Tennessee hung by a thread. In a letter home, Gray confirmed Dickey's observations and added that "the citizens of this portion of rebeldom have lost much of their venom during the past year." Gray also believed that the common soldiers of both armies understood what was happening. Although Johnston still had a large army, Gray believed "at least 1/3 of it will desert—if we can only get one fair fight out of them. The Tennessee, Missouri, North Alabama and Northern Georgia Troops are discouraged and want to quit and only need one more defeat to render a large portion of them unserviceable, hundreds & even thousands of them are coming into our lines as it is."[34]

Gray, like Dickey, had defined Georgia's continuing desertion pattern. One Northern soldier remembered a young deserter who made the short journey across "no man's land" into the Union lines in July 1864. The man had crawled three hundred yards on his belly, a journey that took him two hours and left him exhausted and wringing with sweat. Not every trip was so arduous. In June 1864, twenty men from an entire regiment assigned to picket duty used the cover of darkness to quietly slip into the Union lines. The siege of Atlanta made desertion easy, and Georgia boys took full advantage of the opportunity.[35]

The desertion trend that began in late 1863 continued throughout the summer of 1864 and meant the loss of the Confederacy's best soldiers. William Dickey's brother-in-law, Billy Reynolds, who served in the Army of Tennessee throughout the war, wrote his sister in September 1864. After describing how Sherman had driven Johnston back, he reported: "There has been an exchange of prisoners here to the number of 1500 about 1200 of our prisoners refused to be exchanged and took the oath of allegiance to the Yankee government I am sorry to say the large portion of them were Georgians and most of them were regarded as our best soldiers."[36]

Reynolds assumed these men were prisoners, but it is more likely they had used the cover of darkness or the confusion of battle to slip away from their units and into the Union lines. As deserters they could have been released soon after taking the oath and returned home to an area now free of Confederate civilian and military control. The register also confirms Reynolds's observations that many deserters were veteran soldiers, not conscripts and militia men. Along with names and counties, the register lists each man's rank and distinguishes between conscripts and privates. Of the 3,368 Georgia deserters, 2,947 were privates with only 74 conscripts. Georgia's desertion was an exodus of the "common soldier" and desertion to the enemy among the officer corps rarely occurred. Slightly under 93 percent of Georgia's deserters in the register came from its noncommissioned officers and privates (see table 4).

TABLE 4. DESERTERS BY RANK

Rank	Number	Percentage
Private	2,947	89.4
Corporal	81	2.4
Sergeant	105	3.1
Officers	66	1.9
Conscripts	74	2.1
Nonmilitary	39	1.1
Missing	60	
Total	3,312	100.0

Comparing the dates of desertion in the register with the progress of Sherman's Atlanta campaign shows the continuation of a pattern that began in December 1863. As Sherman proceeded down the state, the chances of safely reaching Union controlled areas increased. Newspaper accounts of May 1864 concede that by the end of that month the Yankees had control of upcountry Georgia. Civilians not wishing to stay had to either seek help from friends and relatives in Tennessee or pass through Union lines to relatives in southern portions of the state still under Confederate control.[37] The path of Sherman's march brought the war from Tunnel Hill, on the border between Catoosa and Whitfield Counties, through Whitfield County, to Resaca in Gordon County. From there the campaign made its way south through Bartow (Cass County in 1860) and Paulding Counties, transition areas that marked the end of the Upcountry and the beginning of the upper Piedmont. By July 1864, when Sherman stood poised on the outskirts of Atlanta, the strain of the steady retreat weakened Confederate morale.

From distant Virginia, John A. Johnson viewed the Georgia situation. His family lived southwest of Atlanta, and the prospects of Sherman's advance left him feeling helpless, emotions he shared with his fiancée: "I have been exposed to danger heretofore, but now danger threatens your happiness." Johnson distinguished between the dangers of combat, which were mixed with genuine excitement and normally lasted only a short time, with the danger that threatened his loved one, a "dread of approaching evil—which is hardest of all to bear . . . at all times before you and it often times happens that the reality is much easier borne than the dread or anticipation." Johnson felt it was natural "that my anxiety should be greater than when the country was in less danger." What troubled him the most was "General J's continual falling back." Johnson explained, "I am like the patient that is having a limb amputated, that may have great confidence in the surgeon before and after the operation is performed but cannot help mistrusting and inwardly cursing while it is being done. The amputation is now being or about to be performed and we must wait patiently to see the result before censuring." Regardless of the outcome, Johnson wrote, "We are now about to see the horrifying effect of the war in the worst form."[38]

Johnson's apt use of analogy explains the devastating effect on morale caused by the Confederate withdrawal. The men of north Georgia serving with Johnston took an active role in the "amputation." From their position as the surgeon's assistants, they could see the doctor had lost his nerve and the patient's death was now a foregone conclusion. With the two armies constantly camped so closely to one another, those who had suppressed the temptation to desert early in the year could no longer resist. The number of Georgians in the Army of Tennessee quickly eroded.

In addition to the seven western Upcountry counties (Whitfield, Walker, Catoosa, Chattooga, Gordon, Dade, and Murray), significant numbers of soldiers from eastern Upcountry counties deserted before Johnston's retreat (see map 2). The Upcountry accounted for 2,058 deserters, or 61 percent of the total Georgia deserters to the Union listed in the register. The counties in extreme north Georgia—Gilmer (203 deserters), Pickens (137 deserters), Fannin (95 deserters), Dawson (36 deserters), Union (69 deserters), White (34 deserters), Lumpkin (69 deserters), Habersham (20 deserters), and Towns (51 deserters)—show release dates consistent with Whitfield, Murray, and Walker Counties in the western Upcountry. Most men deserted and secured their release before Sherman's Atlanta campaign began, but others did so during Sherman's march to Atlanta. Over 60 percent of the deserters from Habersham and Pickens Counties left between December 1863 and May 1864. Among the remainder of the eastern Upcountry, the percentages were even higher, with over 70 percent of the soldiers who deserted doing so before Sherman's Atlanta campaign even began. Not one soldier from Dawson County took the oath after July 1864. Those Upcountry boys who had stayed left when the outcome was no longer in doubt. Only 7 percent of the desertion from the eastern Upcountry occurred after the fall of Atlanta.

The Upcountry counties forming the southern edge of the region—Cherokee (150 deserters), Forsyth (52 deserters), and Hall (54 deserters)—show a pattern consistent with Sherman's movement through the state. Cherokee and Forsyth show some desertion before Sherman's Atlanta campaign, but much more occurred after May 1864. This is the same pattern reflected in Gordon County, where only 20 percent of the soldiers from that county deserted before May 1864. However, those Upcountry soldiers who did not desert during winter camp, including those from Gordon County, definitely did so during the summer fighting.

Those Confederate soldiers who remained through the winter of 1863–

64 left as the Union campaign moved through Georgia. As soldiers from counties in the upper Piedmont felt the brunt of Sherman's march firsthand, their desertion rates resemble those of some of the eastern Upcountry region; some departed before May 1, 1864, but most deserted during the Atlanta campaign. Soldiers from the counties in and around Atlanta—Fulton (102 deserters), DeKalb (27 deserters), Cobb (111 deserters), Campbell (74 deserters), Fayette (13 deserters), Milton (33 deserters), and Gwinnett (47 deserters)—all show the heaviest desertion during Sherman's Atlanta campaign. Cobb and Fayette Counties did not have a single deserter before May 1864. Only Fulton County had more than 5 percent of its soldiers desert before May 1864. Bartow (161 deserters), Paulding (76 deserters), Polk (30 deserters), and Floyd (82 deserters) Counties saw one-third of their soldiers desert before the Atlanta campaign began, but the great majority deserted as Sherman made his way toward Atlanta.

The Union army followed the railroad. After battles at Rocky Face Ridge, Dalton, and Resaca in upcountry Georgia, Sherman's army moved into the upper Piedmont through Bartow County and stopped long enough to fight at Cassville. From Cassville the armies shifted south, to Paulding County where bitter fighting took place at New Hope Church, Dallas, and Pickett's Mill in June 1864.[39] The Georgia soldiers from these counties saw the effects of years of deprivation caused by their own absence as well as the war moving through their homes and communities. Paulding and Bartow Counties, both within the upper Piedmont, shared the culture and economic systems of their Upcountry neighbors. When soldiers from these two counties were faced with the choice of going home to help families and communities ravaged by war or moving on to continue the Confederacy's war, they went home.[40]

Polk and Floyd Counties also had very high desertion figures. As the Confederate army retreated, the men who resided there were given an opportunity to see their loved ones and to understand the direct relationship between the havoc of war and the condition of their families. Despite higher than average slave populations for the region, with between 30 and 44 percent of slaves in their total population, the small farmers of Polk and Floyd Counties shared the family and community loyalties of the Upcountry yeomen. The desertion pattern for both counties shows their soldiers left as the war brought them close to home in the summer of 1864.[41]

Fulton, Campbell, Gwinnett, Milton, DeKalb, and Cobb Counties lay at the center of the upper Piedmont. All six counties had high desertion rates. During the heavy fighting in June and July in and around Atlanta, these

counties were abandoned by the Confederate army. Fulton and DeKalb
Counties became desolate mazes of trenches and gun emplacements during
the Battle of Atlanta and Peachtree Creek. Cobb County underwent a
month-long Union occupation including the battle of Kennesaw Mountain,
then fell under Union control. Milton and Gwinnett, north of DeKalb and
Fulton, experienced heavy Union occupation during this period. As for
Campbell, Fayette and Clayton Counties, southwest of Atlanta, Union cavalry passed through them during Stoneman's raid on the Macon Railroad in
late July. The Union army then maneuvered through the area as Sherman
struck south in the last days of August in order to break the Confederate hold
on Atlanta.[42]

Carroll, Haralson, and Heard Counties lay on the periphery of the fighting in and around Atlanta. All three counties border Alabama and represented the three northwesternmost counties outside the slaveholding plantation belt at the south end of the upper Piedmont.

In these counties neither the Confederate army's location nor the intensity
of the fighting provide any insight into the desertion numbers. Heard
County with ten deserters, and Haralson, with thirteen, did not demonstrate
large numbers, but Carroll County, situated between Haralson on the north
and Heard to the south, had sixty-eight deserters to the enemy. It borders
Paulding County, the scene of heavy fighting and Union activity. Ignoring
for the moment the local conditions in Georgia that may have prompted Carroll County soldiers to desert, examining *when* Carroll County's men deserted provides a clue as to why they left.

The period of heaviest desertion by soldiers from Carroll County came in
July and August 1864 (36 deserters), the two months preceding the fall of
Atlanta when the city was under constant siege. The remaining desertion occurred in the three months following Atlanta's fall (20 deserters). However,
after Hood's army left Georgia, the desertion numbers dropped off. Only ten
men deserted after 1864, all in March and April 1865, the period traditionally
labeled as one of wholesale desertion in the Confederacy. The eight Carroll
County men who took the oath of allegiance in April 1865 did so after Lee's
surrender. The battle for Atlanta, so near home, affected the decisions of Carroll County's soldiers to desert, but none took the oath before the start of
Sherman's Atlanta campaign. Even with a lag time of three months, the earliest would have deserted in April. The more likely explanation is that Sherman's advance made it easy to slip across the lines and into the Union camp.

The story of Carroll County was the same for Heard and Haralson Counties. Despite neither area being in the action, their soldiers were. When the
fighting reached near home, the records indicate that the soldiers deserted.
The soldiers from these two counties directly north and south of Carroll

County deserted between June and September 1864. Two of the deserters in February 1864, one from each county, belonged to cavalry units. Perhaps with a horse, the distances so difficult for infantry men to traverse proved easier.

By the end of September, the vast majority of Georgia's deserters to the enemy had secured their releases. Johnston steadfastly denied the allegations that desertion had decimated his army, but contemporary observers in the Confederate government realized what occurred. As Richmond and Petersburg slowly fell to Grant's siege, the Virginia and the Confederate Congress debated the nation's military options. Georgia Governor Brown had insisted in 1864 that Georgians not leave their state, and the legacy of Sherman's invasion raised serious issues for Virginians. The Speaker of the Virginia House opposed any withdrawal of Lee's army into northern Georgia. Representative Thomas S. Bobcock justified keeping the army in Virginia to fight because of "the desertion of Georgians as the Confederate army fell back into their state, and left their homes in the hands of the enemy."[43] If Lee's army withdrew into Georgia, Bobcock believed its soldiers would imitate those from the Army of Tennessee as Johnston withdrew out of north Georgia.

With the exception of seven other counties, the Georgia desertion story ended with the fall of Atlanta. The only other counties with 10 or more deserters to the enemy were Clarke (11), Newton (12), Bibb (14), Spalding (17), Muscogee (20), Richmond (38) and Chatham (106). Newton, Bibb, and Spalding lie just south and southeast of Atlanta, between that city and Savannah, the terminus of Sherman's March to the Sea. Clarke County lies due east of Atlanta, midway between the city and South Carolina's border. The three remaining counties were home to the three largest urban areas in Georgia: Savannah in Chatham County, Augusta in Richmond, and Columbus in Muscogee County.

Even in late 1864, after most of Georgia's soldiers deserted to the enemy, the register demonstrates a strong relationship between desertion, the Army of Tennessee, and Sherman's invasion of Georgia. After 220 deserters in September, the yearlong trend shrank to 93 in October, 86 in November, and 106 in December (see table 2). Although desertion to the enemy continued, it never reached as high as the lowest figures between January and September. Sherman's March to the Sea, coupled with continued cries from home, kept the trend moving. The decline in numbers was from the Army of Tennessee leaving Georgia.

In late September 1864, John Bell Hood led his army across the Chattahoochee River, destined for Tennessee. The army's 40,000 soldiers was considerably less than the 63,807 "aggregate present" of April 1864, which at that time consisted of hardened veterans with able and experienced officers. As Hood moved north, he took any Georgians remaining in his army with him. Sherman and his sixty-two thousand troops moved unhindered southeast toward Savannah. No place in the South, much less Georgia, was then beyond the reach of the Yankee army, which went wherever it wished.[44]

Newton, Clarke, Bibb, and Spalding Counties either fell in the path of Sherman's March to the Sea or became cut off from the rest of the state as Sherman moved south. All four counties were within Georgia's plantation belt and represented the only rural plantation counties with any significant desertion to the enemy. It is hard to determine how many of the deserters owned slaves, even though they lived in plantation counties. The conflicting data and the absence of significant desertion in counties along Sherman's route to the sea makes it difficult to draw conclusions about why men from these counties deserted. However, the dates of desertion and release of their soldiers appears to have been linked to Sherman's continued presence, both as a destroyer and as a creator of a safe haven to return. Wholesale desertion during the winter of 1864 did not occur among soldiers from these four counties. Only Spalding County demonstrated much desertion activity during the Atlanta campaign. Most desertion occurred after Hood's army had left Georgia and Sherman had burned his way to the sea.

The remaining three counties (Chatham, Richmond, and Muscogee), all with significant urban centers (Savannah, Augusta, and Columbus), represent the most significant desertion numbers outside the Upcountry and upper Piedmont regions. The records reflect that these three counties, together with Atlanta, each contributed more infantry soldiers than any one county. The large enlistment numbers therefore have some bearing on the desertion numbers.

Richmond County borders South Carolina and lies midway between Savannah and the Georgia–North Carolina border. Home to Augusta, one of Georgia's largest cities in 1860, Richmond lies at the eastern most extreme of Georgia's plantation belt. In 1860 slaves formed 39 percent of its total population. Based on the register, thirty-eight soldiers deserted to the enemy from Richmond County. The pattern began in January 1864 and ran through January 1865. Only 5 of the 38 deserters left after January 1, 1865. Consistent with the desertion patterns of all but the six counties closest to Whitfield

County, Richmond's desertion pattern shows heavy desertion during and after Sherman's Atlanta campaign.

Richmond County's desertion rate puts it among the twenty-five highest totals in the state. The dates of oath taking lend some credibility to Richmond's desertion arising from Sherman's presence, both in the destruction wrought and the elimination of the Confederate authority. However, the eastern portion of the state was not freed of Confederate control until late 1864, with over half of Richmond's desertion to the enemy occurring earlier. Richmond's desertion pattern was only partially grounded in Sherman's invasion. The absence of large slave populations contributed to heavy desertion rates. Within the plantation belt, the culture and economy had curbed desertion in those counties, but the smaller size of Richmond's slave population resembled some upper Piedmont counties, more than the plantation counties that lay to its south and west. Consistent with the remainder of Georgia's desertion, Richmond County's deserters were all privates. Unlike yeomen from the plantation counties, the yeoman population within Richmond County most likely held few if any slaves. Like their comrades from the Upcountry and upper Piedmont, when given the opportunity to desert, these men took full advantage.

The city of Savannah lay at the end of Sherman's March to the Sea. In December 1864, it was Sherman's Christmas present to President Lincoln. An examination of the desertion patterns in Chatham County reveals a very clear connection between the Union presence and Confederate desertion. Chatham County's soldiers began to desert in earnest after Sherman's Atlanta campaign started, and they left in greatest numbers after the city fell. Of the twenty-nine who deserted after the Atlanta campaign began, eleven did so in September 1864. Over 70 percent of Chatham's desertion occurred after the fall of Atlanta, and 50 percent of its soldiers deserted when Sherman's destination was no longer in question.

Muscogee County was the only remaining county with significant desertion numbers. Its principal city, Columbus, was situated on the Alabama-Georgia border and flourished as a prominent trade center on the Chattahoochee River. Muscogee lies within the plantation belt and is the largest urban area in the Chattahoochee valley. Within this river valley, almost half the white population was of the poor laborer class. However, despite an apparent weak connection to the slaveholder class, the desertion pattern from Muscogee County reflects one of the realities of Civil War desertion. Without the ability to get safely home or to find sanctuary in "deserter country," desertion was so risky that distance was sufficient to dissuade many men from even trying. Muscogee County's desertion appears to be the result of a total breakdown not only of morale but of the Confederacy's ability to control its army during the last months of the war. Muscogee County was never threatened by direct Union encroachment, at least not until late in the war when Gen. James Wilson occupied the city from his position in Alabama. <u>Muscogee's soldiers came home when it appeared safe to do so and when transportation provided the means to get there.</u> Regardless of which army they were in, by 1865 membership in either army meant they were either in Virginia or in the Carolinas. Without secure control of Georgia by the Union, the journey home was a long one, made more treacherous by Confederate efforts to hold their army together. Considering the large numbers of troops contributed by the county, the desertion numbers are consistent with the general pattern of Georgia desertion to the enemy.

Of the remaining 289 deserters, 88 had no county identified in the register, 5 had names that did not match any known Georgia county, town or city, and 196 were from fifty-four counties, spread out over the plantation belt and Wiregrass/Pine Barrens. A few upper Piedmont counties east of Atlanta, Franklin, Jackson, Madison, and Hart also had deserters listed in the register. Most of the remaining counties had only one or two deserters, although some had as many as nine. The pattern for those remaining counties is insignificant and runs from early 1864 to the end of the war. Thirty Georgia counties recorded no deserters to the enemy.

Although the desertion identified through the register reflects only those men who deserted to the enemy, the pattern seems to hold for those deserting and going home. It is consistent with the sketchy picture in the contemporary records, personal accounts, and postwar muster rolls that provide information on Georgia desertion. Still the corroborating evidence contains numerous gaps. Not every unit compiled muster rolls, and not all of those records survived. Personal accounts tend to limit themselves to isolated incidents or experiences. However, such evidence does reinforce the patterns established by the register. Beginning in the late fall and early winter of 1863, desertion trends reflected in the register hold true for those men who deserted and went directly home without swearing the oath of allegiance.

The muster rolls for Lumpkin County Companies C and D of the Fifty-second Georgia show that in addition to the nine men listed in the register as deserting to the Union and taking the oath, seven men not listed as taking the oath deserted between late September 1863 and mid-December 1863. Two of these were listed as deserting to the enemy, but they never took the oath because neither appeared in the register. Three men, one a prisoner, were listed in the muster rolls as having taken the oath of allegiance in April 1864.

They do not appear as deserters in the roll or in the register. Thirty-three men of the Fifty-second Georgia went AWOL between early October 1863 and the end of December 1863, but never appeared in the register as deserters. The register shows James Grindle took the oath on April 23, 1864, after being exchanged on October 7, 1863. However, William Grindle, perhaps his brother, was exchanged the same day and was listed in the muster rolls as deserting on November 29, 1863, but did not appear in the register with soldiers from Lumpkin County who took the oath of allegiance. While the older studies argue that more men may have gone home than deserted to the enemy, the pattern of heavy desertion to the enemy from late 1863 to late 1864, as depicted by the register, also holds true for Lumpkin County soldiers in the Fifty-second Georgia Infantry who deserted and went directly home.[45]

Throughout the war Georgia newspapers listed deserters on a daily basis. The newspaper reports confirm that some desertion began as early as 1862 and continued into 1863. But these early reports represented only isolated instances. Most notices called for the return of a specific soldier or small group of soldiers. However, by 1864 the notices became more frequent. In October 1864 the *Macon Daily Telegraph* ran half-page notices every other day over the course of two weeks and listed dozens of deserters.[46]

Several conclusions can be drawn from an examination of the newspaper reports on desertion. First, based on the register numbers alone, the newspapers could not possibly have tracked desertion numbers accurately. Between December 1863 and December 1864, over 3,000 Georgians deserted to the enemy, but newspaper notices never approach these figures. Even Union soldiers admitted that newspaper reports failed to grasp the size of the desertion problem. Maj. James Connally, a staff officer in the Army of the Cumberland, said, "The newspapers don't tell one hundredth part of the facts regarding desertion from the rebel army."[47] The *Southern Recorder* indicated an increase in desertion in November 1863 but provided no numbers.[48] Still, the severity of the problem can be inferred from the information in the papers. On August 4, 1864, the *Macon Daily Telegraph* ran an article entitled "Absentee to the Front!" The notice earnestly implored those men absent from Hood's army to return to the front immediately: "Now is the crisis in the fate of Georgia and the history of the War. The state is denuding the farms and plantations of every able bodied man."[49] As the register demonstrates, the Army of Tennessee suffered heavy desertion to the enemy from late 1863 through September 1864 (see table 2). Those who had not left during winter camp would leave during the Atlanta campaign. Such articles echoed the sentiments of Dickey and Gray and confirm the register data: Soldiers from upcountry Georgia and those from the counties along Sherman's path to Atlanta had gone home.

On August 10, 1864, Robert E. Lee issued General Orders No. 64, which the *Macon Daily Telegraph* reprinted, together with a plea to deserters and for amnesty to any man who returned. The newspaper added, "Let the relatives, acquaintances and friends of such persons as have been guilty of the crime of desertion seek them out in their lurking places and read this general order." Moreover, great shame would come to deserters and their families if "they shrink from the manful discharge of their duty in the hour of their country's need and leave their homes to be defended by . . . the unaided courage of others." Failure to respond by returning to their unit also carried the "extreme penalty of law."[50] While the article confirmed the high rates of desertion, it failed to grasp that soldiers deserted because no one remained to defend their homes and they had lost faith in the ability of the Confederate army to protect the state.

While Georgia's media may have missed the mark, the situation did not escape the observations of many of Georgia's citizen soldiers. As Sherman moved toward Atlanta, and particularly after Hood took the army into Tennessee, Governor Brown called up the Georgia Militia to stop Sherman. In October 1864, William Dickey commanded a militia unit near Macon, Georgia, and wrote home to express frustration at being unable to assemble it. He complained that the unit's formation proceeded slowly and that men still sought exemptions. The problem went beyond administrative red tape involving exemptions. Beginning in October 1864, and running twice a week through the middle of the month, the First, Second, Third, and Twenty-first Regiments of Georgia Militia published half-page notices offering a thirty-dollar reward per man for the return of "absentees to their militia units." The notices did not label anyone as a deserter, but indicated that men had either refused to show up or, once having reported, had left without permission. The notices offered men the chance to return to their units and not be prosecuted as deserters. The lists were lengthy, particularly for the Third Georgia Reserve on October 13, 1864.[51] They reflected only militia men absent without leave. Regular soldiers were not listed, but the pattern of desertion, even for these reserve units, shows some consistency with that reflected in the register. What is significant is the counties these men resided in. The First Regiment listed most of its AWOLs from Carroll and Fayette Counties. The majority of absentees in the Twenty-first came from Cobb, Polk, Bartow, Cherokee, Franklin, Hart, Clarke, and Coweta Counties. The militia rolls also contained men who had somehow escaped the earlier drafts, as evident from absentees in Meriwether, Campbell, and other counties in or near the plantation belt. The Second Regiment was almost exclusively made up of Cobb, DeKalb, and Gwinnett men. The Third Regiment, by far the hardest hit by absentees, listed men from throughout central Georgia, including Bibb and Spalding Counties. The muster rolls for the Georgia State Line, another of the local Georgia armies, reflected the same numbers shown in the newspaper notices. As of September 1864, men listed as AWOL or deserters from the First and Second Regiments of the Georgia State Line numbered almost 250 in each unit.[52] Therefore, although the newspapers had different classifications of soldiers, the pattern in terms of both the time of desertion and the residence of the deserters is consistent. The papers also indicate that men who avoided the regular army were unwilling to serve during and after Sherman's Atlanta campaign, for as their homes became threatened, they saw more benefit in staying home than in joining the militia.

Given the pattern in the register, what becomes of the old notions of Confederate desertion? William S. Basinger, a soldier and later the battalion commander in the Eighteenth Georgia Infantry, reflected on the desertion problem in a brief introduction he wrote to the regiment's muster roll:

> It will be observed that a good many desertions are reported. It is impossible now, in all cases to distinguish with certainty between those who deserted to the enemy and those who simply left the colors without leave and never returned. In either case it was desertion. But justice requires a few words of explanation on this subject. By far the greatest number of these desertions, almost all indeed, occurred in Virginia, in the winter and spring of 1864–65, when our outposts were so near those of the enemy that it was impossible to prevent communication between them. There were in the corps a number of men who enlisted with it only for the war. At the time mentioned, these men were constantly receiving letters from their wives and female relations, representing that their families were suffering from want, and entreating them to leave the army at all hazards and go to their relief. At the same time it was understood that the enemy was offering free transportation to their homes to all confederate soldiers who would desert.[53]

The undated piece appears to have been written shortly after the war. It recognized that desertion brought shame on the unit and required some explanation of the high incidence. By characterizing it as an act of personal desperation, in the last days of the war Basinger attempted to preserve the regiment's honor. By March 1865, the problem was greater than just separation from home. Rations were low, the Union policy of inviting desertion and promising transportation was in place, and the general mood of the army was bad, made worse by the absence of furloughs for both South Carolina and Georgia troops.

In March 1865 William Mosely, a private in the Tenth Georgia, watched the execution of eight men from the Forty-eighth Georgia for desertion and indicated in his diary that the stockade overflowed with such men.[54] Mosely's observations, like those of Basinger, describe the last days of the Army of Northern Virginia. While some desertion among Georgia troops then occurred, the register demonstrates Georgia desertion was neither confined to late 1865 nor predominantly in Virginia. Mosely and Basinger's comments reflect old notions of Confederate desertion that cannot be reconciled with the wave of Georgia desertion in 1864. However, Basinger did identify two components of desertion that applied to Georgians: the call from home and the proximity of the Confederate lines to those of the Union.

The quantitative data demonstrates a relationship between Georgia desertion and Sherman's invasion of the state. The large majority of Georgia's deserters to the enemy came from the Upcountry and upper Piedmont, the two regions where most of the fighting took place. As the Confederate army moved into and then retreated through Georgia, the soldiers from north Georgia abandoned the Confederate cause. However, the numbers alone do not answer the more important question of why these men felt compelled to desert in contravention of their duty as soldiers. Returning home to fight presented a clear opportunity to desert. The devastating effects of Sherman's Atlanta campaign also provided a motive, besides removing any military authority that might interfere with desertion. However, something else persuaded many of these north Georgia men to abandon the fight and return home: the wartime experiences of family and community and the deteriorating situation in Georgia that compelled families to call their sons, husbands, and fathers home. It was a call the men from the Upcountry and the upper Piedmont could not and did not ignore.

Families of the nonslaveholding yeomen and poor whites in other parts of Georgia suffered in their absence, and they wrote their men complaining of the hardship.[55] While this study is based primarily on those deserters positively identified from the register, it defines desertion much more broadly. There is nothing to suggest that the pattern of desertion reflected in the register differs from that of men who deserted and went straight home. Either method of desertion still required both opportunity and a safe place to return. Of the thirty counties that recorded no deserters to the Union, thirteen were in the Wiregrass region of southeast Georgia. This least populated region accounted for only 14 of the 3,368 deserters to the enemy. The Wiregrass contributed the fewest soldiers to the Confederate army of any region in Georgia, and its low desertion numbers might be a reflection of its small enlistment figures. However, the plantation belt contributed more soldiers than any other region in Georgia, yet desertion from that region was hardly proportional to its enlistment. Did soldiers from the plantation belt and the Wiregrass regions desert and make their way straight home in such large numbers so as to make desertion from those regions significant? Such an explanation is unlikely because the same factors which so severely limited the number of men from these regions who deserted to the enemy would have prevented them from deserting at all. Were there deserters from regions outside the Upcountry and upper Piedmont? The answer is clearly yes, but the numbers of deserters from Georgia's plantation belt and Wiregrass regions pale in comparison with those from north Georgia.

The only numbers previously compiled that provide any evidence of the size of Georgia's desertion indicate that 6,797 Georgians deserted.[56] The register accounts for almost half of Georgia's total desertion. The same factors that made deserting to the enemy possible also made it possible to desert and go home. The physical presence in the state of the Army of Tennessee and north Georgia's occupation by the Union army made it possible for soldiers from the upper Piedmont and Upcountry to desert. A significant number chose to take the oath of allegiance. But the duel factors of proximity and Union occupation, combined with an acute need at home, makes it reasonable to assume that those men who deserted and went straight home were also predominately from the Upcountry and upper Piedmont.

This, then, is the story of Georgia's desertion. Its focus is north Georgia because it is there that the story unfolds. Men from the Upcountry and upper Piedmont not only heard the call but were able to respond. Most of the non-slaveholding yeomen and common soldiers from other regions of Georgia may have heard the cries from home, but they were simply unable to answer. Then, too, there were those who heard the call but for one reason or another chose not to answer. To fully understand desertion requires looking beyond opportunity and safety to the nature and intensity of the need at home.

CHAPTER FOUR

Calls from Home

As the Union army left Atlanta for Savannah and the sea in November 1864, three hundred miles to the southeast, the full weight of defeat fell upon the city. David Conyngham, a correspondent for the *New York Herald* who served as a volunteer aide-de-camp, watched as General Sherman's men put Atlanta to the torch.

> Winship's iron foundry and machine shops were early set on fire. This valuable property was calculated to be worth about half a million dollars. An oil refinery nearby next got on fire and was soon in a fierce blaze. Next followed a freight warehouse. . . . The depot, turning tables, freight sheds and stores around were soon a fiery mass. . . . The Atlanta Hotel, Washington Hall, and the square around the railroad depot were soon in one sheet of flame. Drugstores, dry good stores, hotels, the Negro marts, theaters, and grog shops were now all feeding the fiery element. . . . The men plunged into the houses, broke windows and doors with their muskets, dragging out armfuls of clothes, tobacco and whiskey.[1]

The destruction Conyngham witnessed in Atlanta continued all along Sherman's methodical March to the Sea. A correspondent from the *Indianapolis Journal* wrote: "So startling is the utter silence that even when a wild bird carols a note you look around surprised that amid such loneliness any living thing should be happy." A Georgia woman said it best: "Thus passed the great Union army, composed of many nations and many kinds of people, through our beloved country leaving desolation and ruin in its track. Many who had always known comfort, even luxury, were poor—some penniless and homeless in a few days."[2]

Sherman's destructive march through Georgia and the Union army's elimination of Confederate control does not totally explain why the men from the upper Piedmont and Upcountry deserted in such large numbers. Matching the dates of desertion with the counties of the soldiers provides a good explanation of opportunity and provides some evidence of motive, but does not address why men would be willing to abandon their sense of duty to nation, state, and comrades. The answer to Georgia's desertion lies deeper than the location of the army. It is found in the experiences of those Georgians who stayed behind, their hardships before Sherman's invasion, their efforts to endure, and their eventual recognition that without their husband, son, father, and brother, they would perish. When the situation became intolerable, Georgians did not hesitate to cry out. When the government refused to acknowledge their needs, first for relief and then for the return of their men, Georgians called directly to the men who could not ignore their pleas.

The *Macon Daily Telegraph* ran the following advertisement on February 27, 1864:

> Men of Georgia! During this terrific war you have been marvelously blessed. Your state has enjoyed comparative immunity from the torch and sword so hellishly used to crimson and desolate others. You have experienced none or very few of the outrages that mark the progress of the invader. Your grass has not withered under his heel; your flowers have not drooped at his breath; your dwellings have not flamed at his approach; your sanctuaries have not shrunk as from a demon at his intrusion; your barns have not been robbed, nor your commerce destroyed, nor your Negroes kidnaped, nor your women insulted, nor your old men kicked, nor your families banished. You know nothing of war except the tidings of conflict on your frontier and the death of your loved ones. You have grown rich on the misfortunes of Kentucky, Tennessee, Mississippi, and Louisiana—R. Afton Holland, Kentucky Relief Society

Holland sought food, blankets, and other relief he believed that Georgians could spare for those less fortunate in Kentucky. However, Holland grossly underestimated, and probably did not understand, what the war had also done to Georgia. True, Georgia had been blessed as one of the southernmost states, experiencing military invasion only in threats on Savannah, Fort Pulaski, and some of the sea islands along her Atlantic coast. However, the absence of significant Union occupation and invasion before 1864 did not mean that Georgia and her citizens had escaped war's hardships.

Georgia began to feel the brunt of the war in 1862. The first eight to ten months of the war produced little hardship because shortages occurred after the depletion of reserves and that took a little time. However, the less of a particular vital resource in existence, the more quickly that resource became scarce. Georgia's human resources also did not disappear immediately. The First and Second Regiments of Georgia Volunteer Infantry were formed in the first year of the war, but most counties, particularly Upcountry counties, lost only small numbers of men until March 1862. The letters and enlistment records indicate early 1862 as the time of large-scale depletion of upper Piedmont and upcountry Georgia boys. Lt. Josiah Patterson of Forsyth County wrote his daughter in March 1862 that he "was pleased to learn that upper Georgia had redeemed itself by the voluntary contribution of so many brave men ready to do or die in the service of the sunny south as well as the defense of their common humanity." Patterson apparently joined almost immediately after the war began and served in Lee's Army of Northern Virginia. The units with the heaviest desertion to the Union did not form until 1862. The Thirty-ninth and Forty-third Georgia, for example, saw their first action shortly after Shiloh, and the Forty-first Georgia did not appear as an active unit until June 30, 1862.[3]

The Upcountry and upper Piedmont sent 287 volunteer infantry companies to the Confederate army. Although the early correspondence between soldiers and their homes revealed little suffering, many letters foreshadowed the hardships to come. Mahalay Hyatte of Ellijay, in Gilmer County, predicted upcountry Georgia's dim future. In January 1862, she described her situation in a letter to Gov. Joe Brown. "I am a poor lone woman I have two sons in the confederate service and have but one son left with me about twelve years of age and has but one hand therefore he is unable to render me any help." Her request was a simple one: "I thought I would ask you if you could help me to some money fifty dollars would do me . . . until I could get some help."[4]

With two sons gone and one physically handicapped, Mrs. Hyatte's situation appeared to deteriorate more quickly than most, but her plight would prove prophetic. The removal of service-age males took half of the workforce from north Georgia's semi-subsistence economy. With the absence of husbands and sons jeopardizing family farms and communities, north Georgia's soldiers understood what their absence meant. Their letters, particularly those from soldiers in the upper Piedmont, portray men vainly trying to perform their family duties by proxy.

The soldiers' letters demonstrate a sense of responsibility to provide much-needed guidance in absentia. In May 1862 Joseph F. Alexander of the Sixtieth Georgia cautioned his wife about the importance of feeding the stock and asked if she had been able to buy any corn. A month later he asked where she had planted the potatoes.[5]

Lt. Joel Crawford Barnett of Morgan County, Georgia, enlisted in a regiment in 1861. In writing to his wife, Annie, in March 1862, he gave specific instructions on planting corn: "Clean up the ditches and ridge up the corn rows and plant about the 1st or 5th of May." Barnett actually did a commend-able job of explaining the planting process, but his letter underscores the im-portance of his physical presence.[6] Despite their willingness to farm, most women found that planting and having planting explained were two differ-ent things. Although Morgan County lay on the northern edge of the planta-tion belt, the Barnett farm appeared to be a family-run subsistence operation without slaves. The smooth operation of the family farm required Barnett's physical labor as well as his knowledge.

The names changed, but the story remained the same. Absent husbands, responsible for the physical and planning aspects of planting, wrote home trying to keep their family farms going and their wives and children fed. Sur-vival depended on the ability of the household unit to provide all or most es-sentials. Writing his wife in the summer of 1863, O. H. P. Chambers tried to guide her through the rigors of clearing and planting. Had she sold any but-ter? Who, if anyone, did the plowing? Did the sugar cane get planted? Ben-jamin J. Moody wrote home fifteen times in the first year of the war. Virtually every one of his letters addressed the mechanics of planting and putting in a crop.[7]

In a desperate plea to Governor Brown in October 1864, Pauline Wheeler defined the essence of the problem for the yeoman. She lived in Columbia County, on the northern edge of the plantation belt, but she owned no slaves. Mrs. Wheeler and other women like her in Georgia knew "how" to farm, but doing the work posed real difficulty. She asked Brown to discharge her son because her and her six children were "almost entirely dependent on him for support." She had already lost her husband and two sons in the war and had another son in Virginia. She told Brown that all of her men had left at the be-ginning of the war. "I possess no slave at all and there is as you know labore on a farm which requires the services of a male such as hauling corn and wood, cutting, going to mill, attending to stock . . . and other numerous things and not having my son with me to do such things I live in a state of perplexity and vexation which is enough to drive me to insanity."[8]

The desperation Mrs. Wheeler expressed in 1864 had not struck the state in full force in 1862, but some men who were far from home could see the danger coming.

W. B. Stanley of Henry County, bordering the southern edge of the upper Piedmont, wrote home to his wife, Anna. His letter is undated, but it falls be-tween two dated letters in late 1862 and early 1863. Stanley's letter clearly de-fined the crisis that loomed just over the horizon: "I want you to rite me as soon as you git thes few lings & rit how you are a long & how your caper for the presen years & rite how your taters is." The weather had been uncoopera-tive, and Stanley was "mity a feard it has bin so dry that tha ant no count but I am in hops that tha are vary good be case you ant got no wheat & the potators will heap you out mity about it." He cautioned Anna to be "careful & tak car of what you have made for I dont no how you will git eny more made a nuther yeare if I dont git to make it for you. I am in hops that I will git to mak it for you if I dont I dont know what you will do." Stanley closed by telling his wife to "do the very best you can & I will do the best I can for you," but he did not hide his fear that he might never "live to see you all eny more."[9]

Stanley's crudely written message could not have been clearer if written in perfect English. If the potato crop failed, his wife and family would not eat. Unless he could get home, there would be no crop next year. In February 1863 Stanley's brother wrote to tell him that he was "gitting willing to quite an come home." If W. B. Stanley ever deserted, it was not to the enemy, because his name does not appear among the eight such deserters in the register from Henry County. Still, Stanley's letter expressed the concern and frustration experienced by Georgia soldiers from the Upcountry and upper Piedmont. If they could not put in the crop, their families would suffer and perhaps starve.[10]

Added to farm and families not being able to survive without their men was a growing fear that many men might never come home. The death toll for the Upcountry and upper Piedmont intensified the anxieties of loved ones. The casualty figures for these counties in comparison with the enlistment figures show that many of the region's men were dead by 1863 and that many were still "at risk." The people back home desperately needed their men to return in 1864 before the war claimed them forever. Some statistics on company enlistment indicate that the Upcountry contributed 114 infantry companies, or 17 percent of the total (see table 1). Although exact casualty figures are difficult to determine, the Salt Census allows for an approximation of both losses and men still at war. For example, 1863 casualty figures can be approximated by looking at the number of soldiers' widows who received salt and widows receiving salt who still had sons fighting. The estimates of the number of men still at war can be calculated by looking at the number of women listed in the Salt Census with their husbands at war, widows who had sons at war, and women who depended on a soldier as their sole means of support.[11]

Estimates of casualties as a percentage of the total infantry soldiers from each county are also only an approximation. Lillian Henderson's *Roster of Confederate Soldiers* contains only infantry companies in the regular army. Militia units or men who fought in one of Georgia's state armies were not listed as Georgia Confederate units. In addition, she left out conscripts, since her work lists only volunteer units. Her roster also omits cavalry units. Because some men actually joined units formed in other counties, their enlistment was not credited to their home county.[12] Therefore, the total number of soldiers is lower than what the Salt Census or more comprehensive enlistment records reflect for soldiers from each county. However, Henderson's figures do accurately reflect the impact of the loss. Deaths run from a low of 5 percent to as high as 38 percent of an Upcountry county's infantry volunteers. The losses are probably too low, because the total widows actually entitled to salt may be underrepresented owing to many not registering. In addition, the men at risk may actually have been greater, because the table does not reflect whether a woman had more than one son at war. Even though the numbers are not as firm as one would like, they reveal a harsh reality. In addition to the death toll, the absence of the men made survival difficult for Upcountry women. In Lumpkin County, according to the Salt Census, almost a third of the 333 women with husbands or sons at war depended entirely on the labor of a soldier for their support. His absence proved crippling, but his death would be unbearable for his family and the community upon which the family would have to depend for its support.

The numbers for upper Piedmont counties are similar to those of the Upcountry. According to the infantry enlistment records, the upper Piedmont contributed 173 volunteer infantry companies, 59 more than the Upcountry, but their percentage of dead was equally high. The regions show roughly the same ratios between widows and total infantry soldiers enlisted. Estimates of casualties as a percentage of total infantry soldiers shows the upper Piedmont death toll ranged from a high of almost 40 percent of enlisted infantry from Jackson County to a low of 5 percent from Fulton County. Like the Upcountry, most families in the upper Piedmont were semi-subsistence farmers, and the war took not only a woman's companion but also her workmate. In Carroll County, 807 families with either husbands or sons still alive received salt allotments in 1863; in 196 families, the husband would never return, even if his son or sons still lived. By 1863, 20 percent of infantry volunteers from Carroll County were dead. Casualties so severely depleted north Georgia's male population by the end of 1863 that the families of the men fortunate enough to survive could no longer risk losing them in combat. A woman from Powder Springs, Georgia, told Governor Brown, when he called her husband to militia duty in 1864, "He is my last and only protection leaving me with eight children . . . to raise and educate myself."[13]

Most of Georgia's deserters in the register came from the Army of Tennessee. That army's military record shows it fought some of the bloodiest encounters of the war. But the frustration felt by the survivors in late 1863 and 1864 was over how the vast majority of men had died. Slow, agonizing deaths, in excessively cold or unbearably hot encampments, claimed two out of every three men who died during the war. When they enlisted, these men had anticipated dying while fighting the Confederacy's enemies. Few foresaw the possibility of dying of a disease.

J. B. Patterson, the man so glad to see that upper Georgia had contributed its fair share of soldiers, testified to the harsh realities. His unit, the Fourteenth Georgia, went east as part of the Army of Northern Virginia. By early October 1861, his regiment had shrunk from its initial compliment of 750 men to 250, with most dying from disease. William Wood of Laurens County also served in the Fourteenth Georgia. His letter of mid-November 1861 confirmed Patterson's observations. Out of the 250 men who enlisted with him, Wood estimated that over half had died by October 1861. The climate change from Georgia to Virginia played havoc with the boys from the lower South. Edwin Bass told his sisters at the end of 1861, "If we are not taken away from this climate, there will not be three men out of ten from Georgia and the other extreme southern states, who will ever see their homes again, and not one of them touched by a Yankee bullet." One of the officers in the Fourteenth Georgia even tried to have the unit reassigned to Georgia because few men thought they could survive the cold winter.

William Wood witnessed the scourge of disease firsthand. Early in 1862, his brother Alex contracted typhoid fever, and William had to watch him die. It would take several letters after Alex's death for William finally to admit his brother's death to his father. In a letter to his wife, William described how Alex's body had been packed in lime and coal for the journey home. Two years later, William died in battle in the arms of his younger brother, Joshua.[14]

As the war dragged into late 1863, Georgia's soldiers from the Upcountry and upper Piedmont were dying in droves, many from disease as they lay in camp. At the same time they knew their families were deprived of food, clothing, and other essentials. The Confederacy proved incapable of bringing law and order to certain counties as bands of irregulars ravaged the countryside, making the plight of families even worse. Attempts to remedy the hardships caused by shortages often deprived those people most in need of essential salt, corn, and grain rations. Those north Georgia men who had hesitated to get involved in the beginning, but nevertheless enlisted, now had second thoughts. As the soldiers in the Army of Tennessee returned to their native soil, many of them finally deserted to make their way home to their families.

Almost twenty years after the war ended, the conflict between home and the Confederacy continued to spark interest. At the dedication of a monument

to the Confederate dead of the University of Virginia in 1893, the speaker
described the conflict as follows:

> If ever there was such a thing as a "conflict of duties," that conflict was
> presented to these men. If ever a strain of such a conflict was great
> enough to unsettle a man's reason and break a man's heart-strings, these
> men were subject to that strain. . . . demanded of a husband and a father
> to choose between his God-imposed obligations to her and to them, and
> his allegiance to his country, his duty as a soldier—[many wives de-
> clared,] that, if the stronger party proved recreant to the marriage vow,
> the weaker should no longer be bound by it—that if he come not at
> once, he need never come—that she will never see him more, never rec-
> ognize him again as the husband of her heart or the father of her chil-
> dren.[15]

For the women back home, their husbands owed them a higher duty than ~Some?~
they owed the Confederacy. Any soldier's failure to understand and respond
to the call would undermine the marriage.

One of the desertion letters most often cited by historians is by Mrs. Edward Cooper.[16] She was married to an Alabaman who, after repeated efforts
to obtain a furlough to return home briefly, left without permission. Voluntarily returning to face a court-martial for desertion, Cooper offered no defense except the letter from his wife. Her letter began by telling Edward how
proud she was of him and that his enlistment in the Confederate army had
only enhanced her sense of pride in him. She assured him that she would
never want him to do anything wrong or to abandon his duty, but then she
wrote, "Before God, Edward unless you come home, we must die!" The situation at home had reached unbearable proportions. Mary Cooper told her
husband how she had been "roused by little Eddie crying. I called and said
'What's the matter, Eddie?' and he said 'O mamma I am so hungary.'" Edward Cooper's daughter, Lucy, fared no better. Mary's letter ended, "Your
darling Lucy, she never complains. But she is growing thinner everyday, and
I repeat, unless you come home, we must all die." Mary Cooper's letter
moved the tribunal members, but they still sentenced her husband to death.
When Gen. Robert E. Lee later commuted the sentence, Cooper returned to
his unit.

Historians have ignored Cooper's testimony on why he returned, which
sheds considerable light on his notion of honor. When Cooper returned
home and his wife apparently expressed joy at his having obtained furlough,
Cooper observed, "She must have felt me shudder," because she exclaimed,
"O Edward, Edward go back! Go back! Let me and the children go to the
grave but save the honor of your name." She did not want her husband to de-

sert in order to return. In his trial Cooper stated, "And here I am, not brought here by military power, but by the obedience to Mary's command, to abide the sentence of your court."[17] If Mary had begged Edward to stay and had reassured him that he would still lose no honor, Cooper might not have returned. What women thought carried enough weight with men that a woman's opinion of her man's honor also mattered.[18] Similarly, with their cry for aid, letters from home carried an implied or expressed promise that a soldier's honor remained untainted in the eyes of his wife, his mother, or his sister.[19]

Honor

★　★　★

Part of the pull from home lay not only in the duty a man felt to his wife and family but in the fear that another man could take his place. If a man failed to respond to one's duty to family and community, his wife would find someone else who could.

Peter Dekle had the good fortune to be stationed in Georgia. His unit, the Twenty-ninth Georgia Infantry, defended the fortifications at Caustens Bluffs, south of Savannah, until 1863. Dekle wrote home often. His letters reflect self-pity for not being able to come home and share the fruits of civilian life, including the company of his wife. Dekle had failed to appreciate the benefits he enjoyed at home until after he had gone to war. "You cant imagine how a pore soldier wants to come home and are the cry among them all the are nun of us ever new what a good home wher until we had to leave it I thought we lived heard but we lived like fatning hogss. . . . I cant tink about the pleasure we have together and I am far of rom you and cant help myuself it goes very heard with me." He realized his wife needed him at home. A letter written a week earlier reveals Dekle's real concern: the fear of being replaced in her affections and in his own home. Dekle had heard some of his comrades "talking so bad about the pore soldiers wifes." He told his wife "to be on your guard and not let no one gaet a holt on you Keepe your eyes open for if you dont they will be some tale on you and I would rather die than to here it from any persons lips." Even more troubling for Dekle was the rumor "that the men at there homes are taken the pore soldiers wifes awy from them and will be more babies there next year than ever were known before."[20]

By September 1863 Dekle appeared ready to subordinate his military obligations to his family responsibilities. His unit left Georgia and spent time in Mississippi. His letter home reflected his strong desire to return to his wife and family and also confirmed the observations of the Confederate military commanders that, once home, many Georgians did not return.

Dekle's last letter began, "Sometimes when I think how long I have been deprived of the pleasure of home and your society and look at the future and see no possible chance of this war ending in our favor I get perfectly disheartened." In his unwillingness to continue fighting we see a diminished faith in the Confederate cause. "At times I am ready to give up but the thought of home and you nerves me on though I must acknoledge that the prosepect is dark and instead of getting better it grows darker. . . . You and the child is all I care for now as for the confederacy that is gone up there is no use in fighting anymore for that if I have to fight I will come home and do my fighting there." Dekle's letter closed by telling his wife that he would not encourage her to write and send it back with the fellow that brought this letter, because "everyone that goes home now stays."[21] Dekle might well have been one of those men who went home and stayed, but he never got the chance, for somewhere between Morton, Mississippi, and Chattanooga, Tennessee, he died.

The fear that a soldier's wife might stray or otherwise lose her affection for him appeared intermittently in many of the letters soldiers sent home. One soldier's correspondence expressed the fear explicitly and feverishly. Col. Tully Graybill, of the Twenty-eighth Georgia Volunteers, then with the Army of Northern Virginia, was from Hancock County, well within the plantation belt in the eastern portion of the state. His fears were hardly peculiar to men of his rank or region, but rather reflected the anxieties of any soldier away too long and grappling with conflicting loyalties. Graybill's correspondence revealed a rift growing between him and his wife over his enlistment in the military. Despite his strong feelings of affection toward her—"my *wife* the best, the dearest of all things on earth"—his commitment to the service obviously troubled her, as Graybill replied to her letters. Mrs. Graybill apparently pressured him to return at every opportunity. "I cannot say at present what I shall do in regard to coming home to stay," he wrote his wife in the spring of 1862. "I cannot think of resigning until the scuffle is over at this place." By that autumn her pleas must have intensified because he wrote, "You cannot possibly feel more anxious for me to come home than I am to go and see you and the children but it is impossible at present." He then reassured her: "Reproach not yourself for any unkindness shown me for I assure you I have never seen it, therefore it has made no impression on my mind." By the spring of 1863, the situation between husband and wife had grown even more strained.[22]

Graybill sought his wife's approval to honor his own sense of military duty. On April 8, he was in a quandary as he wrote, "What shall I do, resign or not? I am still undecided the officers and men have asked me not to resign but I wish to." Apparently Graybill had written often, seeking his wife's opinion on his military obligation, and she refused to comment. He wrote, "I suppose that you are indifferent or think I came in without your consent and

I may get out if I can without your advice but don't flatter yourself that it is as easy to get out of the service at this time as it was to get in." Graybill's letters reflected his inability to reconcile two duties, one to his home and family, the other to the army and Confederacy.

Two days later, Graybill wrote home again. He feared that she no longer cared what he did. "You seem to think you have no influence over my actions." Trying to avoid conflict he asked, "How long or how much influence will I have with you when you come to that conclusion, but let us not talk to each other in this way for I have enough to bear without thinking that my wife cares nothing for me." Graybill struggled to assure her: "I have always intended to make life's uneven ways as pleasant as I could. I know that I have erred and failed in many instances but never through intention and hoping and praying God that you and all the family and I may be able to keep the path of duty."[23]

As the war dragged on, Colonel Graybill feared that he was losing his wife. The letters in the late summer and early autumn showed the same pull from home as well as his loyalty to the Confederacy. He continued to promise her he would get home, but the no furlough policy apparently made it difficult even for officers to return to Georgia. He reassured her that he had not been "weaned from home" and that home seemed "a thousand times more dear to me than before the commencement of this cruel war."[24] Although Graybill's unit was reassigned from its Virginia post to Lake City, Florida, he did not get home.

Graybill wrote from Florida in February 1864. Replying to questions his wife had posed about scarcity of goods and the prospects of selling things, Graybill's gravest anxieties poured forth:

> Now my dear I am going to tell you something that haunts and depresses me, it may be a diseased imagination. Several times last fall and twice since I returned to camp it has seemed as if my spirit, my soul, or my life has left my body and visited other places, once I seemed to meet my mother and when I hastened to embrace her and to receive her caress she smiled sweetly pointed toward heaven and vanished from my sight and her face more beautiful than I ever knew it this occurred on the night of the 14th inst. All the other times I seem to be near you but there was something nearer you and that you seemed satisfied yes happy with, and when you turned your eyes on me there was a look of expression on your countenance that you did not want me to come between you and that object. Oh what a sadness this vision dream madness call it what you will spreads over my future in this life for I feel sure that it cannot affect my happiness in eternity for I am trying to keep my lamp trimmed and to re-

fill my lamp and be ready to meet the bridegroom when he shall appear to enter in and sup with Him and he with me.[25]

Graybill's decision to forsake duty to wife and family had clearly taken its toll. He was overwhelmed by the belief that she no longer wanted him. There is no indication from the register that Graybill ever deserted to the enemy. As an officer, it is unlikely, but his feelings and fears were typical. However, it is clear that his home situation never reached the depth of the hardship the soldiers in upcountry Georgia and the upper Piedmont endured. The call from home was strong, and those who failed to heed it paid their own price. By late 1863, the conflicts between country and home were resolved more on the side of home, as the Confederacy dissolved and demonstrated that the only way a soldier's family could be cared for was by the soldier himself.

The call from home began when some women resisted their men's response to military duty. For those who acquiesced, no matter how grudgingly, the separation soon took its toll. Early in 1862, Samuel Brewer's wife began inquiring when he would return home. Brewer irately repeated that he had enlisted for twelve months. In Virginia, he claimed peer pressure led him to reenlist, and he signed on for three more years. By 1862, reenlistment had become mandatory, but this news must have crushed his wife. When she wrote him in June, she signed her letter "heartbroken." Brewer chastised her for signing off in such a manner. Whether Brewer would have acted on her entreaties can never be known, for he died at Gettysburg.[26]

In May 1862 Martha Moody wrote to her husband from Campbell County, on the southern fringe of the upper Piedmont. Her letter stated that all the men from ages sixteen to thirty-five had now left home, and she listed some of the families whose men had left. Their neighbor "Dave hamel" left, and with him "another family broke up you never saw the like." She told her husband that "thar has bin the mots dethes among the wemin this year I have ever herd of and I dont thinkno wonder if truble can cill any body I dont no way they wont all dye." Martha feared that the longer the war continued, the worse the home situation would become. "I cnt see what will be come ofthe wemin and chilren if peas ant made before what they hav is eat up it looks harde that poor farmers are gone and thare families are left and the speculators are gitng evry thing off of them they can now."[27]

Mrs. Moody did not expressly call her husband home. Like Samuel Brewer, the fortunes of war never gave Moody the chance to desert. After he fell in battle in August 1862, she received $38.52 due him from the Confederate army. Mrs. Moody did not even receive the bounty for her husband having enlisted because he died before the twelve-month vesting period had elapsed.[28]

The pressures from home as represented in women's letters began before Sherman's invasion in 1864. Confederate civilian morale was beginning to waver. Recent scholarship argues that morale at home was tied to the success of the Confederate army and remained strong until final defeat. However, the calls from home suggest otherwise. Women's pleas reached their men in the field and rang with desperation. Emaline Ammons Young of Cedartown in Polk County described the women of north Georgia as "all broken hearted." Young admitted that she was no better "than other women," but she did not think she could stand her husband being gone. In an undated letter, she wrote again in greater anguish, "It is useless for me to tell you I want to see you for language is inadequate to express myself in that respect. Sometimes I feel like I will see you soon, but when I think of the men who left the settlement, a year ago, I almost despair."[29]

Talithra Fowler of Milton County, north of Atlanta, wrote her husband in October 1863. Her letter reflected her rudimentary skills in writing, but her message came through clearly. She had expected him to return: "I look for you the last days very hard it was painc ful to me to hear that you was note a cum ing home." The separation had become unbearable. "I want to see you very bad and I do hopeit wont be long I feel lik I havnt got a friend sometimes it looks lik I am left alone." Her letter ended, "I am thinking of you if I cant see you and be with you. . . . Cum home the first chnce you get." George received a certificate of being unfit for duty in February 1864. However, had he not, he might well have joined many of his comrades and come home the first chance he got.[30]

The call from home that began in 1863 continued after Sherman's invasion. In October 1864 Mrs. M. M. Humpheries wrote her husband to apologize for being unable to get him a detail to come home. She begged him to return, saying, "I think if your superior authority knew my necessities and my situation and a house full of children dependent entirely on me for you are not allowed to come home to our assistance let the consequences be as it may I cant help but think that if they knew their hearts would soften and they would let you come home."[31] Mrs. Humpheries's home county and her husband's unit are unknown, but her appeal to her husband's "superiors" is interesting. If only they knew how badly the home front situation had become, she believed, they would surely let the men come home. Her belief did not reflect the reaction of Confederate authorities, who were barraged by constant and unsatisfied entreaties from Georgia women to bring their men home.

Gen. Robert E. Lee represented the highest, if not the most respected, Confederate military authority at any time during the war. However, Lee afforded no relief for those Georgia women laboring under intense hardship at home. His position represented the inflexibility of a Confederate military system that desperately needed every able-bodied man, but failed to understand the pressures from home. Soldiers and civilians had limits on the hardships they could be expected to endure. Faced with losing their family or farm, soldiers had no reason to continue suffering for the Confederacy. In April 1863, Lee conclusively put to rest any notion that soldiers, once committed to battle, could be allowed to return home. Replying to a letter from an Athens woman, Lee wrote that he had received her request to have one of her sons discharged or furloughed, but he offered no relief: "You have set a noble example in devoting your ten sons to the service of the country and in encouraging them to defend their homes. We need every good soldier we have in the army. If we allowed all to return who are needed at home we would soon have no country and no homes. I sympathize with you in your anxieties and privations, but I trust your kind neighbors in Georgia will not permit you to want while your brave sons are doing their duty manfully against the enemy."[32] Any other mother, wife, or daughter receiving such a letter got a clear message. Their men would not be allowed to return. For women in the upper Piedmont and upcountry Georgia, their neighbors had too little themselves to help others in need. Faced with the reality that only peace or death could reunite these families, many north Georgia women lost hope in peace.

In his November 1863 inaugural address, Georgia's governor called on the state's women to support the war. Joseph Brown reminded Georgians that America would never have won the "first revolution" and secured its independence from Britain without the contribution of the nation's women. He insisted that "without their energetic efforts and moral support of the wives, mothers, sisters and daughters of the Confederate States, our liberties would before this time have been lost." Governor Brown insisted, "With their continued effort and God's blessing upon it, women will avenge the blood of their slain relatives."[33]

The leaders of the Confederate government did not understand Georgia. For Upcountry and upper Piedmont families whose soldiers would soon have the opportunity to give up the fight, revenge put no bread on the table. The Georgia legislature passed a bill in 1864 that provided women with grounds for divorcing their husbands if they deserted the army. To north Georgia women, this law enforced the wrong conduct because divorce might come if these men did not desert. By late 1863, when many wives and mothers had become widows, God already seemed to have withdrawn his blessing from the Confederacy.[34]

From across Georgia, letters poured in begging Governor Brown either to return their men or to exempt them from military service. The letters, starting in 1863 and running throughout 1864, resembled the one Catherine Stephenson of Bartow County sent to Brown in September 1863. After asking that he arrange for the return of her son, Bud, Mrs. Stephenson explained that he had left before turning sixteen, and she offered to trade her husband for him if the boy could return until he turned eighteen. "I love my country and am willing to make a sacrifice for the good of our country, I will give up the father of my children to his god and country for my darling boy."[35] Brown's response does not exist, but he probably declined Mrs. Stephenson's request. This story repeated itself as women, with no one to spare, faced the loss of their means of support. There is no record of a Stephenson deserting to the enemy, but the desertions in 1864 increased in response to women's pleas.

From Athens, located along the southern border of the upper Piedmont, Mary Bennett used simple logic in asking Brown to "liberate my husband he is dooing no good this." Why did she need him? "To help me get bred for my children or will starve to death. . . . Pleas dear governor brown have murcy on and give me my husband as he can doe a little good at hom. . . . I hop you will let my husband come hom in time to make my crop as I can not make it myself."[36] Bennett's note tells the story of a small, subsistence farm, being deprived of an essential part of the workforce and completely breaking down.

North of Athens, in Jackson County, Lucinda Baugh wrote to whomever she could find to obtain the release of her husband from active duty. Her letter was addressed to "Captain James Hudgins, or Major of the Battalion, or Colonel of the Regiment, on the grounds of necessity." The letter found its way to the governor's desk. Mrs. Baugh had three teenagers and two infant daughters whom she could not feed. According to her petition, written in longhand by someone else, Mrs. Baugh had twelve to fifteen acres of wheat that needed plowing, twelve acres of oats, and thirty-five acres of corn. Since all the neighbors had gone to war, without her husband her farm would fail to feed her family.[37] Any hope she had of seeing her husband alive depended on his willingness to choose between his duty to the Confederacy and his responsibility to her and his family.

Elizabeth Kulgar, of Carroll County at the southwestern edge of the upper Piedmont, wrote Governor Brown in February 1864 about what had happened to her family after the departure of her husband. Pvt. John Kulgar served in the Oglethorpe Guards but had apparently become ill. His wife wanted him sent home. She explained, "Thare are six girl children and one baby boy that are not able to help themselves, they are out of corn and cant get any." Her farm was forty miles from any store, and without Mr. Kuglar she had no hope of feeding her family.[38] Her situation was not unique, as some sixty-eight men deserted to the enemy from Carroll County.

Mrs. C. M. Davis of Taylor County, south of Atlanta, explained the inability of the yeoman community to help one another. Her husband had been called to the militia and probably served in or near Atlanta. In 1864 she petitioned Governor Brown to discharge her husband given that she and her seven daughters were totally dependent on him for support. Apparently the family had a healthy crop in the field, but without him they could not bring it in. Her neighbors "were just as bad off." Moreover, Mr. Davis had a sixty-year-old mother with no man to help her, and two widowed sisters, one with two children and the other with five, who also depended on Davis.[39]

From Lumpkin County in upcountry Georgia, Catherine McDonald wrote of a similar condition. She was a fifty-year-old widow and had recently broken her right arm in a fall. Mrs. McDonald had already lost two sons during the war, and her two sons-in-law were in danger of never returning. One languished in a northern prison, and the other remained at the front. Her home situation was a disaster. She had nine children of her own, six grandchildren, and almost no male help. Her only remaining son had just been ordered to the front in the most recent militia call. "If there be any case which can appeal successfully to your excellency's discretion for exemption at least for six months or a year it seems to her this is the case." Mrs. McDonald begged Brown to allow her to "keep the lad at home for a while" and flatly asked, "Is it the policy of the state to subject the widow and her children and grandchildren to suffering and starvation in order to have the services of a mere boy in the ranks?"[40] McDonald's neighbors and immediate family offered no relief because they were in the same condition.

Such letters to Governor Brown reflect not only the plight of these communities but also the need for someone to return to assist everyone in the neighborhood. For the upper Piedmont and Upcountry, the departure of key artisans and tradesman was also damaging to the local economy. William Miller of Lumpkin County provides a good example of such a man. In July 1864, his wife wrote Brown to ask for the return of her husband because his absence had left her "a house full of children . . . almost entirely without provisions [to] subsist." Miller was one of the county's artisans and made wooden barrels, boxes, and "vessels of any kind useful to settlement or farmers." His labor provided the sole means of support for the Miller family,

[margin note: Loss of mill destroyed the econ structure]

and his wife pleaded with Governor Brown to return him to where he "might be able to sustain his almost helpless family and be advantageous to the settlement or citizens of this section as there is no such workman in the neighborhood." She believed he would provide badly needed male support for her settlement because "he has also bin when at home kind and ablidging in everyway that he possibly could be to war widows and helpless families and doing this without half pay of his labor."[41]

This letter requested Miller's return for the sake of "family and settlement now." Fifty citizens of Lumpkin County signed the letter. Unlike the self-contained plantation communities of the black belt, or even the smaller slave-holding yeomen farms where women could depend on the work of even a few slaves, most of the upper Piedmont and upcountry Georgians had lost not only their husbands, essential for agriculture, but also the men whose skills enabled the community to survive. A petition from Barentha Busbee of Macon County reveals a similar blending of personal and community needs. Her husband, a mechanic and cooper by trade, served in the First Georgia Battalion. Her plea shows how desperate the situation could be, not only for an artisan's family but for a community deprived of his abilities. Mr. Busbee believed she and her family would starve if her husband did not come home soon.[42]

In April 1863, seventeen Upcountry women from Forsyth County petitioned Governor Brown to seek the discharge of William Jasper Blackstock. Because Blackstock was the "sole miller" in the county and no corn could be ground without him, the petition stated that many people would suffer or starve if Blackstock were not discharged or detailed back to Forsyth County. From Hart County came a similar request. Martha Teasley wrote Brown to beg for the return of her son. Because George Teasley owned and operated the local grist mill, the community's limited grain supply could not be ground to meal without him. The same situation prevailed in Heard County after M. M. Taylor left home to serve in the state guard. His wife had six children to support and a mother-in-law, and she knew of five other families in the area who had no male to support them. Mrs. Taylor wanted her husband released to help save what grain might be salvaged. Moreover, the local mill had gone down because the men who operated it had gone to war. Without them, Mrs. Taylor wrote, "we are left in a forlorn condition."[43]

Such letters Governor Brown received in 1863 and 1864, when desertion to the enemy escalated among Georgia's soldiers. They reflected severe deprivations on the home front and acute distress. Most of these letters appeared before the autumn of 1864, the point when most historians assume desertion escalated. Although Georgians continued to desert, desertion actually declined after September 1864.

Few letters have survived from Georgia women to their soldiers in the field. Such letters requesting them to desert might have been quickly destroyed for fear of discovery in the event they were captured trying to desert. If the letters to their husbands matched those to Governor Brown in the intensity of their plea, it is understandable how difficult it must have been for soldiers with the ability to desert to resist the calls for help from home.

In 1863 Fannie Dickinson asked the governor to allow her husband to return home to drive the mail. If Brown would do that, she would "get down on my knees & pray for you & and god will bless you forever." Margaret Thompson of Perry had thirteen children. Her forty-eight-year-old husband, Stephen, had been called to war. She begged for his return:

> O most noble governor I would humbly fall on my knees before you if I could be present with you. I was told you had refused to see the ladies. If I had went I had been as one of the foolish virgins. May Lord of glory soften your heart and feel for the poor and kneedy. If you will let my husband come home I'll feel grateful so long as I live if so you may be most successful and when you are called from time to eternity may you be of the welcome to a heavenly home where there is no war nor sorrow there. Expose me not for I am a poor feeble woman. Please send me an answer. If it is in the negative it seems my heart would almost burst. My charge is so great, O may I be resigned to my fate if my request has been amyss pardon me.[44]

If Mrs. Thompson did not move Governor Brown, her words certainly would have moved her husband. This letter and others like it possessed a degree of desperation that could only have driven husbands, fathers, and brothers home. In addition, such a letter offered exoneration to men who chose to desert in the belief that home came before the Confederacy. As common soldiers, Upcountry and upper Piedmont soldiers carried the fight for rich men who did not have to make the same sacrifice. Georgia was on the verge of extraordinary hardship and unexpected disaster, and these hardships precipitated more and more calls from home.

The first shortage of an essential resource in Georgia struck in the early winter of 1862. In a world without refrigeration, food preservation was so primitive that salt was an essential commodity that had to be constantly imported or produced. A man from Banks County wrote the governor to confirm that citizens of that north Georgian county had begun to count the number of soldiers' widows for the purpose of allocating salt to those women. Without salt, there could be no fresh meat, and the salt shortage came quickly. Early in 1862, a Baldwin County man wrote to plead for additional salt. Because the allotment provided to the county did not meet its needs, he requested twenty-five more sacks. In an April 1862 edition of the *Macon Daily Telegraph*, an advertisement appeared offering five thousand dollars from the governor's office for anyone who could devise some way of making salt for the interior of Georgia or who could find a source sufficient to supply that part of the state. The advertisement stated that usually salt supplies existed where coal deposits had been found. Only Dade County met that description in Georgia. The shortage worsened as the Confederate army seized salt destined for Georgia's civilians. A. O. Bacon, an official on Governor Brown's staff, pleaded with Secretary of War James Seddon to return 6,000 pounds of salt that had been seized by the army. His letter is undated, but it appeared about the same time in 1863 that other letters poured into Brown's office from counties across Georgia seeking salt.[45]

Salt epitomized the Southern dilemma, for there was not enough salt to provide for both civilians and the army. There is evidence that the army had exhausted its supply as early as mid-1862. B. J. Moody, a Georgia private in the Army of Northern Virginia, stated flatly: "I can tell you the salt has most give out and I cant tell you how the armey will be kept up without salt I dont thinke wee could live here long without that article."[46] Even if the army survived, without salt there was a serious possibility those at home would not. An Upcountry woman from Chattooga County, with five children and no husband, explained the problem to Governor Brown in 1863. She had several cows and other stock, including enough hogs to make meat for a year. The government had tried to seize her livestock for the army; although she was willing to share what she had "with the poor soldiers," she could not give up all she had.[47]

The salt shortage led to an immediate effort by Governor Brown to alleviate the problem. In the spring of 1862, according to the Salt Census, Brown initiated a program designed to distribute salt rations throughout the state to widows of Confederate soldiers. This program eventually grew to include women who claimed a soldier as their sole means of support, as well as widows who still had sons in the service. As with so many well-intentioned plans, this one failed those people in upcountry Georgia who needed salt most. Preserving slaughtered meat absolutely required salt, but men's absence in war meant they could no longer make the long trek necessary to get it. Women, forced to do their work and that of their husband, no longer produced excess items like butter that they could sell in order to buy salt. Realizing the acute distress the salt shortage caused throughout the state, Georgia's government tried to provide salt for everyone. The salt and grain relief programs required needy families to comply with an administrative procedure in order to receive allotments. The names of those who applied for salt went into a master list, indexed by county and year. According to the Salt Census, families in most of Georgia's counties received salt for both 1863 and 1864. Some even received salt in 1862, the first year of the program. Eligibility depended on timely registration, and the failure to register made a family ineligible for salt or for any other form of government relief.

Registration for salt rations took place in town, with notices of where to register appearing in local newspapers. Anyone who could not read and who lived in rural areas where papers were scarce or who lived too far from the registration site might miss the opportunity to obtain salt rations.[48] Mountains and isolation characterized the Upcountry and the northern upper Piedmont. Rome, in Floyd County, was the only town of any size in the region. The Upcountry had no newspaper of general circulation until after the war. Even if there had been, there was low literacy in a region where the economic cycle subordinated education to the demands of subsistence agriculture. Although the Upcountry desperately needed salt, the administration of salt rations may have left out many citizens. Many of the forms needed to qualify for salt and other types of relief had to be purchased. A newspaper advertisement of July 1863 offered a set of blank forms for three dollars, which was too much for cash-poor residents. Need alone did not guarantee assistance. A family had to have money just to file a claim even after discovering itself entitled to relief.[49]

When a family managed to file a claim, the administrative red tape that accompanied verifying its validity often left destitute families with nothing. One observer noted that various relief funds designed to aid the families of soldiers actually worked hardship on those they were intended to assist. The family of Pvt. B. Blair of Taylor County provides an excellent example. Blair joined a Bibb County unit, the Thomason Guards, a company in the Sixty-first Regiment Georgia Infantry that had been formed eight months before any unit organized in Taylor County. When his wife filed for relief, Taylor County authorities rejected it. Although he served in the Confederate army and resided in Taylor County, she nevertheless did not qualify for aid in Taylor County because her husband had not joined a Taylor County unit. When she applied to the relief fund of Bibb County, the county where her husband joined, she was denied because she did not reside in that county. Mrs. Blair had fallen through a crack created between two relief funds. James Harmon, the clerk of the Taylor Relief Fund, lamented how many families fell through such cracks. Elsewhere in the state, a Washington County woman complained that the county clerks failed to draw names, that women's names had been erroneously removed from the rolls, and that once women were on the rolls, the money and other relief provided came in insufficient quantities.[50]

Why many families did not receive an allotment is open to speculation, but the Salt Census demonstrates that some Upcountry counties did not receive salt rations after 1862 and most did not receive any after 1863. Murray County on the Tennessee border received no salt rations. In May 1863 the Murray County clerk wrote Georgia's commissary general to find out if soldiers' families could get salt, where, and at what price.[51] Although Murray County's inability to secure salt represented the worst situation in the Upcountry, the census shows that the remainder of the region faired almost as poorly. Inadequate communications, difficulty of travel, low literacy, lack of money, and the inability to move through the administrative process all contributed to the Upcountry's receiving few salt rations.

Dade and Whitfield Counties received nothing after the 1862 allotment. One woman's plight is revealing. Elizabeth Wade of Whitfield County wrote Governor Brown in August 1863 to complain: "Last winter our salt was detained in Atlanta until we made application to you. It was then sent to us but not until they had exchanged 'Liverpool' salt for coastal salt. The delay proved disastrous for the meat." Mrs. Wade at least managed to "make application," but apparently many families throughout the Upcountry could not apply after 1863.[52] The counties of Catoosa, Chattooga, Cherokee, Fannin, Forsyth, Gilmer, Gordon, Habersham, Pickens, and Walker received no salt after 1863. Banks County, at the extreme northeast edge of the upper Piedmont, also received no salt after 1863. Only White, Union, Towns, Rabun, Lumpkin, Hall, and Dawson Counties in the Upcountry show salt allotments for 1864.[53]

The salt shortage indicated how the war undermined the Upcountry's family, community, and economic structure. The shortage of salt soon combined with other factors to render Georgia's home front a disaster late in 1863.[54]

The shortage of salt clearly caused severe hardship for Georgia's civilian population because the absence of salt meant that meat disappeared from the diet. Other regions of the state also needed salt. The southeast Wiregrass region relied on a livestock-based economy, and salt, as a meat preservative, would have been essential. However, southeast Georgia is situated closest to the Atlantic Ocean and could obtain coastal salt. The Salt Census indicates that all but five Wiregrass counties received salt rations after 1863.[55] While the upper Piedmont and Upcountry needed salt as badly as the rest of the state, in theory the absence of salt should not have rendered the region totally

Men like Thomas Asbury (right) and his unidentified companion left Floyd County to serve in the Confederate army. Although there is no record of Asbury deserting, at least not to the Union, eighty-two soldiers from Floyd County did take that route home. Photo FLO-151, courtesy of the Georgia Department of Archives and History.

(*Opposite top*) *The Chitwood Brothers—John, Daniel, and Pleasant—from Gilmer County served in the Twenty-third Georgia in the Army of Tennessee. Their unit alone had thirty deserters, and Gilmer County had over two hundred. Photo* GOR-517, *courtesy of the Georgia Department of Archives and History.*

(*Opposite bottom*) *William Thomas Bailey and Henry M. Bailey from Hart County in the Upcountry. Like many families from north Georgia, these brothers enlisted together. Photo* HRT-43, *courtesy of the Georgia Department of Archives and History.*

(*Above*) *Leander Jones of Gilmer County served in the Sixty-fifth Georgia Infantry, one of the Upcountry units with high desertion rates. There is no record of Jones deserting to the enemy, perhaps because he eventually secured duty with the Eighth Regiment and served in Georgia. He was said to have killed a dozen Yankees in one encounter. Nevertheless, many good fighters did desert. Photo* MUR-62, *courtesy of the Georgia Department of Archives and History.*

(Above left) R. Harrison Nations was one of many young
men from Whitfield County who answered the call. He
was unusual, though, in that he enlisted with a unit
outside his home county. Photo WTF-9, courtesy of the
Georgia Department of Archives and History.

(Above right) Thomas Watson of the Sixty-fifth Georgia,
Fannin County, deserted to the Union, then served in the
Union army. He returned to Fannin County after the
war and lived until 1908. Photo SPC-18/79, courtesy of the
Georgia Department of Archives and History.

(Opposite) Perhaps some men did not return home because
they knew that women, such as Nancy Hill Morgan in
Troup County, could take care of themselves. Morgan
organized a militia unit, known as the Nancy Harts,
made up exclusively of women. Photo courtesy of the Nancy
Harts Photo Collection, Troup County Archives,
LaGrange GA.

The maze of trenches and obstacles of the Atlanta defenses provided cover for Confederate soldiers slipping across the battlefield into Union lines. Library of Congress photo B-8171-3643.

destitute. North Georgia relied on grain-based food systems, so without meat, grain products could still sustain the average family. Thus, in the Up-country and upper Piedmont regions, feeding the family should have been possible, even if difficult.

An article appeared in Milledgeville's October 10, 1861, edition of the *Southern Recorder*, entitled "Good Advice to Planters." It encouraged farmers to "Sow Wheat Rye Barley." The article explained that the South needed large grain crops of all kinds and could not depend on any outside source for grain. Before the war, the South's urban centers relied on the northeast United States for flour and other grain-based products. In order to sustain its army and citizenry, the South had to step up grain production.

The spring and early summer of 1862 foretold the fate of Georgia's grain crops. In April, John Ethridge of Macon wrote to his brother in the Fourth Georgia Infantry. His letter contained gossip and other items of personal interest but carried the grim message that "women and children would soon be suffering due to the lack of wheat." Later that month, a soldier stationed at Camp Philips, Georgia, informed his wife, Fannie, that the Georgia wheat crop was failing and that provisions had become scarce all over the state. As the summer of 1862 wore on, the picture became clear. An Atlanta man tried to console his brother, a Pike County farmer. "I am sorry to hear that your wheat and oats have failed. Such is the fate nearly everywhere in the south—not so good in Cherokee as was expected three weeks ago—some portions almost a failure. If the lord withholds the rain as to cut off corn we shall be in very bad condition. I cannot see the end of our troubles."[56] The lack of rain threatened the grain crops, and only time would tell if they survived. An article in the *Macon Daily Telegraph* on July 26, 1862, referred to the general drought conditions throughout the state that were "hurtin corn bad."

What nature did not destroy, man soon did. Lacking the severity of drought, some Georgians were willing to forsake the needs of the majority for their own personal gain.

The corn and other grains that survived the drought often did not reach the families who desperately needed the food. Some Georgians diverted grains to the distillation of liquor. In his letter to Governor Brown, a man described the terrible condition of the residents of Gilmer County because the distilleries took up all the corn and wheat. The writer begged Brown to send someone to tear down the distilleries, which he called "a worse scourge than Lincoln's army." A petition from "Your Friends in Pike City" told much the same story. Two local distilleries operated in the open, "taking corn out of the mouths of women and children and using it to make whiskey to kill their husbands and sons."[57] The distillation of liquor might appear as an incidental drain on the state's grain supplies, but the correspondence to the governor and his actions revealed the enormity of the problem. Brown issued an executive proclamation condemning grain distilleries, making their operation illegal, and promising to shut them down. Hettie Oliver claimed to speak for all Georgia women when she thanked Brown for his action. In March 1862 she observed that she was not "alone in these feelings of thankfulness; hundreds, yes thousands of despairing, heart broken wives, mothers, and sisters will hail it as glad tidings of great joy."[58] The lack of correspondence after 1862 suggests that Brown effectively moved against distilleries in Georgia.

Distilleries

While liquor distilleries had presented problems, a much greater hardship arose from the hoarding of necessities and the inflated prices for wheat and corn. Speculation starting almost immediately after shortages began, appeared immune to government efforts to curtail it, and actually spread into the government itself, which added to the problem and increased the hardships of north Georgia.

Pvt. William H. Lopper of the Fifty-second Georgia wrote his mother and father from his camp at Taswell, Tennessee, in August 1862. Mocking those who said they would "sink their last dollar into the cause of the south," Lopper believed that it was a good time to do so, and he went straight to the heart of the problem. The soldiers knew what transpired at home, and Lopper admitted, "There is much complaint about extortion at home and not without cause. The way things are sold now the poor soldier and his family cannot procure the necessaries of life." He feared that the corruption at home might overcome Georgia before the Northern troops could. "We can successfully battle against those deluded men who are armed and hired to make war on us, but hunger and starvation will overcome us . . . who can withstand the tide of extortion and unpatriotic speculation that like a broad river flows through our land." Flour sold for ten to twenty dollars a bag, while salt went for thirty-five to forty cents a pound: "What soldier at eleven dollars a month can procure a living for himself and family?"[59]

In exchange for the sacrifice of their labor and their skill, yeomen soldiers received only eleven dollars per month. With rampant inflation caused by speculation, who could hope to provide for themselves and their families? Speculation not only caused home front hardship but undermined soldiers' morale. What began in 1862 as frustration in camps and entrenchments far from home would become in 1864 an irresistible pull as soldiers, who learned of hardships at home from letters and newspapers, finally saw for themselves once they returned to Georgia.

Margaret Hudlow of Dawson County described the effects of speculation on Upcountry families. The picture she painted makes it understandable why soldiers from the region took advantage of the return home and deserted. She begged Brown to "assiste us in tellin the speculators how trifling they are treating the soldies wives an that they are whiping our sodiers wors than the yankees." She asked Brown what soldiers would do "when they hear how their familes is having to go an beg an pay one mounths wages for two bushels of corn he cant ceap his family in bread an have eno meat attall. Is this incouraging to a poor soldier who has to lye in ditches and bare all the harships of a camp life?" Ms. Hudlow did not think so, and she added that "many a pore fellow has lost his life and left a helpless family to be sneard at by these speculating villions who will not let them have anything until they get redy." The crop either had failed or was in the process of failing, as "no man has got two bushels of corn." She had four children. Her health was so bad that "I cant spin I have bin nearly eight years that I could not walk a step, my husband is now home badly diseased from the exposure of camp life. . . . Think of this soldiers may fight blead and die for thare rights but will not get them."[60] Mrs. Hudlow offers insights into the devastation of wartime shortage and how demoralizing such news was for soldiers. How could a man from Dawson or any other Upcountry county hear this story and resist the urge to desert?

One of the tragedies of war is the loss of correspondence and other records that might cast even more light on the era. Many soldiers' letters home remain because they were kept safe by their loved ones who often hung on every precious word, but many letters from home have disappeared, having been destroyed in battle or thrown away by soldiers to prevent their capture by the enemy. The concerns they conveyed must be inferred from the soldiers' responses to the hopes, fears, frustrations, and hardships expressed in the letters sent from home. In a letter to her sweetheart, Miss M. Black begged Pvt. Henry Johnson to write. Her July 1864 letter offers some explanation as to why so many soldiers' letters survived and so many letters from home did not. "If you knew that when I receive a letter from you it is carried about my person until another is received and then carefully put away with my most valued treasures. . . . I have never had the strength to ask you before, but would like to know how you dispose of my letters—kindly— with—I hope."[61] Georgia women wrote not only to their men but to their governor. Enough of these letters survive to see the war unfold within Georgia and the tremendous hardship that existed before Sherman entered the state in 1864.

In November 1862 Mrs. Wellborn sat down in an Atlanta residence to write Governor Brown. She was only visiting Georgia from Glennville, Alabama, but her ten eloquent pages constitute a searing indictment of wartime speculation. She had been in Atlanta and other parts of Georgia for several months, so her observations covered the full extent of speculation in the state. Her message was that prewar patriotism gave way to wartime greed, with the soldiers at the front and their wives and children at home suffering the most.

Mrs. Wellborn's letter began almost apologetically, justifying the imposition on Brown's time by her own sympathy for the "suffering humanity." She hoped that he could find it within his power to alleviate the suffering caused by wartime speculation. At the mere talk of lower prices, speculators "ran off all they can to get it out of reach of the city authorities." Wellborn could not understand how Brown or anyone within the Confederate government could expect soldiers to fight for a country that would allow "a set of black hearted Tories to remain at home and perish their families at home." Speculation was ruining the Confederacy. Mrs. Wellborn insisted that "the soldiers who have families and friends at home suffering for food and grain on account of the speculators are swearing vengeance on them, they say when the war is over, they will not lay down their arms until they have been avenged of this wrong, that they will have another war at home." She repeated what others had already told the governor: "It is beyond human reason to expect men to submit to such wrongs any longer than they are compelled to. How can our government expect complete success, while they suffer things to go on in such a manner?"

Mrs. Wellborn reminded Brown that the soldiers knew what happened at home. Atlanta had an abundance of goods, yet the suffering continued. With potatoes selling at two dollars per bushel and salt at one dollar per pound, the soldiers' families could not survive. Wellborn claimed to have seen goods stashed away under the counter to be sold later at much higher prices. She begged Brown to stop it. To her, "necessity knows no law," and it was time for him to intervene.

Speculation existed throughout Georgia. Wellborn described contractors' wives in Columbus who claimed they would be millionaires if the war continued a year longer, with their husbands maintaining their current level of government contracts. Some people boasted of making over a hundred thousand dollars in six months on government clothing contracts. The Quartermaster Department, Commissary Department, and virtually every other branch of government that contracted with private individuals had made such men rich at the expense of the soldiers. Wellborn demanded to know why soldiers had to eat spoiled meat or go without food. Her husband, a soldier, "has been doomed to all the privations and sufferings of thousands of other soldiers."[62]

Mrs. Wellborn wrote of the hardships Georgia's women faced with their husbands, fathers, and sons serving in the army. With wheat crops failing, the demand far outstripped the supply. Unable to pay cash for most goods, much less the drastically inflated prices that necessities brought, the families and communities in the Upcountry and the upper Piedmont slowly began to starve.

One of the most distressing aspects of speculation was the part that the government took in the problem. Government speculation hurt everyone, but yeomen farmers suffered the most. Those who had grown sufficient crops to feed themselves, or perhaps to create a surplus to survive the winter, sold them to government agents for fear that if they did not sell, the government would confiscate them. Many unscrupulous agents took the goods, held them, and resold them. Hungry citizens lost faith in the government. A Stockton resident described what occurred when relief provisions designated for soldiers' families were not distributed. Twelve to thirteen women in the county forced their way into the local depot and seized all of the bacon held in the storehouse. Believing the provisions destined for them had been diverted, these women took matters into their own hands.[63]

Speculation also encouraged other forms of fraud. Some men stooped so low as to traffic in forged substitute papers, which allowed men who could not otherwise escape the service to remain at home, denying any relief to those who had been fighting for at least a year. W. P. Renfroe was arrested in September 1863 on the charge of forging papers or acting as an accessory to forgery.[64]

By the spring of 1864, speculation had become worse. Some men called for a list of speculators to be disseminated throughout Georgia and the army itself. John F. Saunders ran an advertisement in the May 15, 1864, *Columbus Daily Enquirer* entitled "For Posterity." He wanted a "roll of honor" prepared that listed every speculator and the type of speculation he practiced, with a separate list of all government officials who speculated and abused the public trust. With the Army of Tennessee camped in Georgia and moving south, its soldiers could read about those who had profited at their expense.

In the midst of all this speculation, natural disaster struck the Upcountry. Following a summer of drought that had damaged the wheat crop, an early

September frost blighted the corn. In late 1863 the *Southern Recorder* described a bill passed by the Georgia House of Representatives that provided support to certain counties. The bill directed the quartermaster general of Georgia to furnish corn, paid for out of a $2.5 million fund established for county relief, to thirteen counties in upcountry Georgia. Every county except Cherokee, Gordon, Fannin, Union, and Forsyth had been declared sufficiently destitute to be eligible for corn. A total of 77,000 bushels of corn had been allocated to feed indigent soldiers' families. The article concluded, "We are glad that partial relief has been extended, and hope that no portion of the state will be allowed to suffer without food." As the war dragged on and production dropped off, the government made futile attempts to prevent starvation. An act passed by the Georgia legislature in 1864 was designed to end exemptions for those who had previously supplied substitutes. However, out of necessity it omitted grain farmers in 1863 who were the only males on the farm and in the family. Although well meant, it did nothing for families whose men had already departed.[65]

The situation grew more severe throughout 1863 and into 1864. The $2.5 million fund for corn rations increased to $6 million in 1864. A policy that gave money to Georgia families to buy food was made virtually meaningless because of speculation and inflated prices. Governor Brown instituted a massive corn purchase program, with county court judges supervising the distribution. For most of north Georgia, corn became the sole means of survival. In Carroll County 20 percent of the population signed the distribution lists. A Dawson County judge told Brown, "We look to you as the Joseph of our Egypt." Unlike his biblical counterpart, Joseph Brown had unfortunately not stored enough corn to meet the needs of his people. State relief operated in some form throughout Georgia, and the effectiveness of such programs varied not only by region but by county. Virtually all relief efforts fell short of what was needed.[66] By 1863, the families of the Upcountry and upper Piedmont slowly slipped into despair.

Soldiers wrote home to their families and government to express their anxieties over bands of armed soldiers and deserters roaming the mountain counties and preying on the citizenry. The first indications of the problem came from citizens in Whitfield and Gilmer Counties in December 1862. A "Minister of Gospel, Whitfield County," described a local band of partisan rangers who roamed the county, taking horses and stealing corn. "Can there be no relief granted to us Can you not form us a home protection for our wives and children Wee look to you for protection will you grant it to us We must have help or our country is ruined." Later that month, a captain from Gilmer County asked Governor Brown for permission to form a local unit to protect the citizens from wandering bands of deserters who had taken up quarters in the mountains. By October 1863 irregular units were operating as far south as Pike County. Eventually bands composed of deserters, federal escaped prisoners, and brigands found sanctuary in the swamp land of southeast Georgia. A November edition of a Columbus paper described atrocities in White County, located in the eastern part of the Upcountry: "The state of affairs in that section is said to be very bad. . . . It is hoped the authorities will send a sufficient force there to clean them out, root and branch."[67]

The letters do not indicate whether deserters in these irregular units were from Georgia or some other state, and so identifying what army, state, or county these men came from is virtually impossible. However, a June 1863 letter from Gen. Simon B. Buckner indicated that many of the deserters roaming north Georgia may have come from his Army of East Tennessee and not from Braxton Bragg's Army of Tennessee. Buckner told Brown, "Deserters from the army have become so frequent that it appears necessary to take some energetic steps to have arrested and returned to their command all who are absent without leave." The mountains of northwestern Georgia had become a safe haven for deserters, and Buckner believed that "so long as this continues to be the case so long will desertions most surely continue to occur." General Buckner apologized that Brown's state had become connected with the "Army of East Tennessee." Still, he asked Brown to hold all AWOL soldiers until they could be picked up by the army. Headquartered in Knoxville, the Army of East Tennessee operated apart from the larger and more widely recognized Army of Tennessee. Confederate records for June 1862 listed the army as having 13,458 officers and men present for duty. Given the local nature of recruiting, and Buckner's belief that the desertion problem in Georgia stemmed from his East Tennessee army, most of these deserters were probably from east Tennessee. Because the Confederate army occupied the region where their homes lay, wandering bands may have crossed into Georgia and hid in the mountains, before generating the problems Buckner and the local citizenry complained of.[68]

As this problem increased in severity, soldiers lost faith in Georgia's ability to maintain order. Thomas Trammell of the Eleventh Georgia Infantry grew so distraught that he wrote directly to Governor Brown in June 1863. He had been informed by residents of Fannin County and others that deserters were bushwhacking the county's citizenry. He believed it was Brown's responsibility to suppress such activities, and he told the governor that he felt "unwilling to fight longer for a country that will not protect our helpless families." Trammell was not alone in telling Brown, "That is the feeling of most

[handwritten margin note: Bands of deserters]

of the soldiers that is here from Fannin there is three companies here from that county and as you are aware forty percent of them have poured out their blood upon the soil of Virginia in defense of their country."[69]

The register does not reflect that Trammell ever deserted, at least not to the enemy, but of the fifty-five men from the Eleventh Georgia listed, twelve came from Fannin County. The opinions of Trammell and his fellow Fannin County soldiers slowly built up as the war went on. A soldier's willingness to fight depended on the government's ability to maintain acceptable living conditions at home. Wrote J. F. Walker in 1861, "As long as I no my wife and children are cared for and doing well I am willing to stay here and fite in defense of our beloved country."[70] So if a soldier's wife and children lacked the proper care and did not fare well, his obligation to serve crumbled.

The Upcountry and upper Piedmont soldiers' willingness to desert in such large numbers says something important about the elusive concept of Southern nationalism. Modern theories for Southern defeat argue that Union naval and military victories led to the dissolution of Confederate will, created war weariness, and destroyed morale. They specifically point to the fall of Atlanta and Sherman's March to the Sea as the pivotal military events that, when combined with Lincoln's electoral victory in November 1864, sounded the death knell of the Confederacy. By 1865 the Confederacy had lost its will for sacrifice.[71] For many historians, this is the "correct sequence of events." Defeat brought loss of will; loss of will did not bring on defeat. External and not internal forces doomed the South, with the North contributing to Southern defeat.[72]

Georgia's deserters to the enemy came before Sherman's Atlanta campaign began, and most of them had left before the fall of Atlanta. His March to the Sea actually did not drive Georgians to desert. These Georgians demonstrate the problem in trying to articulate a cohesive Confederate will, whether strong or weak. The Confederacy was not one unified whole but several parts that attempted to effect a common goal. Georgia's common soldiers, including those from the Upcountry and upper Piedmont, had lost their will to continue long before 1865, not as the result of any great military defeat but from the long, steady grind required of both soldier and civilian. Granted, some men felt demoralized after the loss at Seminary Ridge. But the defeat was far from a crushing blow. The Confederates fought well at that battle in late 1863, particularly on the Union left, and withdrew in orderly and effective fashion. What undermined the will of north Georgia's soldiers and civilians was the absence of the male population, not its failure to perform on the battlefield. While these feelings surely existed within all of Georgia's common soldiers, those from north Georgia had the opportunity to translate this loss of will into action and the benefit of a Union occupation that made it safe to return home.

The Georgia desertion pattern also calls into question the notion that Southern nationalism was ultimately tied to the performance of Lee's Army of Northern Virginia.[73] Desertion among Georgians began before the spring campaigns of 1864 and had run its course by September 1864. Lee's army remained a formidable force in the field, yielded ground only grudgingly, and was even victorious at Cold Harbor. Grant was nowhere near reducing the Confederacy in the fall of 1864. Morale among Georgians therefore was not bound to the fortunes of the Confederacy's premier army. Any sense of Southern nationalism felt by Georgia's Upcountry and upper Piedmont soldiers came from the government's ability to provide for those left at home when these men went to war. In one sense the argument of external pressure from the North as a major contributing factor to Southern defeat has merit. By not succumbing to early Confederate success and turning a short conflict into a long war, the North challenged the South's internal structure to meet the demands of modern war by not only placing an effective army in the field but by sustaining the civilian population at home. Ultimately Lee's continued success in the field provided little solace to Georgians when the state and Confederate governments proved unable to protect the home front. This crumbling nationalism suffered even more as those who could fight chose not to, and their willingness to forsake military service reached the eyes and ears of those who had done most of the fighting.

When the war began, Governor Brown confidently stated, "They [the yeomen] know that the Government of our state protects their lives, their families, and their property. . . . Every dollar the wealthy slaveholder has made may be taken by the Government of the State, if need be, to protect the rights and liberties of all."[74] If Brown did not fulfill his promise, the soldiers felt no obligation to fulfill their military commitment. This feeling grew more intense as it became evident that the planter class stood to benefit most from the war, yet refused to take much of a role in the fighting.

Despite the isolation of most inhabitants of the Upcountry and the upper Piedmont, they were not ignorant of the world around them. Historians have pointed to low literacy rates in the antebellum South as evidence of their lack of sophistication, but common people possessed common sense. The letters from such people indicate that women understood that their husbands, sons, and brothers had made sacrifices for the more affluent. In February 1864, when the Confederate government instituted another draft in anticipation of heavy campaigning, those Georgians who could escape army service did so. They also avoided the militia call in the spring and summer of 1864. Throughout the war, people had seen their neighbors forsake military duty. North Georgia's men deserted in response to the calls from family, calls strengthened by the knowledge that Georgia's planters had turned their backs on the fight and on those who did the fighting.

CHAPTER FIVE

Faces of Desertion

From Catoosa County, in the extreme northwestern corner of upcountry Georgia, an unidentified writer wrote to Gov. Joseph Brown about the inequity of sacrifices borne by citizens. He described a poor farmer named Suard who sent all five of his sons to war. The only one who returned came home in a coffin. In the same county lived a wealthy farmer named Lee, whose sons all remained safely at home, tending to the farm and the family. The writer could not understand why the poor fought while the rich stayed home. He wondered why he, like Suard, should pay for his patriotism with so high a price, asking, "Must myself and my wife have our hearts torn from us, dripping with patriotic blood?"[1]

Women suffering from their husbands' absence quickly identified those who refused to serve. In September 1862 a Columbia County woman wrote to Gen. H. C. Wayne of Governor Brown's staff. On the back of the letter she wrote: "A Woman complains of the protection given to shirkers in Columbia County." Her letter described able-bodied men in the county, with sufficient wealth and male help enabling them to join the war effort, who nevertheless sought exemptions by applying for officer positions within the militia. In contrast, she said that poor soldiers, who "cannot aspire to militia officers or hire substitutes" are being "compelled to leave wives and helpless little ones to go and fight for the liberty of the Col's Capt's and Lieutenants of the Georgia Militia."[2]

The war seemed to increase such unfairness in Georgia. Slaveholders refused to fight. A rich man's war had become a poor man's fight, with the families of soldiers all losing men. With the absence of their husbands, sons, and fathers, those still at home had fended for themselves. When soldiers returned home to Georgia, they usually found their families destitute and starving.

Laws that exempted slaveholders and allowed wealthy men to hire substitutes were only the most glaring examples of the unequal burdens of the war. Less obvious signs existed in policies that allowed the wealthy to avoid service in the Confederate army. Members of the militia usually served their obligation within the state and remained on active duty only as long as they were needed. For example, Brig. Gen. Hugh Weedon Mercer, the Confederate military commander in Savannah for most of the war, issued General Orders No. 66 in March 1863. The order allowed the militia officers presently gathered in camp to return home to their planting interests, which Mercer deemed "so essential to the welfare of the Confederacy." The militia had been called up in response to a Union threat to Savannah, but when the danger to that city passed, Mercer allowed his officers to return to their plantations.[3]

Most Georgia plantations produced cotton, as the South struggled to feed both soldier and civilian. The inequities of an aristocratic society allowed planters to return home to oversee a crop that even if harvested would not alleviate the food shortage. When north Georgia's soldiers faced the decision to continue fighting or desert and return home, the unwillingness of the rich either to provide for the families of those at war or to join in the fight made it easier to decide to desert.

Actions of rich

A woman from Fort Valley, Georgia, tried to explain this situation to Governor Brown in May 1861. Writing because her "conscience required her to write him," she understood that men must go "to sustain the rights of the country." However, it appeared to her "that all poor men from here had gone and that the rich remains who has slaves it is those in this place that has remained home who is benefited after the war it is the rich they have no mercy on the soldiers families."[4] Before conscription began and the first shots were fired, Georgia's planter class had already shifted the burden of the fighting onto yeomen farmers and poor whites. Lower-class men and women knew it was the planters who benefited the most from the war and yet stubbornly refused to fight. Brown's secession speech promising unqualified support for the families of soldiers in the field haunted him and the Confederacy.[5] Unlike the yeomen, the planter class not only escaped the fight but declined to support the families of those who did. Nonslaveholding yeomen, although not poor, were much less financially well off than planters. They also lacked even the small male workforce that one or two slaves provided. Only so long as they remained at home could the small family farms operate efficiently and feed their members. Without their men, the families and communities declined. In the early winter of 1864, the unwillingness of the affluent to share the burdens of war not only deprived Georgia and the Confederacy of badly needed men but sent a clear signal to soldiers fighting that perhaps their loyalties had been misplaced.

★ ★ ★

As the fighting receded in December 1863, the Union stood poised for its most concerted effort. The Army of the Potomac settled into winter quarters, waiting until spring to renew its struggle with Bobby Lee. With Chattanooga safely in hand, the armies of the Cumberland and the Tennessee camped just north of the Georgia border. Confederate authorities and Georgia officials plainly saw that, as soon as the weather warmed, the Union would resume its campaigns with vigor. The Confederate Congress called for another draft, and in December 1863 Georgia passed a Militia Reorganization Act. Both laws were designed to replenish the ranks of the Confederate army, which had been depleted by fighting in 1862 and 1863. However, despite Confederate efforts to sweep broadly and bring in all able-bodied men between the ages of seventeen and fifty, Georgia's planter class avoided conscription at a time when their efforts were desperately needed. Their refusal to step forward and join those who had been fighting for several years left a bitter taste in the mouths of many north Georgians. The results of Governor Brown's militia call in 1864 confirmed that the only cause still worth the effort was home and family.[6]

The Confederate draft law of February 1864 provided for exemptions of certain "qualified persons." The twenty-slave rule had originally exempted men who owned twenty or more slaves from serving in the military; the 1864 Act to Organize Forces To Serve during the War introduced the fifteen-slave rule. This law also allowed for the exemption of one overseer, or agriculturalist, on any farm that had fifteen able-bodied fieldhands, provided that the person seeking the exemption was the owner, manager, or overseer of the farm or plantation as of January 1, 1864. The law required that each exempt man put up a bond or other security to ensure his obligation to deliver within a year one hundred pounds of bacon or, at the government's choice, an equal amount of beef, for each slave on the farm or plantation of the exempted person. Even this requirement contained a loophole that allowed the exempted owner to prove that such an allotment would be impossible for him to meet and still provide for his family. Upon supplying sufficient proof, he could substitute up to two-thirds of his meat allotment with grain. The exemption also required bonded men to make any surplus available to the government for purchase at the prevailing rate so as to provide for soldiers' families.[7] For most of the war, the upper Piedmont and Upcountry had lived under a severe grain shortage, so the 1864 draft law implied that the plantation belt had not only ample grain supplies but enough surplus to substitute grain for conscription meat obligations.

Georgia kept detailed records of every man who sought and obtained an exemption from the Confederate draft in 1864. The ledger has survived only partially intact, but within its parched and crumbling pages lies further explanation of why north Georgia's soldiers deserted in 1864, why the upper Piedmont showed significant desertion, and why upcountry Georgia deserted in far greater proportions to its enlistment numbers than any other region.[8]

The ledger indicates that when the Confederacy's survival hung in the balance, the planter class, and those who were not planters but who owned at least fifteen slaves, in effect abandoned the Confederate cause for their own safety and that of their families. Those obtaining exemptions ranged from the minimum ownership of fifteen slaves to a high of seventy-nine slaves. Slave ownership allowed Georgia's planters and wealthy farmers to escape the draft, which deprived the South of almost 11,000 soldiers, a full division of infantry, at the time when such numbers would have proved crucial. The exemption not only covered all planters with over twenty slaves but shielded slave-owning yeomen with fifteen or more slaves. Aside from the lack of opportunity and the continued presence of Confederate authority, desertion in the plantation belt fell far below that of the upper Piedmont and upcountry Georgia because some of these men qualified for exemptions and never left home. Such exempted men offered no relief to the wives and families of the soldiers who were still fighting because their obligation to provide meat and other food surplus would not be due until a year after the date of their exemption. The earliest possible exemption would have been after February 17, 1864, so the first obligation to provide meat or grain would be due a year later. Most men exempted apparently secured their exemptions in May or June 1864, so their obligations did not mature until the war was over. For anyone whose obligation came due earlier, the Confederacy no longer controlled Georgia sufficiently to enforce the bond obligations. Therefore, any surplus grown by planters or other exempted slaveholders did not reach the wives and families of soldiers.

Because the exemptions reflected the distribution of slaves throughout Georgia, the Upcountry had none. A few counties at the southern end of the upper Piedmont, including Jackson, Newton, and Walton Counties, listed a handful of exempted men. Among those securing detailed jobs that enabled them to avoid the draft, Upcountry men were few in number. The upper Piedmont did a little better with Gwinnett, Carroll, and Cobb Counties all showing men detailed and exempted from the draft. Yet the vast majority of the men detailed for work at home came from outside the north Georgia area.[9]

Any Georgians who avoided the Confederate draft still fell subject to the Georgia Militia Act of December 1863. This law expressly stated that men drafted under the Confederacy's Conscription Act of 1864 were exempt from the militia act but that any Georgian who did not qualify for an exemption under the militia act could be called up. The state's militia act had several important provisions that distinguished it from Confederate conscription. The

Georgia act did not immediately press anyone into the military service. It divided the state into militia districts with an aide-de-camp for each district appointed by the governor. This aide served as a colonel and assumed the responsibility for compiling a list of every able-bodied man between the ages of sixteen and sixty within his district. The militia list included each man's name, age, occupation, birthplace, and the exemption he claimed. The list enabled the governor to call the militia into service in the event of an emergency that could not be met by the state forces already in service. The militiamen served until the emergency passed and then returned to nonactive status. While in service they drew pay and otherwise lived under the same rules and regulations as regular Confederate soldiers.[10] On the other hand, conscription committed soldiers to service immediately, took them out of the state, and kept them in the service for the entire war. Even the less stringent demands of militia duty proved more than most Georgians were willing to give in the summer of 1864.

While both the Confederate Conscription Act and the Georgia Militia Act provided for exemptions, the latter offered no relief for slaveholders. The Georgia act exempted members of the government, civil servants, members of the judicial branch, and ministers. It also contained a medical exemption that the aide-de-camp of each district had authority to grant. Because the law allowed the governor to exempt such other persons who "in his discretion may deem it absolutely necessary for the public interest to be exempted from the provisions of this act," he received a wide range of requests.[11]

The militia enrollment list explains why men refused to report or why they deserted once they reported. Most men called to duty to defend Atlanta and the rest of the state from Sherman's invasion in July 1864 were either in their late forties or had just turned sixteen, seventeen, or eighteen. When the war began, the youngest had been ages thirteen through fifteen, so they had reached the age of eligibility for military service by 1864. Because the exemptions fell under medical, governmental, religious, or special case categories, farmers had little chance to escape militia service.[12] Again, when the military call came, most who could evade the service tried to do so. Those not qualified for an exemption had little hope of receiving any type of special dispensation and had to either serve or desert. Many refused to show up, and those who did soon deserted when an opportunity presented itself. The most vocal in their opposition to serving in the militia were the men who had been exempted under the 1864 Conscription Act. Despite clear language to the contrary, many felt that Georgia had no right to force them to serve.

William Dickey wrote his wife in late October 1864, complaining that he could not keep those who had reported from leaving camp. "There is a great deal of dissatisfaction growing among the men in the camps. Particularly the bonded men." Dickey explained that many of these men "have gotten it in their heads that Gov. Brown has no business with them in the militia and Judge Richard M. Clark has decided that they are not [exempt] and that has caused the dissatisfaction among them in camp." Dickey estimated that two hundred men had returned home and said that he "would not be surprised if more men left before we get to Atlanta." Many of these bonded men, planters, and wealthier yeomen, claimed exemption under the fifteen-slave privilege and undermined the militia's morale. By November, Dickey wrote, the militia was so restless that everyone talked of going home despite the threat of a court-martial for desertion.[13]

Georgia newspaper notices listed hundreds of men as either deserters or AWOL from militia units. The register listed sixty-eight men from the First Regiment, Georgia State Militia who deserted to the enemy and took the oath. Some of the men Dickey observed leaving had actually deserted to the Union in order to avoid the wrath of the Confederate authorities. Those who lived in areas under Union control could return home safely without fear of capture. This exodus of militiamen punctuated the yearlong wave of desertion among Georgia's troops. The men who deserted the militia knew firsthand of the conditions at home. When their efforts and those of their families had failed to secure their release, detail, or exemption, desertion provided the only remaining road home.

The 1864 letters to Governor Brown from wives and mothers specifically addressed the militia call and its adverse impact on families. Polley Tillery wrote to ask that her husband be excused from the militia. He suffered from a bad leg that so crippled him he could not get to the medical board for an examination to be certified as medically exempt. After admitting that she had consumption and could not provide for herself, Mrs. Tillery begged the governor to "let us stay together what time I have living." Mrs. M. J. Porter pleaded with Brown to discharge her husband from the militia, for he had been discharged twice before and was blind in one eye. Although he was useless as a soldier, he could help her, and she wanted him back home. Mary Hilsman told the governor that his last call "took my father, the only means of support for a wife and five little helpless children." She wanted her husband to stay home and tend to his sick family.[14]

The letters written to the governor after his militia call of July 1864 demonstrated that Georgians' priorities emphasized community and family. With Sherman in control of northern Georgia and besieging Atlanta, most people preferred the protection of a husband or father to that of a state militia. The men whose return these women sought had been gone only a very short time, and some had yet to leave. While their needs should not be denigrated, they nevertheless paled in comparison with the families of Upcountry and upper Piedmont men, serving far from home for over two years. Many men deserted who believed their exemption from the Conscription Act also freed them from militia duty. Some who tried to avoid the militia had never served. Unlike the regular soldiers of the Upcountry and upper Piedmont who slowly embraced desertion, the minds of the militia were clear from the moment Brown called them to duty. In effect, these "bonded" men had already deserted the Confederacy when they chose to invoke the slaveholder exemption in order to stay home. Their willingness to ignore their militia obligations merely reinforced their previous refusal to serve. Militia desertion did not push regulars to desert because most northern Georgia soldiers had already gone, but the response of the planters, wealthier farmers, and some slaveholding yeomen to conscription helped to encourage Confederate soldiers from the Upcountry and upper Piedmont to desert. Some militia members even refused to report for duty.

The faces of desertion encompassed not only those men who appeared in the register but those whose names filled the conscription exemption rolls throughout the war. Historians have ignored what the latter did because of the way they did it. The view that the Civil War either began as or became a rich man's war but a poor man's fight is based on the wealthy paying for substitutes or taking advantage of slave-exemption clauses. James McPherson's examination of class enlistment in the North points to a more equitable distribution between blue- and white-collar workers than had long been believed. While he concedes that the war may have been a rich man's war, the fighting was not limited to the lower classes. James Robertson contends that conscription tainted the war in the South by removing the picture of free men fighting for liberty and replacing it with the belief that the poor did all the fighting.[15]

Southern conscription proved much more devastating than the unequal distribution of the hazards of combat. Georgia's experience supports the view of a poor man's fight but raises questions about how long the rich Southerners continued to support the war. After February 1864, the war ceased to be a rich man's war in Georgia. The significance of Georgia's exemption records lies not just in proving how many men avoided service but in revealing what these men offered in exchange for the privilege of staying out of the fight: money and food. The families of those north Georgia soldiers who did much of the fighting desperately needed the food, but with a year to meet one's obligation and the ability to escape it in part, the rich ultimately neither fought nor supported those who did.

In order to desert, one obviously first had to be in the military. By never joining, Georgia's slaveholders avoided the disgrace that many people associated with desertion. Just as planters with families could avoid the duel and the risk of death because of their family obligations in civilian life, the wealthy avoided military service in the belief that the government acknowledged their greater duty to their families and plantations. Yet it must be emphasized that it is not true that these exemptions ultimately benefited the South. The planters and wealthy slave-owning farmers and yeomen stayed home to protect family and property. The plantation system and cotton economy had never fed the South. By 1860 the South's principal staple crops were rice, sugar, hemp, tobacco, and cotton. Before the war, wheat, corn, and other grain crops had to come from the North's commercial agriculture system, which quadrupled its food production in the forty years preceding the war. From 1850 to 1860, planters put every available acre into cotton.[16] Although their labor force enabled them to grow sufficient food crops to feed themselves before the war, plantations had never been commercial food centers. Thus, conscription exemptions did not enhance the South's ability to feed its army and civilian population. The ability to avoid conscription signified a privilege of the wealthy. At best, the laws that made the avoidance of military service legal could not alter the fact that the wealthy deserted the Confederacy no less than the Confederate soldiers who took the oath to the Union. To brand north Georgian soldiers as cowards while condoning the actions of the planter class is historically invalid.

Even the competing economic and political realities in the South fail to support slaveholder exemptions as anything other than a privilege of wealth. When Jefferson Davis broached the subject of a universal draft, the initial response in the Confederate Congress was outrage. Even those opposed to the draft admitted its necessity, yet blamed Davis for failing to provide incentives for those who enlisted in 1861 to remain beyond their twelve-month commitment. Few Southerners could deny that without an army the Confederacy was doomed. The dispute came not with the draft itself but with the class of men exempted. The first exemptions contained within the 1862 conscription act resembled those within Georgia's 1863 militia act: government officials, ministers, educators, and other essential personnel in transportation, communication, and industry. Despite criticism that Davis retained too much discretionary power to grant individual exemptions, these exceptions made sense. Those excused from the draft formed the essential Confederate infrastructure. However, the exemption for slaveholders was not initially a part of the 1862 Conscription Act. In late 1862, when the slaveholder exemption act passed, claims that it favored the rich followed almost immediately. Davis admitted that the poor fought the country's battles, saying, "It is the poor who save nations and make revolutions." He insisted the rich were also fighting but argued that the only reason for the exemptions was to provide experienced leadership behind the Confederate lines to suppress any slave insurrection.[17]

The slave insurrection argument was weak, and even those from the plantation belt believed slave rebellion was unlikely. Although other subtle forms of slave resistance occurred and did adversely affect the Southern war effort, nothing leading up to the passage of the twenty-slave rule offered any further justification for exempting slaveholders from military service.[18] While fears persisted throughout the war, they never came to fruition (see chapter 6). The political incentive for the slaveholder exemption lay in the appeasement of the South's ruling class that saw conscription as undermining the fundamental principles upon which the Confederacy was founded. The Confederacy sought to limit the central government's intrusion on personal liberty and compulsory service, yet conscription accomplished the exact opposite result by forcing all men, regardless of class, into the service. Governor Brown led the chorus of objectors, saying that "no act of the government of the United States prior to the secession of Georgia struck a blow at constitutional liberty so felt as has been struck by the conscription act." Davis had tried to balance his cabinet appointments and in so doing had excluded some of the South's most ardent secessionists.[19] The slaveholder exemption provided some concession to Davis's critics. However, the South paid a heavy price for allowing its wealthy to avoid service under any guise, and despite economic and political arguments in favor of slaveholder exemptions, the Confederate policy undermined its war effort. While the inequities of service fell upon all of Georgia's common soldiers unable to escape military obligation, such unfairness loomed large in the thoughts of those in the position to turn their discontent into action. This knowledge added support for the soldiers from Georgia's Upcountry and upper Piedmont regions to desert a cause that many felt had long since abandoned them.

Who were these upper Piedmont and upcountry Georgian men who did the fighting, the dying, and most of the deserting? We know little about their specific lives, but what is known of their families makes it possible to draw conclusions as to what brought them home. For some, there is no written evidence of a call from home, yet these men and others like them from the upper Piedmont and upcountry Georgia confirm the yeomen's sense of honor. Just as the people in north Georgia could not allow honor to harm the community before the war, these north Georgia soldiers and their families could not allow honor to destroy their communities during war.

Jesse Cox, a twenty-eight-year-old Floyd County resident in the First Georgia Cavalry, took the oath of allegiance on March 3, 1864, and headed home. On the same day, Jesse's four brothers, Calvin, Jonathan, Joseph, and Richard, also from the First Georgia Cavalry, secured their release and went home with him. One could almost imagine the scene in early 1864, or perhaps December 1863, as the Cox "tribe" slipped out of camp and made their way across the Georgia countryside and into the Union lines. Unlike the failure of the Franklins and their seven cohorts who deserted from the Georgia State Line, the Cox boys successfully negotiated the distance between Confederate and Union lines. There are no letters to explain their motivations, but the personal information gleaned from the 1860 census is revealing.

When the Coxes went to war, they left their fifty-four-year-old widowed father, John. Sarah Cox, their eighteen-year-old sister, performed all the functions expected of the women of the family. Their two younger brothers, James and Riley, could hardly make up for the drastic loss of labor that occurred when five boys, between the ages of sixteen and twenty-four, left the farm in 1862. Although they owned no slaves, the census shows that the Cox family owned seven thousand dollars in real property, a sizable farm, too large for an aging man, his daughter, and two adolescent sons to work alone. Riley, the youngest boy, was only ten in 1860. The Coxes had not been in Georgia long because every member of the family was born in North Carolina.[20] The basic census data reveals how these five boys provided the backbone of the family economic unit, so their enlistment stripped the family of its ability to sustain itself. When the opportunity arose for the Cox brothers to return to those who desperately needed them, they deserted. Armed with their sense of family responsibility, the Cox brothers collectively resolved any remnants of a conflict between home and Confederacy and chose the higher duty.

Lewis D. Abrams, a thirty-nine-year-old private in the First Florida Cavalry, Army of Tennessee, left a wife and five children under the age of twelve in Floyd County when he went to war. Abrams owned little property and no land, having supported himself and his family by working for others. His wife, Sarah, depended upon the state relief programs, which alleviated little of her family's hardship. As the war dragged on, Sarah could not turn to her neighbors for help, as their situation mirrored hers. There are no records to explain Lewis's decision to desert to the enemy and return home in the summer of 1864. All that is known is that with two armies camped around Atlanta in plain sight of each another, Lewis Abrams slipped into the Union lines, took the oath of allegiance on July 20, 1864, and headed home to Floyd County. The fact that the Confederacy needed every soldier to repel Sherman's army no longer mattered to him. In the end, what mattered most was Lewis's duty to aid his family, which had been forsaken by Georgia and the Confederacy.[21]

Leander Cobb, a Floyd County soldier in the Fortieth Georgia Infantry, faced a similar dilemma. Cobb had left a wife and eight children in 1862. He owned no land, and his family depended on his earnings as the local miller to put food on their table. All four of his daughters were under sixteen when he left and his sons were under fourteen. Cobb could not have been in Georgia long because four of his eight children had been born in South Carolina. Supporting nine people presented a challenge for Cobb in peace time, but his family must have suffered terribly in the war. Cobb's regiment dug in for the defense of Atlanta. On July 18, 1864, Cobb took the oath of allegiance to the Union and went home.[22]

Such family sketches of Floyd County deserters recur throughout upcountry Georgia and the upper Piedmont. Albert Allison left his farm in Walker County in 1862 as part of the Thirty-ninth Georgia Infantry. When he left, his father, William, was sixty-two and his mother, Sarah, was fifty-seven. He had only one other brother, Seth, about whom little is known. When Albert's regiment returned to Georgia in December 1863, to camp for the winter, Albert , then a twenty-two-year-old private, slipped through the lines to the Union army, took the oath of allegiance on January 11, 1864, and went home. Without their son, farming must have been difficult for the elderly Allisons, who could have offered little resistance to the bands of irregulars that roamed Walker and the adjoining counties. By 1864 Albert knew his duty lay at home with those who needed him most.[23]

When Walker County farmer James Bankston deserted from the Thirty-ninth Georgia and took the oath of allegiance on February 20, 1864, he did not go alone. His older brother, James, had done the same thing six weeks earlier. Before the war, William had lived with his brother, helping James provide for his young wife, Mary, and their three children. From the records it is impossible to know how these two brothers deserted. Did they go at the same time, or did they plan to go separately, with older brother James remaining a little longer, perhaps to cover his brother's escape? What is clear is that James Bankston left a family in 1862 that needed him and his brother, and when the two men got the opportunity, they deserted.[24]

James Dobson, also from Walker County and the Thirty-ninth Georgia, apparently believed his home situation required his immediate return. The register indicates he took the oath and secured his release from Nashville on December 11, 1863. Barely twenty-one when the war began, Dobson left his eighteen-year-old wife and five-year-old son, Charles, when he went to war. The young Dobson family farmed for a living, so James's absence would have exposed Lucinda not only to starvation but to raiders on the loose in northern Georgia.[25]

James and Isaac Duncan, two brothers in the First Georgia Infantry, also deserted to the enemy and took the oath of allegiance. The Duncan boys represent two of the youngest deserters in the register: James was seventeen in 1860, while his brother Isaac was only fourteen. James secured his release in

December 1863, but Isaac did not take the oath until March 1864. Once the older brother went, the younger brother followed soon thereafter. Within the confines of the Duncan family, their honor remained intact.[26]

The Jay brothers illustrated the power of family action. They served in different units: Rueben in the Thirty-ninth Georgia, John in the Sixtieth Georgia Infantry, and Jasper in the Sixth Georgia Cavalry. Like many of the men in the Thirty-ninth Georgia, Rueben deserted in December 1863. John and Jasper did not take the oath until May 1865, but they were listed as deserters to the enemy in the register. Rueben's early return home may have alleviated some of the strain on their fifty-six-year-old father and fifty-two-year-old mother. With Rueben at home, the Jay family had at least one man who could supervise the farm and protect the four young children left at home. John and Jay may well have known that Rueben had returned home when they both deserted to the enemy and took the oath on the same day.[27]

The three Jay brothers were unusual in the disjointed nature of the family's desertion. In most instances where members of the same family deserted to the enemy, they went at the same time or with short intervals between desertions, like the Bankstons and the Duncans. The Tipton brothers, Samuel and Thomas, left two aging parents and seven brothers and sisters at home in Walker County when they enlisted. The register shows both men took the oath in January 1864. Thomas's unit designation did not appear, but Samuel belonged to the Thirty-ninth Georgia, a unit whose desertion numbers ranked among the highest in either the Army of Northern Virginia or the Army of Tennessee.[28]

In addition to providing some insights as to who these men were and what home meant to them, these stories point up the interplay between family, community, and military service during the Civil War. Recent literature on the social aspect of the war has centered mainly on northern communities to show a relationship between community and enlistment. Both Confederate and Union armies recruited companies from within local communities. Although men from one county could join a unit formed elsewhere, the community continuity seemed to follow these men into military service. The heavy desertion concentrated in specific units formed from specific geographic locations within the state lends credence to the view that these men not only reacted to common experiences in combat, camp life, and the cries from home but that they may have also redefined honor collectively. They avoided abandoning comrades because often their comrades went with them.[29]

★   ★   ★

The families of the soldiers who deserted to the Union, described in the census records, match the descriptions of families in the letters from Georgia's women to their husbands and the governor. A few examples from Floyd and Walker Counties reveal the size of certain soldiers' families and explain why these men chose to desert. Household dependency on the husband's labor to support wives and young children meant suffering from his absence.[30] Some of the family information also explains why no written record exists, because one or both of the parents were illiterate. James Holcomb of Floyd County took the oath and went home on August 10, 1864. His wife, Mary, desperately needed him. The family owned no land, and James's work as a laborer represented the sole means of support for her and their small son, John. James felt the call from home, in part from what he must have seen as the army withdrew south, and from what other soldiers were hearing from their wives. Mary never wrote to James pleading for his return because she could neither read nor write. This did not prevent James from recognizing his duty to her and his son. Leander Burton from Rabun County took the oath in late October 1864. Burton farmed for a living and left his wife, Mary, with only their small daughter, Lucinda. Mary Ann Burton undoubtedly suffered in Leander's absence, but like Mary Holcombe, she could neither read nor write. William Garrett took the oath on Valentine's Day, 1864, returning to his Rabun County home and his seven children. None of his children was over the age of fourteen, and the youngest was only two. His wife could not read or write, but that did not prevent him from responding to his higher duty.[31]

The deserters' families in the upper Piedmont resembled those of upcountry Georgia. John Widener, a private in the Fifty-sixth Georgia Infantry, took the oath of allegiance on September 20, 1864. After he secured his release in Atlanta, he returned to his wife, Amanda, and their three children, ages seven, six, and five. Like many men in Carroll County, Widener made his living as a farmer. With the fall of Atlanta, Widener may have believed that all was lost. When Hood took the Army of Tennessee north, Widener no longer counted himself among its members. Widener had seen the destruction wrought by Sherman's army, and even if his wife had never written, he must have felt the pressure from home.[32]

The families of the deserters from Campbell County reflect characteristics similar to those in upcountry Georgia. Although more people owned slaves than in the Upcountry, the majority of Campbell County did not. Most of these men farmed for a living and had wives and children. As in the Upcountry, brothers deserted from the same unit, only later in the year, during or following the siege of Atlanta.[33]

Perhaps nowhere is the knowledge of a deserter's family more insightful than in Chatham County, an exception to the pattern of Georgia desertion concentrated in the upper Piedmont and Upcountry. As the northernmost county in the Georgia Atlantic rice belt, Chatham falls squarely within the plantation culture. Within Chatham's boundaries lay the city of Savannah, which upon closer examination explains why so many men deserted compared with the figures for the remainder of the plantation and slave areas. By matching deserters to the 1860 manuscript census data, Chatham reflected Irish-born rather than Georgia-born soldiers.

The figures for infantry companies show that Chatham County sent more men to the volunteer infantry than any county in Georgia except Fulton, which may indicate that desertion by those soldiers was not out of proportion to the number of men enlisted. However, the ethnic background of most of these men revealed they were different from those in upcountry Georgia and the upper Piedmont. Virtually none of the deserters from Chatham had farmed for a living. Their livelihood was tied to Savannah as an urban seaport. They were blacksmiths, laborers, bricklayers, policemen, wood merchants, stevedores, tinners' apprentices, watchmakers, dentists, carriage makers, ship carpenters, clerks, tailors, grocers, and mariners. Their wives worked as boarders, seamstresses, shopkeepers, washers and ironers, and general house servants. Many were first-generation Irish and they had been living in Savannah for only a few years after coming from the North or directly from Ireland.

James Booth deserted to the enemy and secured his release on Christmas Day, 1864. Both he and his wife were born in Ireland, and their only son, John, was born in New York City. An Irishman, Michael Boyle, married his wife, Dohra, from Warren County, Kentucky. Their two children, four and six, had both been born in Kentucky. Boyle could not have been in Savannah before 1856, and as a sergeant he represented one of the few deserters over the rank of private. He took the oath and secured his release on September 16, 1864. Dennis P. Brady, a police officer before the war, had been born in Mayo, Ireland. His wife, Hannah, came from Limerick, Ireland. Their four-year-old daughter was born in Detroit, Michigan. A year later, Hannah gave birth to a son. Based on this progression of travel and births, Brady had only been in Georgia since 1857.[34]

Chatham County's desertion clearly falls into a different category than the rest of the state, but this does not mean that concern for family and community did not also convince them to desert. The short time they had been in the state, the close ties they maintained with Ireland, and the fear that Sherman might burn Savannah, as he had already burned Atlanta, made responsibility to home greater than to the Confederacy.

The conflict between poor white laborers and slaves reveals elements of class tension that also may have contributed to desertion among Chatham

County soldiers. Mostly unskilled, and resented because of their Catholicism and propensity toward alcoholism, the Irish in America struggled to survive.[35] They competed for jobs with free blacks in the North and with slaves in the South. It seems unlikely that many Irishmen would fight and die for an institution that offered them little or no tangible benefit. If Irishmen felt some strong ties to the Confederacy in 1861, three long years of war must have weakened any fervor.

Despite their ethnicity and tenuous ties to the Confederacy, Irish soldiers apparently deserted for the same reasons as other Georgia soldiers. Those who did enlist fought long and hard on behalf of a social class that contributed little to the effort. When they returned to Georgia, they had the same opportunities to desert. They fled during the siege of Atlanta or shortly after its fall. Those who deserted later did so during Sherman's March to the Sea or after the fall of Savannah. These men had families and children who had suffered from their absence. Not only did their families experience the shortages that plagued the rest of Georgia, but they must have felt as if they were strangers in a strange land who depended on support from a government that had already shunned many of Georgia's non-Irish citizens. With the exodus of Hood's army from the state in October 1864, Sherman faced no resistance other than from Joe Wheeler's depleted cavalry, a few militia, and some cadets from military schools. Neither Georgia nor the Confederacy protected the families of these soldiers, and some portions of the Confederacy actually posed a threat to the welfare of those who remained at home. As recent immigrants, Irishmen shared few of the notions of honor and duty to the South that had created conflict in the minds of many Georgians. Irish culture prevailed, so when it became apparent that Savannah would be left to Sherman's mercy, these Irish-Americans deserted to the enemy and went home. With the Confederacy effectively eliminated from the state, they had no fear of being arrested as deserters.

Wartime hardship at home and the responsibility to wife and family caused Georgia's soldiers to desert. Some of those who fought clearly believed that home and family fueled desertion. Melvin Dwinell, a first lieutenant in the Eighth Georgia Infantry, survived the war. In September 1865, he wrote to his brother, Albert, from his home in Rome, Floyd County. Albert lived in Vermont and fought for the Union during the war. Both Melvin and Albert had grown up in Vermont, but Melvin moved to Georgia in the 1850s, bought a small weekly newspaper, the *Courier*, and made upcountry Georgia his home. Melvin tried to justify the Confederate cause and explain the reasons for the terrible war that had split his family. The South gradually lost the ability to sustain the effort, according to Melvin, who saw Georgia's soldiers slowly lose heart, not as a result of defeat on the battlefield but because they could not ignore the desperate calls from home. "Our soldiers were caused to desert on account of the suffering of their families at home more than by all other causes combined."[36]

Georgia was a state where a significant portion of the population opposed secession and remained outside the sphere of people who benefited directly from slavery, yet these people joined their fellow citizens in the quest for Confederate independence. Fueled by the rhetoric from both the wealthy planters and the government that the South would spend every dollar necessary to provide for and support their families in their absence, men from upcountry Georgia and the upper Piedmont filled the ranks of Georgia's volunteer infantry and cavalry and left their loved ones in the hands of the government.

Once these men departed, they quickly left for places many had never heard of. Who could have known that the last sight many of these men would see was an obscure little church near Pittsburgh Landing, Tennessee, that many would not survive the bloodletting along the winding banks of Stones River, or that they would starve or perish from disease inside the rotting confines of Vicksburg, Mississippi? Some Georgians found their way even further north into Virginia, with an unfortunate few going all the way to Gettysburg, Pennsylvania, where many died. By the winter of 1863–64, those who survived such combat experiences had to endure the hardship of camp, fight off disease, and live without adequate food and clothing.

Alton Holland, the well-meaning representative for the Kentucky Relief Fund, was wrong. Despite the absence of the Union invader before 1864, Georgia suffered terribly. By late 1863, Georgia soldiers in both armies knew their families needed them desperately. Calls from home, both directly from wives, mothers, sisters, and daughters, or indirectly through newspapers, rumors, and other men's letters, pulled Georgia's soldiers home. Those in the Army of Tennessee returned to their native soil to see the destitution that had overcome their communities. As Sherman pushed his way toward Atlanta, Georgians whose homes lay along the route deserted and went home. Even some men serving in distant Virginia began to take advantage of the protection and transportation afforded by the Union desertion policy. These were not "poor" men who had led unfulfilling lives before the war. They were hardworking farmers whose livelihood demanded the full efforts of every member of the family.

These are but a few of the soldiers who were able and willing to desert, but they were not the only ones whose families suffered and who felt a higher duty to home. Common folk and nonslaveholding yeomen occupied both the plantation belt and the southeastern portions of the state. However, a wide gulf existed between the desire to desert and the ability to successfully do so. The plantation belt and nonslaveholding areas of south Georgia experienced desertion but in much smaller numbers. Most of the south Georgia desertion experience was centered around its swampy terrain, which provided sanctuaries for deserter bands and escaped federal prisoners. Such men were too far from home to successfully return, but unwilling to go back either to prison or to the army. While they represented deserters hiding in south Georgia, many cannot be identified as south Georgians. Some of these deserter bands roamed areas from Mobile, Alabama, to Macon, Georgia, making it unlikely they were south Georgians. Distance made desertion from the army difficult for soldiers within the plantation belt and south Georgia. Most desertion from both regions took the form of men who refused to serve. The advertisements for men to return or join their militia units set out in chapter 3 accounts for much of this activity and does show some plantation belt desertion. It is also true that slaveholders were not the only ones who evaded the draft. Common folk who did not qualify for exemptions nevertheless refused to serve. Some even found their way to the deserter havens of the Wiregrass swamps. However, while this type of desertion occurred, it represents a small part of the total picture.[37]

Among men who enlisted and went to war, the difficulties inherent in deserting from places as far away as Virginia and safely negotiating the distance home to south Georgia or even the plantation belt, reinforces the notion that although the need may have existed, the means simply were not there. Most of south and central Georgia's soldiers found their way into the Army of Northern Virginia.[38] Aside from its two ill-fated sojourns into Maryland and Pennsylvania, and James Longstreet's transfer to Georgia, Lee's army never left Virginia. Even had Georgia's Wiregrass soldiers been able to desert and return home to areas safe from Confederate control, which this study concludes they did not, their desertion would hardly have been significant. Southeast Georgia represented less than 10 percent of the state's population in 1860 and contributed slightly over 8.5 percent of its infantry. Although many of its citizens suffered in the same way those in north Georgia did, their suffering did not contribute significantly to Georgia's desertion story.[39]

Georgia's deserters had distinctive characteristics. The semi-subsistence yeomen of northern Georgia who answered the call but eventually abandoned the Confederate cause represent the traditional definition of desertion. As soldiers they left the army without permission, intending never to return. However, these men were not Georgia's only deserters. Those who lived and prospered within the plantation belt and never answered the call to arms also deserted the Confederacy as surely as did the upper Piedmont men and upcountry Georgians. Desperately short of soldiers, the South needed every able-bodied man. With the full knowledge of what they were doing,

Georgia's wealthy slaveholding class etched their names into the exemptions rolls, forgoing military service in defense of the Confederate cause for which they stood to reap most of the benefits. A third group of Georgia soldiers, men from the plantation belt, not only stepped up when called to duty but remained in the service until either death or defeat brought them home. They did so despite calls from home that, although compelling, did not move them to abandon their duty as soldiers.

CHAPTER SIX

Unanswered Calls

The conditions in Georgia during the war make it easier to understand why so many men from the Upcountry and upper Piedmont deserted. Yet the more populous plantation belt counties supplied more soldiers than any other region, and their desertion rates were among the lowest in the state. Only Chatham, Richmond, and Muscogee Counties demonstrated significant desertion. Why did men from the plantation belt remain at war when those from the Upcountry and upper Piedmont deserted? Part of the explanation may have been the absence of a significant Union presence throughout most of the plantation belt. With Confederate civilian and military authority still intact, it may have been unsafe to return. Yet Sherman's March to the Sea cut directly through the eastern portion of the belt, and still those counties did not demonstrate high numbers of deserters to the enemy. The picture is all the more puzzling because some of the women from these areas did try to get their husbands to return. Many wrote Gov. Joseph Brown seeking exemptions for their husbands, but when this failed, they wrote directly to their men.

There are several reasons why men from the plantation belt did not answer the call from home. Although Sherman's march proved severe, it was also rapid, which reduced its long-term severity. More important, as Sherman moved southeast, the Army of Tennessee left Georgia for Tennessee. This made it more difficult for any plantation belt soldiers who wanted to desert to do so. The nature of the suffering by some of the families and communities in the plantation belt differed from that experienced in the Upcountry and upper Piedmont. The perceptions of these men of their families' hardships also differed. Aside from the poor whites and nonslaveholding yeomen, they did not see the plight of their families as a struggle for basic survival. Consequently, the notions of honor held by many of the slaveholding men and women in the plantation belt compelled the men to remain in the Confederate army and the women to encourage them to fight. Proximity to home and the Union army's occupation provide part of the answer to Georgia's desertion story. But to understand why desertion was virtually nonexistent among Georgia's more affluent, one must look to notions of class. Although slaveholders could be found in most of Georgia, including the upper Piedmont and Upcountry, by far they were most heavily concentrated in the central and southwest portions of the state, thereby giving class in Georgia a distinct regional quality.

At its core, desertion measures the morale of both the army and the civilian population. In situations where neither lost hope, the continued belief in the Confederacy explains in part why some soldiers from black belt counties did not desert. The Fifty-seventh Georgia Infantry exhibited one of the lowest desertion rates, with only six deserters listed in the register. Its ten companies came from Thomas, Wilkinson, Crawford, Washington, Laurens, Baldwin, and Houston Counties, all squarely within the plantation belt.[1] On March 7, 1864, the entire unit, acting through a committee, published a written resolution from Savannah, Georgia, which announced that every man had reenlisted.[2] Although the Confederacy gave them no choice by requiring reenlistment, their unified position was important. When desertion among Georgia soldiers escalated early in the spring of 1864, this unit chose to recommit itself to the Confederacy. They apparently took this momentous step with the full support of the women in their lives. A printed message signed by Mrs. Seaborn Jones and Mrs. Martin J. Crawford, delivered to the unit on the night of February 1, 1865, by a young lady identified only as Miss B of Columbus, Georgia, declared:

> Soldiers of the Army of Tennessee: The ladies of Columbus, fully aware of the severe reverses which have befallen you in Tennessee, but appreciating the matchless valor so often displayed by you to undergo privations of no ordinary character cherishing the heroic and chivalric bearing exhibited by you on every field, from Shiloh to Franklin, bid you god speed in the proud task you have assumed. The country may become demoralized, but the women and the army will ever be undismayed and undaunted. Human courage approaches perfection only when it can calmly look into the face of danger. It has been your fortune to exhibit this high type of manliness in a marked degree. Confronted by a foe almost always numerically superior, you have disputed every inch of territory with him and retired only when bravery availed nothing. Thank god the spirit that animated the martyred dead who have fallen in the contest for freedom still lives within you. We have no fears for the future. Our honor and welfare are in [the] keeping of brave hearts and strong arms. Debarred from sharing with you the dangers of the battlefield our

prayers shall follow you, and history, in recording your virtues, will write in letters of living light: they Endured and Conquered.[3]

The pluck of these Georgia women matched the perseverance of the regiment and expressed an undying belief in the Confederacy. The address came when only two months were left in the war and with much of the South lying in ashes. From the tone of the message, it would have been unthinkable that Mrs. Jones, Mrs. Crawford, or any of the other women responsible for the address would have sent their husbands letters imploring them to abandon the fight and return home. Some of the men from the plantation counties who went to war remained in the field with the support of the women. There was no conflict for those in the Fifty-seventh, for duty to home and duty to the Confederacy merged. For these women, their honor and welfare demanded their men not return home. This commitment displayed by the Fifty-seventh could have been based on class, a message delivered by wealthy women imploring the common soldiers of the region to continue the fight. However, while reenlistment might have become mandatory, nothing compelled these men to remain in such a symbolic show of unity. The plantation belt was home to Georgia's wealthiest residents. Although some of the affluent avoided service, others did not. Since most soldiers were privates, the wealthy members of the Fifty-seventh were not the only ones to openly affirm their loyalty to the Confederacy.

A sense of duty among the plantation belt women appeared almost as soon as the war began. Mrs. J. C. C. Blackburn from Barnesville, in Lamar County, wrote Governor Brown in May 1861 in response to an address he made outlining ways all citizens could aid the war effort. She enclosed a gold watch and asked him to use it "to the best advantage . . . to our brave volunteers who are risking all in our defense." Mrs. Blackburn continued: "While our sex are not allowed to mingle actively in the time of conflict, we can work for those who go away pray God's kind protection upon them when absent, thus proving that the blood which honored the women of the revolution has lost none of its patriotic fervor in us." Mrs. Blackburn made it clear that for her, and perhaps women similarly situated, the war was as much a matter of honor for them as for their men. A woman's honor therefore could only be served and protected by men going to war. Such notions of honor were common among Georgia's planter class and, to a lesser extent, its wealthy farmers and slaveholding yeomen. Historian Bertram Wyatt-Brown has suggested that a man's obligation to fight stemmed from a duty to defend his women. Failure to do so exposed him to scorn not only from his peers but from women. Some men from the plantation belt thus fought because of their women, not in opposition to their wishes. Those men who embraced the planter's notion of honor feared that their women would be ashamed of them if they did not fight.[4]

This close connection between women's honor and the call to war found expression in letters from some plantation belt soldiers to their families. Edwin Bass and his brother Johnny enlisted in 1861 from Terrell County, located in the extreme southwest corner of the plantation belt. In a letter written two weeks after the war began, Bass tried to explain the importance of the war to his sister and mother. His letter remains a clear statement of the relationship between the war, men's service, and women's honor.

Edwin's letter opened solemnly: "I must speak to you and ma and all the rest about a matter that must so deeply interest us all. And Stir our hearts with deep emotions of sorrow." Bass believed everyone understood that the South was "threatened [with] destruction by an inveterate enemy that is willing to show no regard for humanity nor the rights of our section. And People." More important, "the young and brave chivalrous sons of Georgia and the South" had been summoned to their country's defense, forcing men to leave "home and the endearments that binds us to our families to defend the rights and interests of our mothers and sisters and homes." Edwin's letter brimmed with a confidence, so endemic early in the war, that the South would undoubtedly prevail. However, there was more at stake than the survival of the Confederacy. "Our interests and rights my mother and sisters must be defended and fought for too," and Edwin and Johnny Bass could not "remain inactive and contented at home while others more ready than we are fighting for you and us." Edwin insisted, "We are the ones to fight for you and we are the ones who will fight for you. . . . None, will shoulder their muskets, to use them against their enemies who has [more] to fight for than Johnny and myself." Bass insisted that he and his brother were the only ones who could adequately defend the honor of the family's women, and they could not "look on inactive at the contest." The issue was one of personal and family honor, and honor required not only that the Bass boys go to war but that they go with the blessings of their women. "I want all to join in bidding me go and fight bravely like a soldier, and not let our family want for a brave and patriotic heart and arm to fight for them. . . . Write to me immediately and give your consent."[5]

Bass's letter gives no indication of his wealth or class, but the duty Bass spoke of bound husbands and wives, sons and mothers, brothers and sisters. He described a duty to home and family that required him and his brother to go and fight. Failure to go to war would constitute a breach of this duty to defend the honor of their women, which would also stain their honor as men. Perhaps the most important aspect of this duty lay in the need for Bass's mother and sister to acknowledge that his actions met with their approval.

No letters from Edwin Bass or his brother after December 1861 have survived. In his last letter, Edwin revealed the extent to which disease had decimated his unit, but gave no indication that his fervor for the cause had waned.[6]

The honor and duty motivating men to stay in the service rather than desert appeared in various writings throughout the war. For some, duty to the Confederate cause remained strong even after the war had ended. Martha Virginia Stevens left among her writings a poem that expressed both men's duty to fight and the contempt women felt for those who did not. Her husband served in Company A of the Twenty-eighth Georgia Volunteers, formed in Washington County. The poem shows how a soldier's loyalty to the cause may have come from a personal sense of duty to his home and family, particularly his duty to women:

> I think I hear the ladies say
> young men you'll have to go away
> you would not go and fight for me
> therefore you'll have to let me be
> the single men they are so slow
> the married men they had to go
> leaving their weeping wives behind
> almost distracted in their minds,
> you would not go and fight for me
> therefore you'll have to let me be
> And as it is my guard and shield
> my valentine is on the field.[7]

This short piece suggests that the duty that drove some men to enlist arose in part from a very personal sense of responsibility to defend the honor and safety of their women. In order to be their "guard and shield," these men had to remain "on the field." Women scorned the advances of any who remained behind and shirked their duty. Leaving one's wife sad and weeping and leaving her without the means to survive created different hardships. The former generated loneliness and apprehension for their men's safety, a feeling clearly experienced by all women from the plantation belt whose husbands went to war. The latter left women with the prospect of suffering if they could not provide for themselves and their families when their men went to war. While emotional anxiety created hardship, it did not break civilian or military morale. Few women of the wealthy yeomen and planter class within the plantation belt struggled simply to survive in the absence of their husbands, sons, and fathers because these women enjoyed the benefits of a slave workforce that remained intact. In many cases a strong male presence also remained on the plantation. The twenty-slave rule, later reduced to fifteen, exempted any male overseer or owner from conscription laws in every Confederate draft. Although the militia law did not provide for slave exemptions, many simply refused to go by the time Brown felt compelled to call exempted men into the militia.

As men from upcountry Georgia began to abandon the Confederacy in late December 1863, some women wrote letters to reaffirm their dedication to the cause and their belief that going to war upheld the honor of those at home. Ivy W. Duggan, a soldier in the Forty-ninth Georgia, wrote letters for a hometown paper that were published in a "Letters from the Front" column. In late 1863 Duggan quoted another soldier who feared that the women at home had given up. Duggan's letter did not survive the war, so we do not know which newspaper he wrote for, but a woman wrote back anonymously to Duggan, and her letter vehemently denied that Georgia's women had conceded defeat. Duggan had made reference to a Confederate officer's belief that "all the women at home are whipped." "I deny it," she wrote, adding that there were without doubt men and women at home who were "ready to cry 'hold, enough' at the fire of the first gun." However, she believed that for every woman who felt that way, "you will find three among the men." Were the women defeated? "Never, never!" she insisted. The "idea of subjugation, or submission to Yankee rule," was loathsome, and the women of Georgia "detest the cowardly sulkers, and whinning puppits who would force it upon us." Any man "who would stand by and quietly do nothing, waiting for his neighbors to do all the fighting, undergo all the hardship, is not worthy of the esteem of any."[8]

This woman's response to Duggan's letter not only reaffirmed her convictions about honor but claimed that men, not women, had lost heart. Before, during, and after the war, a small segment of Georgia's women expressed a deep conviction that military service directly reflected on a man's honor. Fighting served as a means to protect women's honor, and duty required men to be at war. Bravery and perseverance in the face of hardship were admired qualities.

Letters from women expressing this belief could reinforce the men's commitment to the cause by strengthening their will to fight or dissuading anyone who might have contemplated deserting his post and dishonoring both himself and his family. For men among Georgia's more affluent class, this burning conviction must have come partly from the security of being able to provide for one's self and family in the absence of their sons, brothers, fathers, and husbands. The ability of wealthy women in plantation areas to sustain themselves allowed them the luxury of maintaining their sense of honor, a luxury that did not exist for most common folk throughout Georgia.

Most women in the plantation belt were not of the planter class. But the notion that honor took precedence over all else was more prevalent in this region of Georgia where the planter class enjoyed an immunity from the hardships that plagued the Upcountry and upper Piedmont. A letter in the spring of 1863 from Mary E. Gross of Macon County, located in the heart of the plantation belt, reflected a strong sense of support for the war coupled with the luxury of a lifestyle far removed from the struggle to survive. Her letters to Pvt. William M. Jones of the Fiftieth Georgia showed a sadness common to women on the home front. The inevitable casualties of war left many families in mourning. Still, Mary's letters encouraged nothing but William's complete devotion to military duty. Her letters described a community untouched by the horrors of war and the shortage of essential goods. Gross spoke of weddings and other social occasions, expressing regret that Jones was missing these festive occasions.[9]

Although Gross's letters did not preach the importance of honor and duty, her encouragement to Jones reflected the belief that his place was at the front. On a deeper level her letters revealed something about not only Georgia but the South itself. People experienced the war differently depending on their wealth, the location of their homes, and the economic structure of their family and community. Those who still enjoyed the leisure of social gatherings, weddings, parties, and other diversions had experiences different from those who could no longer feed their children, whose crop had failed, and who lived in counties where law and order no longer prevailed because they were exposed to wandering bands of men who took what little food remained. Women like Mary Gross and J. C. C. Blackburn could afford to continue to carry the banner of Southern honor. Although they suffered the loss of companionship and experienced both the fear and the reality that their men would never return, conditions at home had not reduced them to desperation, and their morale remained so strong that they tried to impart their strength of purpose to their men in the field.

Some of the soldiers from the plantation belt shared the understanding these women showed of the connection between honor and service. Capt. David Pope served with the Tenth Georgia in the Army of Northern Virginia. His frequent letters home to his wife in Worth City reflected many of the same desires, fears, and apprehensions that characterized Upcountry men, but without the fear that his family suffered in his absence. One month after returning from a visit home during the Christmas holidays in 1863, Pope wrote to Martha with a severe case of post-holiday depression. After returning to duty, he had felt "a great disposition to go home again" and could not remember ever having a "greater ambition in that particular." Pope told Martha that he "longed and sighed for one day at home or even a single peep into the family circle again." He could not imagine how he could endure "until the appointed time for getting home." What really upset Pope was that "they have invariably shut off furloughs in the spring and to know it they refuse to let me go on the first of April."[10]

The comforts of home stood in stark contrast to the cold, dreary surroundings of camp life in Virginia. Pope's feelings are completely understandable, but his longing for home shows no indication he would even consider deserting. His letter also reflected no anxiety over his wife and family's situation at home. Pope's family lived in Worth County, far south of any Union threat. While Pope enjoyed a furlough visit home for Christmas, men from north Georgia had already begun their exodus from the army. Many of these Upcountry and upper Piedmont soldiers had not seen their families for over a year.

Within a month, Pope regained his composure. His next letter to Martha reaffirmed his sense of duty to his military service, an obligation he believed she and other women shared. "When I think of the undying patriotism of the women, me thinks I can hear you in my imagination say, I would rather know that my husband died at his post than for him to be a coward and remain with me." Once again this notion of honor, shared by both spouses, comes through in the letters home. With his family apparently safe, removed from the reality of battle and spared the home front hardships suffered by other parts of the state, Pope wrapped himself in his family honor and stayed in the field as duty demanded.[11]

Other men in the plantation region shared Pope's notion of honor. In the spring of 1862, Lucias T. C. Lovelace of Troup County told his father of his willingness to remain true to his military commitment. Lovelace served in the Fourth Georgia Infantry. Of the ten companies in his regiment, only Company F came from a county outside the plantation belt. All eleven Fourth Georgia deserters to the enemy came from Company F.[12] The dangerous journey home over a long distance to an area still under Confederate control may explain why men from the plantation belt did not desert. However, Lovelace did not speak of a fear of capture, but told his father that he would reenlist after his yearlong term expired: Some "were dissatisfied with being kept here, but if it is best, I shall be willing to stay; for I want to do everything that will aid our cause on." His own morale surely gained strength from the knowledge that in addition to his father, who remained at home, he had two brothers still in Troup County to attend to the family's needs. It is unclear whether the Lovelace family owned extensive property or slaves, but Lucias could remain at war with the knowledge that his family was safe.[13]

Even after Gettysburg and the severe emotional letdown that came from being driven off Northern soil, some Georgia soldiers expressed a belief in the continued success of the cause. J. W. Shank, speaking for himself and his comrades, believed the South would prevail. He told his superior officer, Col. J. B. Smith, "This army would be glad to meet Meade's army again in battle. This army cannot be whipped." Shank suggested, "It would do some of 'those blue people' in Georgia good, . . . if they could go through this army and see the spirit and determination that pervades it." Shank admitted that some of the men at home had begun to believe the Confederacy might lose, "but no such idea is entertained amongst the soldiers."[14] Shank came from Columbia County, where Colonel Smith lived, and the idea of desertion did not even occur to him. Coming from the eastern portion of the plantation belt, on the Georgia–South Carolina border, Shank probably did not understand that the despair of some Georgians came not from the fortunes of battle but from the living conditions at home.[15]

For some men, loyalty to home and dedication to the Confederacy prevented them from abandoning their duty even after they became prisoners. Joseph Bogle, a private in Company I of the Fortieth Georgia, served throughout the Atlanta campaign. Captured near Atlanta in the summer of 1864, Bogle spent the rest of the war imprisoned at Camp Chase, Ohio. He believed that the poor conditions and hardships imposed on the Confederate prisoners represented the Union's intention to break their morale. Years after the war, Bogle wrote that "the faith and loyalty of the Southern soldier underwent a more severe test in prison than in the field." The temptation to abandon the cause never subsided once prisoners were given the opportunity to take the oath of allegiance to the United States. A soldier had to "only hold up his hand and say I swear, he could get out of it all and stay north of the Ohio River until the war is over." Bogle indicated Northern officials constantly encouraged Confederate soldiers to take the oath. Bogle was one of the younger soldiers in prison, and a Union officer apparently took it upon himself to convince the young Confederate to abandon the cause. Finally, Bogle told him that "I had a widowed mother down south, that I was not willing to disgrace her, or even let her be ashamed of me if I could help it; moreover I had taken a solemn oath on my enlistment to be true to the south."[16]

Bogle had enlisted in Bartow County with the rest of the Fortieth Georgia. Despite the conditions at home, he refused to desert even after it became clear that the war had ended for him. Believing he would have to remain in the North until the war ended, Bogle may not have understood that the Union offered transportation home. The inability to return home may have influenced his decision. If he could not have helped his family immediately, the disgrace of desertion may have been too great for him to leave. He wrote his memoirs thirty-six years after the war ended, so he may have over-emphasized his loyalty to the lost cause rather than his inability to return home. However, his stance was atypical of Upcountry soldiers. The Fortieth Georgia had one of the highest rates of desertion.[17]

Even with Sherman at the gates of Atlanta, some men clung to their honor and cursed those willing to desert. Virgil White worked in the Atlanta trans-portation office but championed a soldier's duty. For White, honor flowed from his pen with the ease of a man who felt no war hardships and endured no family suffering. As Sherman's army approached, White wrote home to his wife, Mollie, complaining that some Confederate deserters were serving as scouts for the Union army. White knew of two such men who had served in his father-in-law's company the previous fall. Virgil believed that men who "desert their country in this hour of trial deserves a traitors doom and al-though they escape that, I know they cannot escape the vengeance of heaven which will be soon to fall upon them sooner or later." Desertion tainted a man's honor and placed a "stigma upon their offsprings," and he could not understand what would drive a man to such an act. "I would sooner die a thousand deaths with the enemy's ball than to tarnish the little moments committed to my charge in such a way and have them pointed at as the sons of a denigrated father a traitors sire." He encouraged his wife "not to de-spond, true our condition is bad, but woman never shows herself so great as when she unflinchingly bears the adversities of life. Although she does not merge forth into battle yet by her example she wields a powerful influence in every conflict." Virgil expressed no doubt that "a love of liberty permeates through your whole being." He insisted that she "not give way to evil fore-bodings but be cheerful while passing through the eventful crisis which now hangs over our country."[18]

White's letter describes honor as an ideal shared between husband and wife. He must do his duty, while her duty required enduring the hardships cheerfully. Turning one's back on the Confederacy placed a stain on a man's honor that he would pass down to his children. Virgil encouraged Mollie to remain strong, implying that if she did not, her weakness might well under-mine his resolve. Virgil's concerns were not misplaced. Unlike families of common soldiers across the state and the women of Georgia's Upcountry and the upper Piedmont, Mollie White appeared to suffer only from a lack of luxuries and the separation from her husband. Morale on the home front re-mained strong or broken, depending on the living conditions, and those cir-cumstances differed sharply for the more affluent residents of the plantation belt and those of north Georgia.

White could afford the luxury of honor. He did not desert, because his concept of honor did not create a conflict between competing duties. With wife and family still safe, both husband and wife could embrace the Confederacy's cause as a shared quest, and they believed that the strength of the civilian morale actually bolstered the army's morale. White did not have to serve until late in the war, and after reporting for duty, he remained in Georgia where he could easily provide his wife with the security and protection she required. In August 1864, White told his wife that he had made arrangements to bring her to Atlanta. Stating that "this thing of living an old bachelor is detestable," he added, "Not many weeks will pass before I bring you under my strong arm for protection and support."[19]

White bemoaned living the life of a bachelor, but for soldiers such as those in the Army of Tennessee, battle and camp life did not amount to bachelorhood. They represented a daily threat to their lives. Men in the Upcountry could not go home or bring their wives and families to them. White could afford to condemn desertion when he served close to home and knew his family did not suffer. However, for men whose presence at home became the only way to save their loved ones, desertion seemed a far more honorable course to take.

Besides being able to fight unhindered by concerns for those at home, other factors kept some Georgia soldiers from deserting. While Southern honor and dedication to the Confederate cause motivated some men, particularly those among the upper class, some soldiers stayed in the army out of a debt to those who fought and died at their side. Survival in combat can create an obligation irrespective of one's class that requires honoring those who have given their lives. Blanton Fortson, a private in the Sixty-third Georgia Infantry, felt this way. Still with his unit in June 1864, he wrote his mother, "I would tell all who should visit the works from Rocky Face Mountain near Dalton, to Paulding County, tred lightly, this is sacred ground, made so from the many gallons of southern blood it has drunk and the many mangled bodies it contains."[20]

The duty to fallen comrades intensified with the knowledge that those who lived would always be able to bear witness to what happened. Almost thirty years after the war had ended, two veterans of the Forty-second Georgia exchanged correspondence as the occasion of their unit's reunion approached. Lt. Col. L. P. Thomas asked Capt. J. M. Mitchell, "Do you feel older now, old friend?" Over the course of three decades, the battlefields had changed, but the memories remained intact. "The battlefields . . . look lonely; small trees that grew on them, have changed and grown into giant oaks, and the whispering breezes only tell of our efforts to save our beloved

Southland." But Thomas knew that neither he nor Mitchell would ever forget the fighting at Resaca, "where we lost so many of our brave boys, over 100 going down in that brave charge. . . . I was therefore, in position to know who did their duty, and it always gives me pleasure to speak of them."[21]

Both Thomas and Mitchell were from Gwinnett County. They served in Company A of the Forty-second Georgia, a unit composed entirely of soldiers from the upper Piedmont and upcountry Georgia. Both Gwinnett County and the Forty-second showed high desertion rates. Of the fifty-eight men from Gwinnett County who deserted to the Union, eight were from the Forty-second. Thomas and Mitchell's sense of duty to their fallen comrades, coupled with their leadership positions as officers, may have kept them from deserting as conditions worsened. As officers, their notions of personal honor may have more closely resembled those of Georgia's wealthier classes. Perhaps their families did not suffer in their absence. The eight men who deserted were all privates for whom the duty to comrades in the army may have given way to home responsibilities.

For some men, the bonds they had formed within their military unit created an obligation to their comrades that substituted for their families. Lt. Josiah Blair Patterson of the Fourteenth Georgia seemed driven by his commitment to the cause. Of the ten companies in Patterson's unit, only three came from upcountry Georgia or the upper Piedmont, so the majority of the unit enlisted from counties within the plantation belt or in Wiregrass counties along its southern border. Patterson lived in Forsyth County in the Upcountry, the area of heaviest desertion to the enemy. However, his letter home in 1862 applauding "upper Georgia's" contribution to the war effort suggests his beliefs were shaped more by where he originally came from than where he lived when the war broke out. Although Patterson lived far from the plantation belt, he had come to Forsyth County as an adult from Abbeville, South Carolina. His fervor and sense of honor appear much closer to that of the planter class than of the folk from upcountry Georgia.[22]

In one of his earliest letters home, Patterson expressed a level of commitment rivaled by few men whose correspondence has survived to provide insight into their feelings. Patterson longed to come home, but explained that his desire for the comforts of family came second to his duty to the Confederacy. "I feel I belong to my country that if my wife and daughter were but men they too would be by my side bravely defending their insulted and invaded country. I feel that in acting I have but proven myself to be worthy of their love and affection." His duty to family did not exist separate from that to his country, and this obligation required his absence. Moreover, Patterson believed his family understood this sacrifice and consented to it. With a son approaching maturity, Patterson had not left his family without some male support, a situation shared by few of his Upcountry neighbors.[23]

Despite the realization that his comrades died every week from sickness, Patterson's convictions grew stronger as the war continued. Part of his fervor seemed tied to a belief that he could rely upon Georgia's state and county relief funds. Southern relief programs often fell so short of their purpose that it is impossible to determine whether Patterson's family benefited, but his dedication to the cause did not waver. Weeks after his first letter, he wrote home again to tell his wife, "If you need anything do not hesitate to apply to the fund contributed by the Court for the benefit of families. . . . I may possibly pay you a visit sometime this winter as a recruiting officer I will not leave here now however, until things become more settled and I can return without the least fear of dishonorable charges." Patterson's belief that his honor was tied to his military service clearly showed. He had already become totally committed by December 1861, when he wrote from Manassas Junction to tell his family, "No my Dear wife and children. Dear as I love you Dear as your embraces may be sweet as your childish prattle and infant smiles I tell you Nay. If my government were voluntarily to discharge me honorably today I would yet forego the comforts and joys of life to do her service."[24] Not even the government could let Patterson go home with its full permission. His own sense of honor, grounded in a responsibility to his family and state, left him only three routes home: death, defeat, or victory.

Sometimes Patterson's letters appear to be written in response to his family's wishes that he return, but he would not return while the battle raged. Not even a brief taste of home's comforts could sway him. As an officer, he secured a furlough in early 1862, something most private soldiers from Georgia never experienced. Judging from a letter written in February, his family felt slighted by his departure. When he returned to duty, he wrote home to stress the importance of his military obligations. Patterson explained that he left home not because he wanted to but out of "a sense of duty to men who had intrusted to my care and keeping their highest earthly interest their lives." He added that he could never forgive himself if the lives of his men "had been sacrificed in defense of their country me at the same time enjoying the comforts of home and the smiles of my loved ones in conscious security." Although his departure from home may have been abrupt, he reminded his wife and children that he had two families, "for each man in my company is a son and a brother in whose defense I would peril my all."[25]

Patterson's devotion had transferred his feelings of civilian family and community to the Confederate army. His morale came to be grounded in a sense of esprit de corps, driven perhaps in part by his rank, but nevertheless a bond existed between himself and his unit. His fervor appeared almost out of place in the Upcountry, but his later letters provided the answer to why he could feel such a zealous devotion to his military duty. Patterson's outlook resembled that of the wealthier men from the plantation belt because his lifestyle more closely resembled theirs.

Patterson represented that small segment of the population in Forsyth County who owned slaves. With a slave workforce and an older son still at home, Patterson had no doubt that his family could always count on dependable labor. Steeled with the knowledge that his family could endure in his absence, Patterson's letters reflected a will that certainly must have been among the strongest of the South's soldiers. Unlike David Pope, Patterson returned to duty in February 1862, freed from the pull of home, ready for the task ahead that he felt everyone should share. "Let every man be up and to doing his whole duty. Let every wife encourage her husband and man him for the coming strife. Let mothers emulate the Roman matron and when asked for her jewels point the country to her sons."[26]

Patterson's slaveholding status and economic security directly affected his outlook on the war. His letter home of August 1863 removed any question about the difference between his family and those Forsyth County families around him. Within the neatly folded pages of his letter, Patterson had enclosed $150 that he hoped would "enable them [family members] to live more bounteously than you supposed." Patterson did not want his family to suffer, even though it was everyone's duty to "practice a rigid economy." He admitted that in Forsyth County "the poor families generally are hard run and do not have the variety and abundance to which they are accustomed," but the poor had to understand that "this is one of the contingencies in every revolution." Although Patterson felt sympathy for their plight, he blamed "the greedy avierous money maker," and he could only "hope the day will come when a just retribution will be visited upon all such amassed money in this war by extortionate speculation."[27]

Patterson's letter suggests why some men did not answer the call home. At a time when salt was scarce or nonexistent, when the wheat crop had already failed, with the Upcountry corn crop in the process of failing, and when most of the Upcountry, including Forsyth County, stood on the verge of total destitution, Patterson's family "lived more bounteously than you supposed." A hundred and fifty dollars represented more than thirteen months' salary for the average Confederate private. Lieutenant Patterson could afford the burdens of "honor."

The most revealing aspect of this letter is Patterson's observations on the rest of the families in the county. Not all of them were poor before the war, but by 1863 they did not enjoy the "variety and abundance to which they were accustomed." This point is crucial to understanding Georgia's desertion. Although the small, nonslaveholding yeoman lived well when his family economic unit functioned as a whole, his absence destroyed the effectiveness of the family economy. To say those families were "hard run" understated the situation. The privates in Patterson's unit, and others from north Georgia, did not have the luxury of insulating their own notions of honor from what occurred at home. For them, economic necessity required their return home.

Patterson's high morale stood in contrast to the soldiers of north Georgia. Some of the more affluent soldiers from the plantation belt did not desert because they had the support of women who did not need them home simply to survive. Men and women shared a common concept of honor, even if it placed different burdens and responsibilities on each.[28] Their economic station strengthened their morale in support of the Confederacy. However, in his fervor to embrace the Roman matron example, Patterson forgot another Roman lesson, one that should have been more important to him as a leader. Julius Caesar, despite his rank, slept in the field with his men and ate their food. He shared their hardships because only by doing so could he measure their morale and know what they were capable of doing. Roman soldiers rarely enjoyed family ties; therefore, when Caesar felt their military hardships, he could take the full measure of the man. The Civil War soldier, however, left a family at home when he went to war. Without the ability to share the battlefield hardships as well as the anxieties the common soldier felt for the well-being of his loved ones, a commander lacked the ability to truly understand the plight of his men.

Patterson's last surviving letter reaffirmed what the register and other supporting sources reveal about Georgia's desertion. By the spring of 1864, Georgia's Upcountry soldiers were deserting after losing faith in a cause that had left their families destitute. Writing from Virginia in March 1864, Patterson lamented that he had not seen home for fourteen months and that he was "very anxious to see my loved ones." But Patterson believed that Forsyth County was "considerably tinctured with disloyalty" and that the common folk entertained "a deep seated hatred for the *original* secessionists." Patterson reaffirmed that he belonged "emphatically to that original panel," and if he was a traitor, then "all states of the Confederacy have solemnly in convention decreed treason."[29] Patterson remained committed to the end, whereas most of north Georgia's residents lost faith and its soldiers deserted. Patterson and his family, who survived the war and continued to live in Forsyth County, may have felt awkward among so many families who had starved for most of the war.[30]

For Patterson and men with the wealth to hold honor above all, desertion was an unacceptable act because they could not honorably leave the fight even under the protection of an honorable discharge. Lt. Col. J. C. Mounger, Ninth Georgia Regiment in the Army of Northern Virginia, was such a man. Living in Clarke County, on the northern edge of the plantation belt, Mounger owned at least twenty slaves. All the Mounger men answered the call to arms in 1861, and many served as officers, which indicated their status as community leaders. Mounger reached his fifties in the war, and despite his age he endured the early rigors of war well.

In May 1863, his son was killed in action. At the end of the month, he tendered his resignation as regimental commander of the Ninth Georgia. In a carefully written letter to his brigade commander, he explained his decision. Mounger was fifty-four years old and had served almost two years. He had "not had a well day since the Battle of Antietam or Sharpsburg." During that battle Mounger received "four severe wounds in the left arm and shoulder" and had never fully recovered. Every male member of the Mounger family had gone to war, leaving "my wife and three daughters, two of them quite young to manage and controul my Negroes all of which require my attention." Mounger explained that his son, Capt. T. T. Mounger, had fallen near Chancellorsville, and his "wife & one child and aged and infirmed mother-in-law had no white male on the place the mothers only son having been killed at the battle of seven pines & her son-in-law (my son) being killed as stated leaving them to manage and controul about twenty Negroes."[31]

There was no Confederate draft in 1861. The prompt enlistment of Mounger's sons showed the family's commitment to the cause, and the elder Mounger could have remained at home. He apparently owned enough slaves to have avoided the draft in 1862 and every year thereafter, but the enlistment of every male member of the Mounger clan compelled him to serve.[32] Mounger reflected on the hardships of the previous two years, particularly the recent loss of his son. For a man who worked, lived, and socialized in a world where reputation held real value, relinquishing his command struck his sense of honor. Once he had penned his resignation, he had only to see to its delivery. Mounger's resignation letter never reached brigade commander Gen. G. T. Anderson. Mounger died in Longstreet's ill-fated assault on the Union left at Gettysburg, Pennsylvania, on July 2, 1863. His letter remained with his personal effects when his sons, John and Tom, gathered them up and sent them home to their mother.[33]

Why did Mounger not send his letter to Anderson, resign his commission, and go home? Despite hardship and personal loss, nothing within the letter justified resignation by a man of Mounger's rank and standing. Although Mounger's personal loss clearly evoked sympathy, many families with men at war had been touched by death. Mounger appeared absolutely overwhelmed by the loss of his son. Since both had served in the Army of Northern Virginia, they probably saw one another frequently. Mounger felt an immediate emptiness, but with time to reflect he knew his son's death did not justify his resignation. Nor were Mounger's wounds, although clearly a hindrance, exceptional. Many men suffered from the pain of wounds that lingered throughout the war. He had only to walk among his men to realize that his wounds represented a symbol of his honor, not a reason to relinquish his duty. Finally, Mounger's family, although certainly in need of him, appeared in no danger. Mounger's resignation letter was the muffled cry of a man whose rank and status did not allow him openly to weep. After expressing his anguish in the only way he could and reflecting on his resignation, Mounger must have realized that there was no duty higher than his military obligation. Instead of destroying his letter, he placed it among his private effects, to be recovered and sent by his sons to the widow.

Had Mounger resigned and returned home, he would have been the only one of the Mounger men to have survived the war. He understood that his wife grieved for the loss of family and loved ones. Still, the situation at home for the Mounger family never sank to the depths of the small farmers of northern Georgia. Lucie Mounger, the widow of one of the Mounger sons, grieved from so much death. Her letters expressed sorrow over the loss of her husband and the other members of the family. However, her letter to Edwin Mounger in September 1864 indicates that she had sufficient meat and corn and could safely rely on other members of her family and a network of local friends to sustain her.[34]

The economic structure of the plantation belt and its community network provided the support necessary for families like the Moungers to endure. Letters from women in Liberty County in 1863 demonstrated that the planting process continued unhindered by the war, and the plantation belt enjoyed an abundance in goods unavailable to north Georgia. Salt, that most cherished of scarce commodities in the Upcountry, existed in such quantities that some Liberty County women sent as much as a year's supply to friends and loved ones at war.[35] The families of north Georgia's common soldiers had no such support network, and the steady deterioration of the situation at home eventually destroyed family morale. By late 1863 only the return of their men stood between them and destruction. The price of personal honor proved too great. Unlike the soldiers from the slaveholding classes of the plantation belt, Upcountry and upper Piedmont Georgians deserted.

The letters to and from soldiers of the plantation belt testify to the relative prosperity enjoyed by families in this region. As late as October and November 1864, at the very end of the heavy wave of Georgia desertion, some of the people south of Atlanta lived far better than their northern neighbors. This is clear not only from the lack of complaints coming out of the region but from the observations of the Union army as it moved through the plantation belt on its way to Savannah. Soldiers on General Sherman's March to the Sea confirmed the disparity in food and necessities between the plantation belt and north Georgia. During the Atlanta campaign, Sherman rarely strayed from the railroad, his lifeline for supplies. When he did wander away, he did not go far for very long. Yet during his March to the Sea he and his sixty-two thousand-man army lived entirely off the land and ate well. The Confederate army not only left the state but made no effort to scorch the earth along Sherman's path. Sherman himself stated:

> The skill and success of the men in collecting forage was one of the features of the march. Each brigade commander had authority to detail a company of foragers. . . . This party . . . would proceed on foot five or six miles from the route traveled by their brigade and then visit every plantation and farm within range. They would usually procure a wagon, or family carriage, load it with bacon, cornmeal, turkeys, chickens, ducks and everything that could be used as food or forage. . . . Often I would pass these foraging parties on the roadside . . . loaded with hams, bacon, bags of cornmeal, and poultry of every character and description.[36]

Had Sherman not burned through the region, these counties could have sustained the inhabitants long after the war. David Conynham, a news correspondent traveling with Sherman's army, summed up the situation after Savannah had fallen to the Union army in December 1864: "We passed through in our march over forty of the wealthiest counties of Central Georgia . . . supporting our army on the country."[37] The prosperity that had been evident in letters of Patterson, Pope, Lucie Mounger, and countless other inhabitants of the plantation belt had fed the Union army. Because Sherman only marched through a strip between Atlanta and Savannah, the remainder of the plantation belt was untouched by war. For the nonslaveholding yeomen of the region and the poorer soldiers, the absence of the Union army made their return impossible. However, some of its soldiers continued to fight without the weight of suffering families at home and remained with the Confederate army long after those less fortunate, men from upcountry Georgia and the upper Piedmont, decided that their family came before the Confederacy.

★ ★ ★

While morale remained strong for wealthy yeomen and planter families throughout the plantation belt, some women finally subordinated the Confederate cause to their own personal needs at home. Because the rigors of life without their husbands, sons, and overseers proved greater than some women could manage, the wives, daughters, and mothers in north Georgia's yeomen families were not the only ones to ask their men to come home. Some slaveholding women of the plantation belt experienced hardships peculiar to the plantation culture, which they felt necessitated the return of their men. Like the women of north Georgia, plantation belt women called upon the government and their men for help, but their calls often fell upon deaf ears.

One of the most striking qualities of the letters from slaveholding women of the plantation belt lies in how their hardships differed from those of Upcountry and upper Piedmont women. Mrs. John Green of Burke County wrote Governor Brown in December 1863 to seek the return of her husband and other men from the county. Her letter reveals different fears and arguments between these women and their north Georgian counterparts. Mrs. Green believed it was the governor's duty "to see to it that one class of citizens are protected & not left to meet a fate worse than death, by the withdrawal of all the white-males, from the planting interest." She had done her research well, telling Brown that based on "the last census I observe that the largest slave population is in the county of Burke and of course the production of food must be in the same ratio." However, food production did not directly relate to the size of a county's slave population. Most plantations grew cotton as a cash crop. This did not occur to Mrs. Green, and she asked Brown, "How then is the army to be fed & this vast population sustained, if the planters owning, controlling and directing this force are withdrawn from their avocation, and forced into the service?" She was willing to put up with some adversity, but admitted that she was "no Spartan mother to be willing that my children should endure *all* things for my country." Mrs. Green's real concern was for neither country nor soldiers but for her own personal safety. "For what should life be worth if the women & maidens be left entirely to the tender mercies of the Negro race?" This plantation woman had little empathy for her north Georgia counterparts and believed that Upcountry and upper Piedmont women were actually better off than the slaveholding women in the plantation areas. North Georgia's women lived "where there is a sparse population of blacks, where the whites have been accustomed to perform almost the entire amount of labor." Women from those regions could "make a bare subsistence for themselves," because they were "inured to the hardship incident to that mode of life." Where "slave labor preponderates," she argued, "few or none of the women of our day have the practical knowledge sufficient to husband up every resource and to manage the various crops efficiently and profitably."[38] Requesting the return of her husband and other men from the county to act as overseers and local police, Mrs. Green appealed to the governor on behalf of the women in Burke County.

Mrs. Green based her request on a fear of slave uprisings, the destruction of property, and the killing of whites. The South had not experienced a slave rebellion of that nature since Nat Turner in 1831, although the Harpers Ferry fiasco had reignited fears of insurrection.[39] The departure of most white men from the county heightened her fears. Her concern for the plantation lay in the efficient and profitable management of the crop, which was a far cry from being unable to put in a crop at all. Mrs. Green implied that the release of her husband and the men from Burke County should have taken precedence over men from "some sections of the state where there is a sparse population of blacks."

Mrs. Green feared that she and other women could not control the slave population. She refuted the notion that black slaves would remain loyal in the absence of masters and overseers. As whites watched the blacks for any sign of resistance that might signal rebellion, the tone in the voices of house servants or congregations of fieldhands carried new meaning. The American Revolution served as a reminder and added fuel to the fears of slave insurrections with the British actively inciting slave rebellion in the Southern colonies. Despite a clearly stated Union policy against slave insurrections early in the Civil War, Southern fears died hard. Benjamin Butler warned Southerners in Maryland not to use poison against his troops or he would incite a slave rebellion. Despite Lincoln's clear language to the contrary, Southerners viewed the Emancipation Proclamation as encouraging slave insurrections. Fears, however, did not reflect reality. In the absence of the slaveholding men during the war, violent rebellion by the slave population did not occur. Slaves understood the possibility they might soon be free, but they chose to wait and watch rather than to risk rebellion.[40]

Despite her fears, Mrs. Green enjoyed the benefits of a full complement of slave laborers. She underestimated the importance of male labor to the Upcountry and upper Piedmont family-based economy. Although northern Georgia's women could and did work well during their husbands' absence, men were required for such tasks as planting and harvesting. If Mrs. Green's letter reflected the views of the affluent in the plantation belt, such people never understood how the war had affected north Georgia.

Other plantation women requested the return of their men and expressed similar fears of slave insurrections. Mrs. Mitchell Jones of Brooks County, in the extreme southern part of Georgia's plantation belt, informed the governor of an insurrection plot. The local police force uncovered a scheme by Brooks County slaves and those in the Florida County immediately to the south. According to Mrs. Mitchell, the conspirators had already met and soon would "begin their horrid work of murdering men, women and children." The slave leader belonged to her husband, whom she wanted to be detailed from his post in Atlanta in order to come home.[41]

Mrs. Francis B. Tillery of Columbia County, located on the northeast edge of the plantation belt, informed Brown that blacks had threatened to kill all the women and children and take possession of their homes after the white men had gone. Mrs. Tillery's husband still lived at home, but she feared the recent militia call might take him. Her fears of a slave insurrection appeared almost as an afterthought. They came at the end of her letter, after she had claimed that her husband had been afflicted for fourteen years and was unfit for duty. Perhaps she raised the possibility of slave rebellion in the hope it would strike a nerve with the governor.[42]

While Mrs. Tillery's claim of a pending uprising appears rather transparent, the most telling evidence that the specter of slave insurrection was exaggerated is that such fears never came to fruition early in the war. An anonymous letter from a farmer in Washington County to Brown in February 1862 informed the governor that "there are some neighborhoods in our Co. that will be shortly left entirely destitute of white men and exposed to the ravages of Negroes without any control at all." The farmer believed that "some white men should be left in the neighborhoods to carry on the farms and raise corn for the soldiers."[43] The farmer initially justified leaving white men home because the citizens feared the "ravages of Negroes," yet he concluded that raising "corn for the soldiers" required that able-bodied men remain at home. It is hard to believe that the writer thought slaves posed a serious threat to rebel.

Confederate anxieties early in the war led to the hanging of some slaves suspected of arson. When many of Georgia's white men left home to fight, hysteria spread. It is hard to determine how real the slave control problem was because the evidence is sketchy and uncertain. J. William Harris maintains there was a steady and perceptible increase in slave insurrection, violence, and rebellion as the war continued, but he provides little or no evidence. Many Southerners never believed slaves posed a threat. "Our Negroes will remain quietly and faithfully at home and cultivate our land," remarked one Georgia newspaper editor at the outbreak of the war. James Harris Hammond, a Georgia planter, agreed, saying, "Slaves will remain peacefully on our plantations."[44] While passive resistance may have increased, accompanied by isolated instances of violence, slaves did not rise up in rebellion. White fears expressed early in the war never came to fruition, and this helped the Confederate government and its soldiers dismiss such fears made later in the war.[45]

In their letters, few planter or slaveholding women claimed their lives or those of their families were in jeopardy, but many complained that they could not control their slaves. Typical were letters from Elizabeth Clark and Nancy

Colbert. Mrs. Clark explained to Brown that, by January 1863, both her sons had gone to war and left her alone with two daughters. She sought Brown's help in keeping her overseer out of the army. Mrs. Colbert, a sixty-nine-year-old widow, complained that she felt so surrounded by slaves that she begged Brown to let her son return. With only one white man in the entire settlement, Mrs. Colbert needed additional male help to keep the "blacks down."[46]

Such letters testify to the hardship inherent in managing the large slave populations without a master in charge. Yet there is no indication that the welfare of the plantation was threatened. Such calls are weak, compared with the entreaties of those unable to feed themselves or their families. Moreover, many of these complaints were identical to those made by plantation women during peacetime, when the master absented himself for an extended period.[47]

Military duty was enforced in the Confederacy, and because desertion carried the death penalty, it involved considerable risk. Any employee would have been unlikely to risk his life to return to his job. Although many overseers developed close working relationships with their employers, deserting to manage another's plantation hardly matched the call from one's own wife or mother to return home. Overseers were also unlikely to hear the calls from the plantation women. Most requests for an overseer exemption or work detail went directly to Governor Brown.

Although far short of rebellion, the war did cause some plantation women to lose control over their slave populations. Striking increased in the plantation belt the longer the war went on as slaves became conscious that the South might lose the war. But strikes did not mean total disobedience. Slave resistance took many forms: less responsiveness, more assertive attitudes, and refusal to perform certain tasks were practices that might never have occurred if the master or his overseer had remained on the plantation.[48] Instead of requesting the return of their husbands, most plantation women sought the return or exemption of the overseer. Some letters show how women realized that their need for a male on the plantation might be inadequate to secure an overseer's exemption or return from duty. Lucinda Culbreth tried to secure the exemption of her overseer, W. T. Robinson. She needed him to manage more than fifty slaves. Because Robinson represented one of the few white men left in the area to look after soldiers' wives, she argued a community rather than a personal need. From tiny towns like Land Hills and Davidson, in Baker and Jones Counties, women wrote the governor seeking the return or exemption of their overseers and said nothing of their husbands.[49]

A key to such unanswered calls lies in the lives led by slaveholding women before the war. Anne Firor Scott decries the Southern belle as a delicate woman unfamiliar with the rigors of work. Such women not only worked on the plantation but made vital contributions to its daily operation.[50] Bell Irvin Wiley contends that the managerial and organizational skills developed in the antebellum years served the slaveholding Confederate women well. They shouldered admirably the burdens of running plantations. In some instances women controlled plantation power through domestic struggles with overseers who had been hired by absent husbands.[51] Drew Gilpin Faust concedes that women may have provided key managerial and organizational functions, but she argues that few could provide the bare necessities of living without their slave labor force. Even with slaves, the women of the planter class and slaveholding yeoman farmers had to cope in the absence of their husbands. They did cope, and in the process the South's upper-class women changed. Myths of the South, particularly its dependent, helpless ladies, died with Confederate military defeat. The Confederate soldiers from the slaveholding regions returned home to women no longer able to rely upon the notion of their men as protectors, as more women survived the war by managing affairs for themselves.[52]

The replies of husbands at war to complaints by their wives about slave management points up more differences between these women and the hardships of upcountry Georgia and the upper Piedmont. Many women complained that their husbands did not appreciate their hardships. Madison Kilpatrick avoided military service until Georgia's last militia call in 1864. Kilpatrick served in the Fifth Georgia Militia, defending Atlanta during Sherman's advance to Savannah. His letters showed little worry for his home. He had left his father on the plantation, so his wife had some male support. Kilpatrick's advice to his wife and her concerns about slave discipline showed that he was not worried enough to return. "Tell the Negroes to stay at home and not to be led into any difficulty for there will apt to be hanging done. If the Negroes are unruly tell them I have been a good master, have waited on and cared for them when sick and now they must fight for you and the kids."[53]

Some women realized their hardship did not require the return of their men. Julie Pope Stanley remained on her family's plantation in Clarke County after her husband, Marcellus, left for war. The letters between her and her husband do not indicate how long he was gone. Mrs. Stanley's first letter to voice any concern came in August 1864. When Governor Brown activated the last of Georgia's militia to help defend Atlanta, Mrs. Stanley wrote to her husband, concerned for the future of the family plantation. She had been out to the plantation, "found the Negroes were doing badly," and had written to Governor Brown "to detail Mr. J.——to come home to stay." The last militia call depleted the plantation of its remaining white men. Up to that time, "the Negroes did very well, but now there are so few white men in the neighborhood and they do not visit the plantation at all, the Negroes do as they please." Mrs. Stanley had not written her husband for over a week because she was certain "you would come home when you heard of the danger we were in and . . . now I am afraid that my letter might not reach you at all, it seems the Yankees can go anywhere and everywhere over the state without hindrance."[54] Stanley expressed concerns similar to those of other women of the plantation belt. Her letter reflected the rigors of plantation management in the absence of husbands and the need for overseers, but such fears had been expressed before the war.

In Georgia and South Carolina, absentee masters were the rule rather than the exception. Among plantations with more than one hundred slaves, only 30 percent employed overseers, but the percentage employing overseers was even lower on smaller plantations. Over 75 percent of the plantation owners who did not employ overseers had no sons or other males who could assume the role of management. Historians used to assume this meant that blacks actually ran plantations in the absence of white male authority figures. Historical scholarship during the past twenty years has exposed how this faulty assumption ignored the role of women in managing plantations. Women, not slaves, actively oversaw slave management before the war, and they often complained of the hardships inherent in plantation management and slave control. Even on those plantations with overseers, disputes often occurred between the plantation mistress and the husband's overseer. Some women regarded the overseer as a burden and often felt themselves almost enslaved to slavery.[55]

The antebellum work experience of Georgia's plantation women helps explain why their pleas to both husband and the government went unanswered. Their hardships did not approach those suffered by women and communities in the Upcountry and upper Piedmont. For husbands suffering the hardships of war, the pleas of wives must have sounded no different than their complaints before the war when the husband was absent from home. John T. Swan served with Phillips Legion in the Army of Northern Virginia. Swan was from Newton County, situated immediately east of Atlanta on the southernmost edge of the upper Piedmont and the northern border of the plantation belt. Swan's economic standing is unclear, but he believed his family faced no real difficulty in his absence. He wrote bluntly, telling his wife, Bettie, "I know that you are not satisfied but I can't help it at the present." He assured her, "It grieves me to think that my lovely companion is so dissatisfied and I can't help it. I hope the time will come when I can return to

Female hardship (handwritten margin note)

you to stay." However, Swan did not hide his belief that she enjoyed the better part of the separation. "My present task is much harder than yours—though I guess you think the same way by me. . . . Bettie I hope you will not have as hard a time as before. I will try to be with you this time if there is a chance."[56]

Swan's letter, one of fifty-five he wrote during the war, came as many upcountry Georgia and upper Piedmont soldiers had begun to desert to the Union from camps in north Georgia. Swan focused more on his wife's emotional well-being. His letters reveal that he returned home on furlough sometime in October or November 1863, when they took full advantage of the opportunity, because Bettie seems to have become pregnant. He wanted to be with her for the birth, but clearly felt that the war had cast him a far harder lot than his wife. Even after being captured in February 1864 and then imprisoned at Fort Delaware, Swan did not desert.[57]

Carroll County, in the southwest corner of the upper Piedmont, offers strong evidence that slaveholders did not have to desert to provide for their families. Carroll County had 307 male slaveholders in 1860. Of the sixty-eight men from Carroll County who deserted to the enemy, only two owned slaves in 1860. Less than 1 percent of the county's slaveholders deserted to the Union despite having a clear opportunity to do so when the army camped in and around Atlanta in July and August 1864. Carroll County's non-slaveholders used the same opportunity to desert at that time. Only nine slaveholders owned twenty or more slaves, which provided them with an exemption from the draft in 1862; eleven more owned more than fifteen slaves, which would have allowed them to avoid the 1864 draft. Carroll County's low desertion numbers among slaveholders reflect men who did not desert, because their slave ownership provided the labor necessary for their families to survive, rather than men with so many slaves that they were exempted from service.[58]

Although the war virtually emptied northern Georgia of its male population, many plantation belt men did not have to leave. Every draft offered an exemption to either the slave owner or the overseer. Even service in the Georgia militia did not take men away for a long time, with plantation men receiving releases to return home as soon as a crisis had passed. The final militia call of 1864 took some men, but others refused to show up, claiming the same exemption that freed them from conscription also released them from the militia. The calls from the wives of planters and more affluent yeoman farmers in the plantation belt never reached the desperate level of those in the northern part of the state. Despite the notion that nonslaveholding women were better equipped to endure the hardships of war and the absence of the men, most upper-class women knew better.

Catherine McDonald of Winchester, Virginia, understood why north Georgia's soldiers deserted. Different social and economic classes perceived the Confederate government and its cause differently. "To those whose education and habits of life made them enthusiastic, or whose pride acted as an incentive for them to endure and suffer, as was the case with the higher classes, It [Confederate government] wore no such aspect [despotism]." However, for "those who had but their poor homes and little pieces of ground by which they managed to provide but little bread for their families," one government was as good as another. To force such men into the army who could never "be free from the apprehension that their families were suffering" was oppressive.[59]

Once men from upcountry Georgia and the upper Piedmont left for war, many did not return home alive. The plantation belt had more men remain at home and the wealth to employ others to help bring their men back home. Dr. John M. Gullet of Dawson, Terrell County, ran the following advertisement in the *Macon Daily Telegraph* on December 2, 1864, addressed to "the Parents and Friends of Sick and Wounded Soldiers": "I have made several trips after sick and wounded soldiers, and have never failed to get them home when alive and not able to do service. All those who desire their friends hunted up or cared for can be accomplished on liberal terms by applying to me. The citizens of Dawson and surrounding country can secure my services in the practice of medicine on liberal terms and I respectfully refer you to the following named gentlemen." Gullett's services offered the hope that loved ones could be returned home through legal, honorable channels. Soldiers in the field must have known that men like Dr. Gullett existed. For those capable of paying, home could be but a medical discharge away, complete with transportation.

Dr. Gullett's services may have been atypical, but in an environment where hardship and fear of the unknown sparked women to call for the return of their men, anything that helped to allay fear served to lessen or remove the motive for desertion. If a soldier knew he could secure his release through men and services offered from his own county, he would not have to compromise his honor in the knowledge that those at home had actually sanctioned his return by helping to facilitate his release. What seems clear is that such a service would have been far beyond the financial means of north Georgia families.

One of the most interesting differences between the plantation belt and the northern regions of Georgia was in the reactions to Sherman's invasion. The desertion patterns in upcountry Georgia and the upper Piedmont tied to

Sherman's Atlanta campaign did not continue in the plantation belt. Desertion itself fell off drastically, but what remained showed a connection with Sherman's advancing army in Richmond and Chatham Counties, the two large urban areas that Sherman threatened. However, the soldiers from the rural slaveholding counties along Sherman's path to the sea did not desert as the Union army moved through and past their homes. The different desertion patterns depended on which class one belonged to within the plantation belt. For those nonslaveholding soldiers within the region, men whose situations more closely resembled the families of northern Georgia, the lower incidence of desertion stems from the lack of opportunity and the continued Confederate civilian and military control of their home counties. While this class formed a large portion of the region's population, proximity and Union occupation do not completely explain the actions of all the plantation belt's soldiers. Some men's continued commitment came from their perceptions of the severity of the situation and their women's reactions to the Union army.

Sherman's March to the Sea affected forty of Georgia's most prosperous plantation belt counties. Despite the destruction of homes, crops, and infrastructure, there is virtually no record of atrocities committed by Union soldiers against Georgia's civilians. Much debate surrounds how Sherman intended to treat Southern civilians. His orders indicated that foraging was to be done with a minimum of pillaging and wanton destruction, but he understood Union commanders could not completely control the conduct of their enlisted men. Sherman also expressed the opinion that such places as Atlanta served as key points of rebellion and merited destruction.

As the Union army moved toward Savannah, when foraging operations did get out of hand, excessively destructive conduct often led to quick reprimands. Burning and pillaging occurred almost daily, but Southerners admitted that they had no knowledge of outrages committed against civilians. Moreover, unlike the north Georgia citizen who was left destitute by the hardships of war, the foraging operations through the plantation belt still left families with enough to get through the winter. During the Atlanta campaign, Union and Confederate armies foraged north Georgia to the ground in large part because both armies moved slowly. It took two months for Sherman to reach Atlanta. Corn crops, already scarce and barely sufficient to feed the struggling population, were consumed before they were ever harvested. North Georgia supplied two armies with food and had so little to begin with that by the time the war passed through, it had even less. In contrast to upcountry Georgia, the March to the Sea came after harvest and was done by a mobile column. The plantation belt had enjoyed a relative abundance before Sherman's arrival and could still feed itself after his departure.[60]

Eyewitness accounts confirm that the pillaging and destruction had limits.

Mrs. Mary Mallard of Liberty County described what happened when the Union army came through in December. She described rude conduct on the part of some Union soldiers, but even those who came into their homes did not harm the inhabitants. Enlisted men showed no hesitation in taking anything in sight, even if it meant starving the inhabitants, but their officers intervened to prevent the looting process from depleting the food supply. It appears that Union soldiers and Southern civilians both knew that Sherman's direct orders forbade the physical mistreatment of civilians. The women in Liberty County did not hesitate to remind Union officers of this directive.[61] Some women even questioned whether a man's presence at home would have made matters worse when Sherman's army moved through. Louise Cornwell of Jasper County described the scene as the Union cavalry moved past her home. "All day they were passing. . . . My mother, niece and myself were all the family. My younger brother who lived with my mother was in General Lee's army, and for once I was glad there was no gentleman in our house, for he would have been no protection, and perhaps been treated badly."[62]

Some men from the plantation belt knew that war had come to their doorsteps, but they expected their women to endure. Letters from plantation belt soldiers showed genuine concern for the safety of their families but no willingness to abandon their military duty. The letters also reveal the disparity of conditions between plantation counties and those in the north. As Sherman's army stood poised outside Atlanta in August 1864, John H. Boyce wrote to his mother in Troup County, southwest of Atlanta, far beyond the path of the Union army. Boyce served in the Twenty-seventh Georgia, Army of Tennessee, and had personal knowledge of the situation in Georgia. Boyce had no way of knowing when, or if, the Yankees would reach his home county, but his letter exhibited no fear for his family's safety, much less his intention to come home to protect it.

Boyce acknowledged receiving a letter from his father, who had apparently been home recently. Although Sherman's march did not take him through Troup County, Union cavalry roamed the area. Boyce wanted his mother to write him soon and "tell me how you felt when the yankeys come to hour house and what you and the negros done and if the yankeys did take anything or knot and what they done in towan and if they burnt any thing any whare about." Boyce understood his mother was scared "as white as coton," but her fear did not move him to come home. What Boyce really wanted was to "hear you awal talk about the yankeys." He could not understand why no one had written him for the past two weeks.[63]

Boyce had the same opportunity as other soldiers to desert by slipping across the lines, taking the oath, and going home. However, he had no intention of going home, legally or otherwise. His family clearly owned slaves. Whether he felt secure in the knowledge his wife and family could provide for themselves in his absence with their slave labor force, or his status as a slaveholder made the idea of desertion abhorrent, or both, cannot be determined from his letter. He only wanted to hear what everyone had to say about the Union invasion. While he conceded that everyone must be frightened, he also knew his father was at home, and his letter gave no sign that his family suffered in his absence. It is also possible that Boyce drew strength from the knowledge that other women within Troup County had not only remained strong in the face of adversity but had taken an active part in their own protection. Nancy Hill Morgan of LaGrange, in Troup County, organized a militia unit made up exclusively of women. Christened the "Nancy Harts" after a revolutionary war heroine, the company drilled regularly and served as a deterrent to stragglers and escaped prisoners.[64]

While Boyce's letter implied that his family had to face the Union invaders without him, the letter from H. T. Howard to his wife was more explicit. He served in the Sixth Georgia Militia outside Atlanta; the possibility that Sherman's army might pass through his county concerned him but created no conflict between duty to home and duty to the Confederacy. According to Howard's wife, Union cavalry had been seen but did not immediately come through their county. When the Union riders did appear, she feared for the safety of herself and the family home. Howard had apparently seen "some few letters from home, which gave a distressing account of the yankey depradations in our county." Despite knowing that his wife was frightened and the Union army was active near his home, the best Howard could offer was to "hope for the best." He showed no intention of deserting, and when his request for a furlough to come home was rejected, he felt "compelled to remain and leave you in the hands of your enemys."[65] The concern simply did not rise to levels high enough for some of Georgia's plantation belt soldiers to desert. With no furlough or other legal excuse to come home, Howard remained at war.

After Sherman had come and gone, men from the plantation belt seemed reluctant to return if doing so meant desertion. The severity of the hardship caused by Sherman's March to the Sea varied depending on whether the army passed by or actually stopped on one's doorstep. Some correspondence, for example, left the impression that Liberty County had suffered terribly during Sherman's March to the Sea. A series of letters from one woman to her husband reveals her home front hardships and the attitudes of soldiers from the wealthier classes. Lt. John Stark served in the Twelfth Georgia Militia. His wife, Victoria, wrote him from Thomasville, Georgia, in January 1865 and openly expressed her own despair. She saw Georgia as overrun and believed the Confederate cause was lost. "The catalogue of crimes committed in the dear old county is too numerous to relate, suffice it to say Liberty County is desolate and ruined and I know if Savannah is held, it will be impossible to live there much longer." She was "sorry to hear of so many deserters from the county." She could not "blame them much, though, for it seems like we do not accomplish much to bring about peace."

Mrs. Stark wrote again two days later and told her husband, "I am so disheartened about our cause. I feel like you do now, that I want the war to close and let us live together again." It is unclear from which county she believed mass desertion had occurred. Liberty County soldiers did not desert to the enemy, but Chatham County men did so in December 1864. Lieutenant Stark apparently stayed to the bitter end, despite letters from his wife that all but sanctioned his desertion.[66]

Even though his service obligations only bound him to the militia, Stark must have told his wife he would not return until the war's end. In the war's final months, her plight did not justify his return. Her pleas grew stronger, for she "did not know what will become of our family, if you are not allowed to come home to make something to buy us bread to eat: and how shall our taxes be paid." She admitted that the slaves had behaved well in his absence, but she still wanted him home. Stark refused to desert and did not believe Victoria's concerns over taxes and his inability to generate income while at war justified desertion. Her call, like that of so many other plantation women, went unanswered.[67]

Some men went to war and remained there with the support of those at home. Duty to the Confederacy merged with responsibility to family and community. The conflict facing soldiers from upcountry Georgia and the upper Piedmont forcing them to choose between cause and home did not occur for everyone, including men from the plantation belt. Within the protective cocoon of the plantation system economy, planter and wealthy yeomen alike had the luxury of keeping personal and family honor. Women clearly suffered emotionally from the absence of husband, son, or father, but they did not face starvation. They too had the luxury of encouraging the protection of their husbands' honor. For plantation women who felt overwhelmed by the absence of their men, their call to the government and their men went largely unanswered.

Soldiers throughout Georgia took their military duty seriously, for desertion carried severe consequences, legally and personally. Even when presented the opportunity to leave the army under seemingly honorable circumstances, some men of the plantation belt refused. As Georgia's desertion wave began to ebb in late 1864, soldiers with families in the path of Sherman's unopposed march still refused to desert. Most men from the plantation counties through which he moved remained in the army. Planters and wealthy yeomen formed a small but nevertheless significant portion of the plantation belt, but most soldiers from the region were yeomen. However, even among yeomen the ownership of slaves seemed to make a difference in the decision to desert. Carroll County provided a clear example of the different reactions of slaveholding and nonslaveholding yeomen. With only a few slaves, a small yeoman farmer's family could manage in his absence, and judging from some of the correspondence, these men believed that their families could survive. Thus while notions of honor and duty peculiar to the upper classes in the plantation belt accounted, at least in part, for the low incidence of desertion among affluent soldiers from that region, the ownership of even a few slaves made it possible for lower-class farmers to remain at war. For soldiers of any class who nevertheless felt the urge to desert, it seems clear they resisted out of an inability to reach home safely.

While the letters from soldiers and their families help to understand why Sherman's March to the Sea did not create more desertion, they do not provide a complete answer. Given only scattered sources from participants with limited ability to write, and given the loss of many records, the truth may never be known. However, it is possible to speculate why Sherman's march from Dalton to Atlanta caused so much desertion, while his unopposed march to Savannah did not.

With but a few isolated exceptions, the entire war was fought in the South. Even during periods where the Confederacy enjoyed military success, the Union still remained camped and active in the South. Thus, while most soldiers could not know the precise extent of Union activity in Georgia, they had years of experiencing Union occupation. For example, Winchester, Virginia, changed hands over seventy times.[68] Despite instances of looting, such as at Fredericksburg in 1862, Sherman's destruction of Mississippi during his Meridian campaign in 1864, and Sheridan's harsh treatment of the Shenandoah Valley in 1864, Southern soldiers realized that stories of mistreatment of women and children were largely unfounded. If one's family situation did not necessitate returning home, why desert solely because Sherman occupied Savannah, which he did not burn?

By December 1864, Georgia desertion had run its course. The men from upcountry Georgia and the upper Piedmont had left in large numbers during winter camp and the four months of the summer when Sherman approached and took Atlanta. With their families safe beyond the Union advance and supplied well enough to prevent starvation, plantation belt soldiers with sufficient wealth and slave populations clung to honor and duty. For those small slaveholders whose families could survive in their absence, the consequences of desertion and the possibility that capture meant execution overrode the urge to leave. Proximity and Union occupation clearly explain why fewer common soldiers and nonslaveholding yeomen from the plantation belt deserted. Even with declining morale at home driven by the eroding economic conditions, these men simply could not get home, and if they could, home remained a perilous place for deserters. However, the forces that undermined the morale of the families of common soldiers throughout Georgia, particularly the Upcountry and upper Piedmont men, did not eat away at the spirit of those in the more affluent classes in central and southwest Georgia. Even when the call went out for the return of a husband, son, or father, the soldiers and women knew they could not respond. Most calls from those whose spirit did waver went unanswered.

Conclusion

With the surrender of the Confederacy's two main armies in April 1865, the commitment of its soldiers to the government and its military ended. In the years after Appomattox, soldiers were reluctant to talk about desertion. The image of ragged butternuts making their way home or into Union lines ran counter to the emerging image, fostered by the Lost Cause apologists, of valiant soldiers fighting to the last. As the North and the South struggled to justify the greatest of American tragedies, both sides drew solace from the glorification of bravery and the sacrifices made by the soldiers who had fought for the Union and Confederacy. Stories of human frailty appealed to neither the victors nor the vanquished. Desertion carried the taint of cowardice and had no place in the war's folklore.

This study has shown that desertion did not necessarily reflect cowardice. Moreover, the ability of Georgia's soldiers to endure hardship and face death early in the war contributed to Georgia's desertion wave in 1864. Trouble back home, not the fear of death on the battlefield, drove Georgia's soldiers to desert. The Union, understanding the close connection between Southern soldiers and their homes, constructed a policy designed to exploit it. The Union desertion program did not attract cowards because the weakhearted had left long before 1864. Seasoned Georgia soldiers accepted the Union desertion alternative that year because their responsibility to family gradually overcame their duty to the Confederacy. They returned only after the situation in Georgia became unbearable and when they realized that their sacrifice had not been matched by other Georgians, particularly the wealthy and slaveholder classes, who stood to benefit most from the war and contributed the least to it.

Georgia did not follow the traditional patterns of desertion. Ella Lonn pointed to the fall and winter of 1864 as the period when desertion escalated, but this was not the case in Georgia. By late 1864 Georgia's desertion wave had almost run its course. Bessie Martin's findings for Alabama desertion did not apply to Georgia. Georgians did not desert to the enemy in separate waves, and they did not desert during the same periods she identified for Alabama soldiers. Furthermore, there is no indication that widespread desertion among Georgia troops began in 1862. Most of Georgia's desertion came from units that did not form until March 1862, and few saw action until late that spring. It took time for north Georgia to become completely destitute and for its soldiers to comprehend the situation. Finally, James McPherson's belief that early 1865 witnessed wholesale desertion may be true, but not for Georgia's soldiers. The register reveals that Georgia's desertion to the enemy had all but stopped by 1865.

Desertion among Georgia Confederates was concentrated in the Army of Tennessee. Most men from north Georgia counties with the heaviest desertion rates joined units that fought in that army. It retreated into Georgia in late 1863 and camped there for the winter. The men from Georgia's extreme northwest counties deserted before Sherman's Atlanta campaign began, at a time when they were close to home. The remainder of Georgia's desertion occurred between May and October 1864 when the invasion of Georgia threatened the counties where these men lived, and many deserted as the army passed by their homes. With the Union desertion policy in place, Georgia soldiers from the upper Piedmont and upcountry Georgia had to travel only short distances to desert. They returned home to counties cleared of Confederate authority after taking the oath of allegiance to the Union. When the Army of Tennessee left Georgia in late September 1864, Georgia's desertion rates declined drastically. Sherman's March to the Sea did not spark desertion among Georgians, at least not to the same extent as had his earlier campaign for Atlanta. The perception that soldiers returned home driven by fears of the Union army moving unhindered through the plantation belt does not convey a true picture of Georgia desertion. Most of Georgia's desertion began and ended before Sherman ever left Atlanta.

What does a study of Georgia soldiers who deserted to the Union reveal about Civil War desertion? Desertion studies fall into two categories: broad studies, like Ella Lonn's, that examine desertion in both armies over the course of the war, or the narrower contemporary scholarship that examines a particular unit or specific region. By using specific numbers that tie soldiers to specific counties, this study does both and demonstrates that while each model is useful, only by combining the two approaches can scholars get inside Civil War desertion. Georgia's experience demonstrates a broad desertion pattern partly connected to major events of the war. At the same time it shows how community and family, areas typically passed over in broad studies, influenced desertion.

Previous studies have argued that most men went directly home and did not desert to the Union, but those studies are based on estimates of desertion derived from records that may reflect not desertion but death, capture, or temporary absence. Soldiers absent from their units, with no other explanation of their whereabouts, were presumed to have deserted and gone home. There was no way to prove these men deserted or where they went. This study provides precise numbers and clear proof of desertion. It also supports conclusions based on the wartime observations of soldiers and government officials about Confederate desertion that may not be reflected in the numbers of those deserting directly to the enemy. This study clearly identifies almost half of the traditional estimates of desertion among Georgia troops. Desertion was driven by the proximity of the state's soldiers to their homes and the Union occupation that made their return safe. There is nothing to support a belief that men deserting and going straight home, electing not to swear an oath to the Union, would have done so in a pattern any different than that demonstrated in the register. Regardless of whether one chose to renounce the Confederacy, desertion remained dangerous. The same factors that made it safe to desert to the Union would have made it safe to go straight home. This study is therefore more than just an examination of clearly identifiable deserters. It provides a broader explanation of Georgia's desertion patterns, an explanation supported by the actions of almost half of Georgia's deserters.

When the patterns set forth in this study are compared with the observations made by both soldiers and civilians at the time, they point to the possibility that the frequency of desertion to the enemy may have been greater than previously imagined. Desertion to the enemy may also have been more common than desertion, going directly home, and remaining there. Secondary studies of the Army of Tennessee refer to claims made in early 1863 that soldiers from the Army of Tennessee would soon be leaving. However, the sources show desertion did not occur until August and September 1863, when the Union finalized its policy on deserters.[1] Soldiers' statements cited by historians as evidence of large-scale Confederate desertion indicate desertion to the Union, not reports of men deserting and going directly home. Gen. Ulysses S. Grant observed Confederates deserting into his lines in 1864. William Dickey of the Confederacy and M. B. Gray of the Union both described the exodus of Confederate soldiers near Atlanta. Dickey watched them leave, but Gray knew that many had come into the Union lines and not gone directly home. Union soldiers in Tennessee saw how Confederate soldiers were "coming to us constantly" in September 1863. Their observations do not indicate from which states these men hailed, but their statements are consistent with the register, showing that high desertion to the Union began in August 1863.[2]

Traditional estimates of Confederate desertion reflect conduct other than desertion and fail to account for soldiers who returned and may even count desertion by the same man twice. For example, Gary Gallagher states that as many as two-thirds of Confederate deserters were only AWOL and returned to their units.[3] Whether true or not, the possibility that so many presumed deserters may have returned undermines the historiography of Confederate desertion. Other studies that mention desertion, even if only superficially, seem content with unverified statements that there was "plenty" of desertion from this place, or that region, or that "lots" of these soldiers deserted. Claims that as many as 278,000 out of 500,000 men listed on the rolls were absent and unaccounted for not only lack any kind of proof but are inconsistent with the limited work that has been done on Civil War desertion. The only confirmed Confederate deserters were those who deserted to the enemy and took the oath of allegiance. But for those studies such as Ella Lonn's that provide actual numbers, there is no evidence that her numbers reflect men who deserted from different regions, or who deserted at different times, than those shown in the register.

Desertion became a reality for north Georgia's soldiers as the war began its third year. Despite their best efforts to farm by proxy through correspondence home, nothing could replace their labor. War was hard on all of Georgia's soldiers, but war came harder to those whose homes and communities had slipped into such destitution that they could no longer justify the continuing sacrifice. North Georgia's communities were ill equipped to meet the demands of modern war, which required the full-scale mobilization of the entire male population for the duration of the conflict. North Georgia had a surplus of men who could only be spared for short periods.[4] When the war took them away for more than a year, their families and communities suffered. When natural disaster struck the state's grain crops, only Georgia's government stood between the people and starvation.

Despite Gov. Joseph Brown's best efforts, the families of upper Piedmont and upcountry Georgia soldiers suffered. Bessie Martin's work concluded that the Alabama counties receiving the most aid were the counties most in need; the high numbers of deserters from the counties receiving the most aid indicated that the soldiers from those counties returned home because their families were destitute.[5] Georgia counties most in need of government aid often received the least. The disparity between their needs and the inadequacy of the relief caused soldiers from these northern counties to desert. A closer examination of Alabama's desertion might reveal the same thing. Everyone welcomed whatever assistance they could get because the war had taxed the resources of even the most affluent. Those people who were able to feed themselves still took advantage of whatever relief they could to ensure their future sustenance. The receipt of aid indicated not only need but the ability to work within the administrative process. North Georgia received less aid, particularly salt, because the citizens in those counties did not know what to do or, for one reason or another, could not register. To make matters worse, no one in Georgia knew how long the war would continue.

A prominent theme of Confederate defeat focuses on the lack of unity among the Confederate states. This study supports a failure of Southern nationalism and the notion that Southern morale was not necessarily tied to the performance of the Army of Northern Virginia. Governor Brown's efforts to keep Georgians at home after Sherman's invasion, his attempts to bring back soldiers already stationed out of the state, and his undermining of Confederate military authorities all point to conflict between Confederate goals and Georgia's needs. Arguing that conflicts within the Confederacy were exaggerated, James McPherson points to Governor Brown's efforts to raise and equip regiments, to provide aid for soldiers' families, and to organize other relief programs as proof that Georgia acted with the Confederacy in good faith.[6] However, the aid never reached many of Georgia's families who needed it most. Most of the regiments raised in 1863 stayed in Georgia, and the government proved to be a source of corruption rather than a reliable source of supply. Because Brown never solved the problem of irregular bands terrorizing the population, Georgia's soldiers lost faith in his ability to maintain order at home.

Governor Brown undermined the Confederate effort by his inability to provide for the families of Georgia's soldiers, but the greater problem stemmed from the situation in Georgia itself. Regional divisions and conflict hurt the Confederate cause. The last dollar of the planters' wealth did not go to sustain the families of north Georgia's soldiers; that money and surplus food stayed in the plantation belt. When the Confederacy badly needed troops in 1864, Georgia's planter and slaveholding class took full advantage of the exemption policy and refused to fight. The only consideration they gave for this immediate relief from military duty was the promise to provide meat and grain within a year. The war in Georgia became both a poor man's war *and* a poor man's fight. Soldiers were expected to fight and provide for their families, but nonslaveholding yeomen soldiers could not do both. Those from north Georgia were in a position to do something about the plight of their families, and when the opportunity presented itself, they did so.

Georgia's desertion story reveals diverse ideas of honor between social classes, and because of the heavy concentration of the planter class in Georgia's black belt, it also points to differences between geographic regions. Granted, even in the plantation belt nonslaveholders lived and worked among the slaveholding population. But that does not mean that notions of honor and the relationships among men and women of the upper class are irrelevant to the actions of those soldiers. Bertram Wyatt-Brown's evaluation of Southern honor among Georgia's elite holds true among most of Georgia's affluent plantation belt soldiers. Civilian honor extended to the battlefield, with women from the slaveholding class understanding that a man's honor and their own required him to enlist and stay in the army for the war's duration. For the wealthy farmer and planter class, the economic conditions in the plantation belt allowed these men and women the luxury of maintaining such notions of honor. A stable slave labor force, even if less cooperative in the absence of the male population, enabled the slaveholding population within the plantation regions to weather the hardships of war at home. The planters in the region did not suffer from a lack of meat, salt, grain, and other necessities. Exemptions allowed some men to stay home. Even after Sherman moved through Georgia on his March to the Sea, many of the citizens in the counties that he passed through were able to survive. In addition to the lack of opportunity that prevented nonslaveholders in Georgia's central and southern regions from deserting, the combination of Southern honor and the economic structure of the slave economy accounted for the lack of desertion among the slaveholding classes from the plantation belt.

In north Georgia, honor had a very different history. Georgia's Upcountry and upper Piedmont people resembled their revolutionary forefathers. They had difficulty conceptualizing a duty beyond home, family, and community. Although individual reputation was important to them, it yielded to the needs of the community. When war rendered north Georgia communities destitute, the soldiers from that region deserted honorably. Desertion was acceptable for north Georgia's soldiers because of the duty to their homes and families, an obligation recognized by their comrades, many of whom joined in the desertion wave. Among north Georgia's soldiers, desertion gathered momentum from the collective redefinition of honor that recognized war had limits. The success of Lee's army could not feed north Georgia, and the loyalty to the Confederacy held by men from this region was tied to the government's ability to protect their families, not the success or failure of its most respected army.

This study recognizes how the traditional explanations for desertion also contributed to Georgia's desertion. Events on the battlefield and the long periods spent idle in camp took their toll. Georgia's soldiers wrote letters telling of disease, malnutrition, and death, and many men expressed a homesickness that intensified as one-year enlistments became permanent commitments to fight until the war ended. By adding the horrors of the battlefield, it is easy to understand why men deserted. However, desertion carried such harsh penalties for both soldiers and civilians that the aversion many men felt for the war was insufficient to make them desert without a strong pull from home.

The call from home came from Georgia's women. It was sometimes desperate and persistent. It began as an effort to secure the return of their men legally through appeals to the government and the military leadership. When such requests went unanswered, Georgia women wrote directly to the soldiers to explain their plight and demand their return. Some letters written directly to soldiers were shared with their comrades. Newspapers sent to the front carried the same message: Georgia's soldiers owed a greater duty to home than to the Confederacy. In one respect Georgia's nonslaveholding yeomen women, whether in north Georgia or in other portions of the state, were no different than the slaveholding women of the plantation belt, in that women in both classes acted as the keepers of men's honor. Yet unlike the wealthy in the plantation belt, honor among common folk required that the men return home. Soldiers from north Georgia not only heard the call but were willing and able to respond.

Desertion among Georgia's soldiers reflected less a lack of commitment than a gradual exhaustion of will. North Georgia had responded to the enlistment call in 1862, and by the end of 1863 most men still living had fought in every major engagement from Perryville to Chattanooga and countless smaller battles along the way. Without their initial commitment, Georgia's soldiers could not have sustained the necessary effort to fight for as long and as hard as they did. Georgia's desertion did not undermine Confederate morale. It measured the morale of Georgia's soldiers and civilians and reflected the depths to which it had already sunk. For many nonslaveholding soldiers in central and south Georgia, the loss of morale could not find the same expression as it did for the men of north Georgia. The great distance and continued Confederate control made desertion a far less viable option. Obviously men from these regions deserted. The register lists several hundred. Did the desertion from these more southern regions take the form of going straight home? It is unlikely that men who were unable to desert to the enemy because their distance from home made it difficult and their homes remained dangerous would have found going straight home either easier or safer.

While the desertion of 3,368 Georgians must have damaged the Confederacy's war effort, it was far less damaging than the approximately 11,000 Georgia men who took exemptions in 1864 under the Confederate Conscription Act. These men who were able but refused to fight undermined morale in Georgia. The men who secured exemptions not only deprived the army of their service at a point when soldiers were desperately needed but they also did nothing for the families of the men who remained in the field.

When the people in north Georgia discovered those in the southern part of the state had escaped the draft, any lingering conflict between duty to home and duty to country was resolved.

Georgia's story is only a part of Confederate desertion. Much remains to be explored. Because Virginia contributed more soldiers than any other state in the Confederacy and the war was fought from start to finish within its boundaries, did Virginia produce the most deserters? When did they desert? What forces drove their desertions? North Carolina has been the focus of most of the Confederate desertion studies. After Virginia, North Carolina contributed more troops than any other Confederate state. Do North Carolina's deserters to the enemy reinforce or undermine the notion that North Carolina had more deserters than any other Confederate state?

Other Confederate states experienced Union occupation during the war. Tennessee fell first and came almost completely under Union control by the end of 1863. The register did not begin recording deserters to the Union until August 1863, but official correspondence reveals that Tennessee soldiers were deserting to the Union in 1862. Did this trend continue throughout the war? Did certain areas of the state contribute most of Tennessee's desertion? Union operations in Mississippi served as a precursor to Sherman's invasion of Georgia and South Carolina. The register began recording deserters to the enemy seven months before Sherman's Meridian campaign. Did Mississippi soldiers, whose homes lay along the path of Sherman's march, desert while the Confederate army was in Mississippi, as did those from Georgia during the Atlanta campaign? How many Mississippians took advantage of the fall of Vicksburg to take the oath and return home? States such as Texas and most of Arkansas remained free from Union control during the war. Did the continued Confederate presence and great distance from the war front discourage men from those states from deserting to the Union and going home?

Many of the answers to Confederate desertion lie at the other end of the spectrum. Much work remains in exploring the role community played in desertion. What did these deserters' individual communities look like? In Georgia, for example, how isolated were the Upcountry communities? How far away was a man's nearest neighbor or the closest town?

Despite these unanswered questions, desertion to the enemy during the Civil War helps to refine the traditional military definition of desertion. It involved more than escaping military service, because swearing the oath of allegiance represented an embrace of the Union cause. The Union's lenient desertion policy returned thousands of the Confederacy's best soldiers to their Southern homes as loyal citizens. Many of Georgia's deserters to the Union returned to communities that had resisted secession from the beginning. Georgia's deserters provided badly needed relief to a region that learned that the war had been a mistake. Equally important, Georgia's deserters to the enemy provide evidence of a clear pattern that would seem to apply for men who deserted but rejected the notion of swearing allegiance to the Union.

President Abraham Lincoln's hope for the rapid reconstruction of the South seemed within reach, but his vision died with him. Congressional reconstruction treated Southerners as conquered people, alienating civilians as well as soldiers who had taken the oath of allegiance in the belief that they could return to the Union as full citizens. Whether or not the men who deserted to the Union remained reconstructed or resisted, the Northern efforts to completely remake Southern society after the war is immaterial to this study. In an area so rife with uncertainty, the Georgians and other Confederates who deserted to the Union may be the only verifiable Confederate deserters of the war. The Union policy to reconstruct Confederate soldiers may have ultimately failed, but at least it documented Confederate deserters beyond the obscure estimates in traditional scholarship. Desertion reflected the resolution of conflicting loyalties within complex social relationships that in the end were not acts of cowardice but decisions made by men who simply chose home over the Confederacy.

Appendix: Methodology

The Register of Confederate Deserters lists each deserter's full name, rank, regiment and company, home state, county of residence, and physical description in height, skin complexion, eye color, and hair color. The record is contained in two volumes, assembled in alphabetical and chronological order. Because the register represents a compilation of records gathered from all Union military districts, the names were not listed in strict alphabetical order. Since all men did not desert at the same time, they were grouped together alphabetically, with earliest deserters followed by later deserters. Avery might precede Aaron if Avery was in a group that deserted earlier. Both books are double paged: the page on the left contains name, state, county, rank, and unit designation as well as certain physical characteristics. The page on the right provides date of desertion, date and place of release, and the signature of the Union commander authorizing the release. Each page spread is considered one page; thus, the first book has 423 pages of names with most pages having forty-six deserters to a page. The second book has a full 389 pages of deserters with a similar number of deserters per page. Officers are listed at the start of each letter of the alphabet and rarely occupy more than one full page. Thereafter, enlisted men are listed as described above. Based on the number of pages and the names per page, the register contains over thirty-five thousand deserters, slightly less than 35 percent of the total estimate of Confederate deserters.

There was no sampling of the source. Every Georgian in the register was identified. After running frequencies to match individual deserters to specific counties, units, and the dates of desertion, I organized the information by county so that any duplicate names could be removed from the total numbers. The organization of individual deserters by county facilitated two other important inquiries. First, by looking within each county at the date of a deserter's release, I could determine whether men from the same county deserted at the same time. Second, by organizing men by county, I could trace each man more efficiently in the 1860 manuscript census to discover something about his family background.

There were 3,368 Georgians, slightly less than 10 percent of the total Confederate deserters listed in the register. They came from 102 counties, but as this study shows, most were from the upper Piedmont and Upcountry sections. Their patterns of desertion show a clear connection between the Confederacy's retreat into Georgia and the invasion of the state by Sherman. The unit designation demonstrates a heavy concentration of deserters to the enemy from units in the Army of Tennessee. The data also suggest what both older desertion studies and more recent general studies claim: desertion occurred most frequently among the lowest ranking soldiers of the army.

The source created several problems that could not be overcome with precise certainty. First, much of the handwriting was so ornate that it was sometimes difficult to distinguish certain letters in a man's name. Second, there are many examples where the soldier in question gave responses that the person transcribing the information must have written down based on the pronunciation. For example, cross-referencing some names with census data or postwar muster rolls revealed such things as "Cader" for Decatur or "Rayburn" for Rabun County.

In almost every case, the date of desertion is missing. The desertion dates are based on when the deserter took the oath of allegiance and obtained his release. For this study, I arrived at the desertion date by calculating the amount of "lag" time that must have occurred between actual desertion and release. This is done in chapter 3.

The deserters whose manuscript census information appears were also not the result of any sampling. The information that appears was extracted from alphabetized manuscript census records at the Georgia Department of Archives and History. Not every county in Georgia alphabetized its 1860 census records. I went through the records and researched every deserter's name from Campbell, Carroll, Chatham, Floyd, Towns, Rabun, and Walker Counties. The information gleaned from the census has been used not to make any statistical conclusion but to more accurately tell the stories of some of the deserters' home front situations.

The manuscript census itself created certain problems. Because the information is organized by head of household, many times I had to investigate several households with the same surname to find a deserter within his parent's household. Because census listings are based on residence in 1860, no one who came to Georgia after 1860 appeared in the census, even if they claimed that county as their residence. However, even though I was not able to identify all of the deserters in the alphabetized manuscript census records, the family sizes and property holdings of those I could match provided insight into why they deserted.

Notes

INTRODUCTION

1. Joseph Hodges, Co. C, 8th GA Vols. to sister Mollie, July 17, 1862, Civil War Miscellaneous Correspondence (microfilm)(hereafter referred to as Miscellaneous Correspondence), Georgia Department of Archives and History (GDAH), Georgia Record Group (GRG) 3–2728, drawer 283, box 28. Hereafter, microfilm records held by the Georgia Department of Archives and History will be cited as GMRG, drawer, box, GDAH.

2. Ella Lonn, *Desertion during the Civil War* (1928; reprint, Gloucester MA: Peter Smith, 1966); Bessie Martin, *Desertion of Alabama Troops from the Confederate Army: A Study in Sectionalism* (1932; reprint, New York: AMS, 1966).

3. *Official Records of the War of the Rebellion of the Union and Confederate Armies*, 70 vols., 128 bks. (Washington DC: Government Printing Office, 1880–1909)— hereafter cited as OR; Thomas Livermore, *Numbers and Losses in the American Civil War* (Boston: n.p., 1901); Frederick Phisterer, *Statistical Record* (New York: n.p., 1883).

4. Lonn, *Desertion during the Civil War*, 3–20. For Lonn's history of the Confederate salt shortage, see Ella Lonn, *Salt as a Factor in the Confederacy* (New York: n.p., 1933). For works citing Lonn and the causes she identified, see James M. McPherson, *Battle Cry of Freedom* (New York: Oxford University Press, 1988), 873; James I. Robertson, *Soldiers Blue and Gray* (Columbia: University of South Carolina Press, 1988), 136; Bell Irwin Wiley, *The Life of Billy Yank: The Common Soldier of the Union* (Baton Rouge: Louisiana State University Press, 1991), 277.

5. Robertson, *Soldiers Blue and Gray*, 38–39; William C. Davis, *Jefferson Davis: The Man and His Hour* (New York: HarperCollins, 1991), 452–53; Martin, *Desertion of Alabama Troops*, 40–44, 121–59. See Colonel Fowler, superintendent of army records for the State of Alabama, comp., *Records of Alabama Commands, 1861–1865* (n.p.: n.d.).

6. McPherson, *Battle Cry of Freedom*, 820–21.

7. Albert Castel, *Decision in the West: The Atlanta Campaign of 1864* (Lawrence: University Press of Kansas, 1992), 52.

8. McPherson, *Battle Cry of Freedom*, 694 n.11; Katherine A. Giuffre, "First in Flight: Desertion as Politics in the North Carolina Confederate Army," *Social Science History* 21, no. 2 (summer 1997): 245–63. William E. Emerson, "Leadership and Civil War Desertion in the Twenty-fourth and Twenty-fifth Regiments of North Carolina Troops," *Southern Historian* 18 (fall 1997): 17–33.

9. See the appendix for a detailed description of the source and methodology.

10. John A. Campbell to John C. Breckenridge, March 5, 1865, *Southern Historical Society Papers*, 1876–1959 (hereafter referred to as *SHSP*), 52 vols. (Millswood NY: Krause Reprint, 1977), 42 (1917): 53.

11. Martin, *Desertion of Alabama Troops*, 13–25. The legal definition of desertion can be found in *The Statutes at Large of the Confederate States of America* (Richmond, 1864), vol. 1, sec. 6, p. 62; *Rules and Articles of War for the Government of the Army of the Confederate States of America* (Atlanta, 1861), Art. 10, and in Gen. P. G. T. Beauregard, General Orders No. 35, March 2, 1863, headquarters,Department of South Carolina, Georgia, and Florida, and Gen. Robert E. Lee, General Orders No. 16, February 16, 1862, headquarters, Army of Northern Virginia, cited in Martin, *Desertion of Alabama Troops*, 13.

12. William C. Davis, *The Orphan Brigade: The Kentucky Confederates Who Couldn't Go Home* (Garden City NY: Doubleday, 1980), 147–50. See also "Two Specimen Cases of Desertion," in *SHSP*, 8 (1880): 28–29. For expired enlistments in the 1st Maryland, the Army of Northern Virginia, see *SHSP*, 10 (1881): 52–53, 219–20.

13. Special Orders No. 170, Headquarters of the Army, Washington DC, 1861," *OR*, 2d ser., 3:52.

14. Gary W. Gallagher, *The Confederate War* (Cambridge: Harvard University Press, 1997), 31–32, 180.

15. Richard Beringer, Herman Hattaway, Archer Jones, and William N. Still Jr., *Why the South Lost the Civil War* (Athens: University of Georgia Press, 1986); Frank L. Owsley, *States Rights in the Confederacy* (Chicago: n.p., 1925); Paul Escott, *After Secession: Jefferson Davis and the Failure of Southern Nationalism* (Baton Rouge: Louisiana State University Press, 1978); Grady McWhiney and Perry D. Jamison, *Attack and Die: Civil War Military Tactics and the Southern Heritage* (Tuscaloosa: University of Alabama Press, 1982).

16. George C. Rable, *The Confederate Republic: A Revolution against Politics* (Chapel Hill: University of North Carolina Press, 1994), 300; William H. Freehling, *The Reintegration of American History: Slavery and the Civil War* (New York: Oxford University Press, 1994), 220–52; James M. McPherson, *Drawn with the Sword: Reflections on the American Civil War* (New York: Oxford University Press, 1996), 128–36.

17. Flavius Vegitius Renatus, *In Re Militari*, in *Roots of Strategy*, ed. Gen. T. R. Philips, trans. Lt. John Clarke (Harrisburg PA: Stackpole Books, 1985), 1:172.

18. Emory M. Thomas, *Robert E. Lee: A Biography* (New York: W. W. Norton, 1995), 308–9, 347–50.

19. Ulysses S. Grant to William Seward, August 19, 1864, *OR*, 1st ser., 37:517.

20. See Maris A. Vinovskis, ed., *Toward a Social History of the Civil War* (Cambridge: Cambridge University Press, 1990); Reid Mitchell, *The Vacant Chair: The Northern Soldier Leaves Home* (New York: Oxford University Press, 1993); Judith Lee Hancock, "The Role of Community in Civil War Desertion," *Civil War History* 29 (June 1983): 123–34.

21. Drew Gilpin Faust, "Altars of Sacrifice: Confederate Women and Narratives of War," *Journal of American History* 76 (March 1990): 1200–1228; Drew Gilpin Faust, *Mothers of Invention: Women of the Slaveholding South in the American Civil War* (Chapel Hill: University of North Carolina Press, 1996); Catherine Clinton and Nina Sibler, eds., *Divided Houses: Gender and the Civil War* (New York: Oxford University Press, 1992); LeeAnn Whites, *The Civil War as a Crisis in Gender: Augusta, Georgia, 1860–1890* (Athens: University of Georgia Press, 1995).

22. See Faust, "Altars of Sacrifice."

23. Bertram Wyatt-Brown, *Southern Honor: Ethics and Behavior in the Old South* (New York: Oxford University Press, 1982); John Hope Franklin, *The Militant South, 1800–1861* (Cambridge: Harvard University Press, 1956). Men's honor and the violent consequences of affronting this honor are recurrent themes throughout Franklin's book. James McPherson cites examples of Union soldiers remaining at war for the sake of their personal honor in *What They Fought For, 1861–65* (New York: Doubleday, 1995), 29.

24. Thomas Bigbie to Ant [*sic*] Ann, December 15, 1863, in *In the Land of the Living: War Time Letters by Confederate Soldiers from the Chattahoochee Valley of Alabama and Georgia*, ed. Roy A. Mathis (Troy AL: Troy State University Press, 1981), 82.

25. See Reid Mitchell, "The Northern Soldier and His Community," 80, and Thomas Kemp, "Community and War: The Civil War Experience of Two New Hampshire Towns," 37, both in Vinovskis, *Toward a Social History of the Civil War*; James K. Newton to father and mother, May 6, 1862, in *A Wisconsin Boy in Dixie*, ed. Stephen E. Ambrose (Madison: University of Wisconsin Press, 1961), 18–20.

26. For eyewitness accounts of executions for desertion, see Thomas Owens, "Penalties for Desertion," *Confederate Veteran* 2 (1894): 235.

1. SEEDS OF DESERTION

1. Lt. Charles C. Jones to Rev. C. C. Jones, July 25, 1862, in *The Children of Pride: A True Story of Georgia and the Civil War*, ed. Robert Mason Myers (New Haven: Yale University Press, 1972), 938.

2. Dr. John S. Law to Rev. C. C. Jones, December 19, 1860, in Myers, *Children of Pride*, 636.

3. William W. Freehling and Craig M. Simpson, eds., *Secession Debated: Georgia's Showdown in 1860* (New York: Oxford University Press, 1992), viii–ix.

4. Julia Floyd Smith, *Slavery and Rice Culture in Low Country Georgia, 1750–1860* (Knoxville: University of Tennessee Press, 1985), 15, 36. For a more detailed description of the rise of the cotton belt, see James C. Bonner, *A History of Georgia Agriculture, 1732–1860* (Athens: University of Georgia Press, 1964), 47–59.

5. Michael P. Johnson, *Toward a Patriarchal Republic: The Secession of Georgia* (Baton Rouge: Louisiana State University Press, 1977), 67–69, 87; Bertram Wyatt-Brown, *Southern Honor*, 176.

6. David Williams, *A Rich Man's War: Class, Caste, and Confederate Defeat in the Lower Chattahoochee Valley* (Athens: University of Georgia Press, 1998), 14–18.

7. Williams, *A Rich Man's War*, 17–24, 43–51, 62–73, 76, 101; Freehling, *Secession Debated*, xxi.

8. Merton Coulter, "The Myth of Dade County's Seceding from Georgia in 1860," *Georgia Historical Quarterly* 41 (December 1957): 352–53, 358.

9. Stephen Hahn, *The Roots of Southern Populism* (New York: Oxford University Press, 1983), 16–17.

10. Frederick A. Bode and Donald E. Ginter, *Farm Tenancy and the Census in Antebellum Georgia* (Athens: University of Georgia Press, 1986), 3.

11. Brown, *Southern Honor*, 54; Catherine Clinton, *The Plantation Mistress: Women's World in the Old South* (New York: Pantheon Books, 1982), 108–9.

12. Elizabeth Fox-Genovese, *Within the Plantation Household: Black and White Women of the Old South* (Chapel Hill: University of North Carolina Press, 1988), 102–4.

13. Clinton, *Plantation Mistress*, 18, 29, 165, 168; Anne F. Scott, *The Southern Lady: From Pedestal to Politics, 1830–1930* (Chicago: University of Chicago Press, 1970); Anne F. Scott, "Women's Perspective on the Patriarchy in the 1850s," *Journal of American History* 61 (June 1974): 52–64, 54; Whites, *Crisis in Gender*, 5.

14. Bertram Wyatt Brown, "Honor and Secession," in *The Coming of the American Civil War*, 3d ed., ed. Michael Perman (Lexington MA: D. C. Heath, 1993), 246–47; Clinton, *Plantation Mistress*, 107–09.

15. L. H. Ansley, *Reminiscences of L. H. Ansley, 10th Georgia Cavalry*, in Miscellaneous Correspondence, GMRG 3–2715, drawer 283, box 16, GDAH.

16. Unsigned letter to Ivy W. Duggan, December 31, 1863, Miscellaneous Correspondence, GMRG 3–2723, drawer 283, box 24, GDAH; Brown, *Southern Honor*, 33, 43–44.

17. For Appalachian studies outside Georgia, see Wilma Dunaway, *The First American Frontier: Transition to Capitalism in Southern Appalachia, 1700–1860* (Chapel Hill: University of North Carolina Press, 1996); Durwood Dunn, *Cade's Cove: The Life and Death of a Southern Appalachia Community, 1818–1837* (Knoxville: University of Tennessee Press, 1988), John C. Inscoe, *Mountain Masters, Slavery, and the Sectional Crisis in Western North Carolina* (Knoxville: University of Tennessee Press, 1989); Mary Beth Pudup, Dwight B. Billings, and Altina L. Waller, eds., *Appalachia in the Making* (Chapel Hill: University of North Carolina Press, 1995).

18. David Williams, *The Georgia Gold Rush: Twenty-niners, Cherokees, and Gold Fever* (Columbia: University of South Carolina Press, 1993), 57, 65, 118; James Alfred Sartan, *The History of Walker County, Georgia* (Carrollton GA: Thomasson Printing and Office Equipment, 1972), 1:41–42; Charles H. Shriner, *History of Murray County* (n.p., 1911), 14.

19. Coulter, "Myth of Dade County," 363; Andrew Cain, *The History of Lumpkin County for the First Hundred Years, 1832–1932* (Spartanburg SC: Reprint, 1978), 57–63.

20. Smith, *Slavery and Rice Culture in Low Country Georgia*, 33.

21. Jonathan D. Sarris, "An Execution in Lumpkin County: Localized Loyalties in North Georgia's Civil War," in *The Civil War in Appalachia*, ed. Kenneth W. Noe and Shannon H. Wilson (Knoxville: University of Tennessee Press, 1997), 133.

22. Hahn, *Roots of Southern Populism*, 27.

23. George Gordon Ward, *The Annals of Upper Georgia Centered in Gilmer County* (Carrollton GA: Thomasson Printing Office and Equipment Co., 1965), 118–22.

24. *Fayette County: The History of Fayette County, 1821–1971* (Fayette County Historical Society, 1977), 24.

25. Cain, *History of Lumpkin County*, 241.

26. Memoirs of Jim Kugler, Carroll County, Georgia, Pvt., 56th GA Inf. (unpublished), Miscellaneous Correspondence, GMRG 3–2730, drawer 283, box 30, GDAH.

27. Lucien E. Roberts, *A History of Paulding County* (Dallas GA: n.p., 1933), 27–28; Smith, *Slavery and Rice Culture in Low Country Georgia*, 33.

28. Roberts, *Paulding County*, 28; Ward, *Annals of Upper Georgia*, 118–22.

29. James C. Bonner, *Georgia's Last Frontier: The Development of Carroll County* (Athens: University of Georgia Press, 1971), 50, 54, 56–57; Cain, *History of Lumpkin County*, 79, 91, 97, 105. For a description of Union County's gold mining, see *The Heritage of Union County, 1832–1994* (n.p.: Walsworth, 1994).

30. Act of the General Assembly, February 10, 1787, in *Georgia Voices: A Documentary History to 1872*, comp. Spencer B. King Jr. (Athens: University of Geor-

gia Press, 1966), 169; Dickson D. Bruce Jr., *Violence and Culture in the Antebellum South* (Austin: University of Texas Press, 1979), 92–94.

31. Bertram Wyatt-Brown, *Honor and Violence in the Old South*, abridged ed. (New York: Oxford University Press, 1986), 60–61.

32. Hahn, *Roots of Southern Populism*, 23, 29; Bode, *Farm Tenancy and the Census in Antebellum Georgia*, introduction. See also Christopher Clark, *The Roots of Capitalism, Western Massachusetts, 1780–1860* (Ithaca NY: Cornell University Press, 1990) for a study of northern farm economy and the family as an economic unit.

33. Hahn, *Roots of Southern Populism*, 29–33, 72. Even the reliance on merchant goods that did exist was slight. See Hahn, 72 n.56.

34. Hahn, *Roots of Southern Populism*, 36–37, 51–58; Eugene D. Genovese, "Yeoman Farmers in a Slaveholder's Democracy," *American Historical Review* 49 (April 1975): 336–38; Williams, *Rich Man's War*, 16.

35. Johnson, *Toward a Patriarchal Republic*, 3–4, 60.

36. Williams, *Rich Man's War*, chaps. 4 and 5.

37. For a comparison of the two main Confederate armies, see Richard M. McMurry, *Two Great Rebel Armies: An Essay in Confederate Military History* (Chapel Hill: University of North Carolina Press, 1989); Lillian Henderson, ed., *Roster of the Confederate Soldiers of Georgia, 1861–1865*, 6 vols. (Hapeville GA: Longino & Porter, 1955–62).

38. Mark Boatner, *The Civil War Dictionary*, rev. ed. (New York: David McKay, 1988), 829; Albert Castel, *Decision in the West*, 111, 552; *OR*, 1st ser., 21:1121; James Longstreet, *From Manassas to Appomattox: Memoirs of the Civil War in America* (New York: Konecky & Konecky, 1992), 553.

39. Stewart Sifakis, *Compendium of the Confederate Armies: South Carolina and Georgia* (New York: Facts on File, 1995), 147–69.

40. Dade, Gordon, Walker, Catoosa, Whitfield, Fannin, Murray, Union, Towns, Rabun, Habersham, White, Hall, Lumpkin, Forsyth, Dawson, Gilmer, Pickens, Cherokee, and Chattcoga.

41. Bartow, Floyd, Carroll, Polk, Haralson, Heard, Campbell, Paulding, Cobb, Milton, Fulton, Fayette, Clayton, DeKalb, Gwinnett, Walton, Jackson, Banks, Franklin, Hart, and Madison.

42. Johnson, Emanuel, Bullock, Tattnall, Appling, Wayne, Pierce, Charlton, Ware, Montgomery, Berrien, Irwin, Coffee, Clinch, Echols, Lowndes, Brooks, Colquitt, Worth, Wilcox, Pulaski, Laurens, and Telfair.

43. Chatham, Bryan, Liberty, McIntosh, Glynn, and Camden.

44. These figures match the numbers provided in several of the local county histories and correspondence during the war, like the Muscogee letter. Fayette County claimed to have sent 1,131 men to the war. Henderson, *Roster of the Confederate Soldiers of Georgia, 1861–1865*, indicates six companies from Fayette

County. Union County shows two companies, and its local history specifically identified them as Company B of the 23d GA, Army of Northern Virginia, and Company G of the 52d GA, Army of Tennessee. Cavalry units did not appear in the *Roster*, but the local history claims that Union County contributed Companies B, F, and I of the 6th GA Cavalry. The *Roster* lists Lumpkin County as providing three infantry companies. Lumpkin County's local history identifies them as Companies C and D of the 52d GA Infantry, and Company E of Phillips Legion, which was a regiment in the Army of Northern Virginia. Gordon County's local history does not state the precise numbers, but it indicates that the county sent troops in July, September, October, and December 1861 and in March and September 1862. *The History of Fayette County, 1821–1971*, 344; *Union County: A Pictorial History of Union County* (Union County Historical Society, n.d.), 1:29; Cain, *History of Lumpkin County*, 158–65; *Gordon County: 1976 Bicentennial History of Gordon, Georgia* (Calhoun: Georgia State Historical Society, 1976), 115–34; From Your Most Humble Servants Several Joe Brown's Men, Citizens of Muscogee County to Joseph Brown, February 19, 1862, in Adjutant and Inspector General's Correspondence (hereafter referred to as Inspector General's Correspondence), GRG 57–1–3, box 16, GDAH. Hereafter nonmicrofilmed records from the Georgia Department of Archives and History will be identified as GRG, box, folder (if appropriate), GDAH.

45. Robert Gross, *The Minutemen and Their World* (New York: Hill & Wang, 1976), introduction; Fred Anderson, *A People's Army: Massachusetts Soldiers and Society in the Seven Years' War* (Chapel Hill: University of North Carolina Press, 1984), 28–29; Donald Higginbotham, *War and Society in Revolutionary America: The Wider Dimensions of Conflict* (Columbia: University of South Carolina Press, 1988), 268.

46. Higginbotham, *War and Society*, 296; Clark, *The Roots of Capitalism*, 317.

47. John J. Cheatham, Athens GA, to James Hunter, Confederate secretary of war, May 4, 1861, F. Kendall, Greenville (Meriwether County)GA, to Jefferson Davis, September 16, 1864, both in *Free at Last: A Documentary History of Slavery, Freedom, and the Civil War*, Ira Berlin et al. (Edison NJ: Blue and Grey Press, 1997), 5, 151–52. Both men advocated using slaves in the military, either as soldiers or as support units, to prevent their rebelling or falling into Union hands. See chap. 6 infra for discussion of slaveholding women and their wartime concerns. See also Clinton, *Plantation Mistress*, 30–33.

48. Whites, *Crisis in Gender*, 6; Booker T. Washington, *Up from Slavery* (1900; reprint, New York: New York Limited Editions Club, 1970), 9. For examples of nonviolent resistance, see Williams, *Rich Man's War*, chap. 6.

49. Hahn, *Roots of Southern Populism*, 86–87; Gross, *The Minutemen*, 35–36. For an in-depth study of the notion that yeomen and planters shared a common vision of republican independence, held together by the mudsill of slavery, see

Lacy K. Ford, *The Origins of Southern Radicalism: The South Carolina Upcountry, 1800–1860* (New York: Oxford University Press, 1988).

50. President Woodrow Wilson, speech in Washington DC, May 12, 1917, *Words on War*, ed. Jay Shafritz (New York: Prentice Hall, 1990), 461.

2. PREPARING FOR THE PRODIGAL SON

1. Much of the material in this chapter appears in Mark A. Weitz, "Preparing for the Prodigal Son: The Development of the Union Desertion Policy during the Civil War," *Civil War History* 45 (June 1999): 99–125.

2. Samuel M. Bird is 1 of 257 deserters to the enemy from Walker County identified in the Register of Confederate Deserters, 1863–1865 (microfilm), RG M598, roll 8, National Archives, Washington DC. His personal information is taken from Jessee June Griffin, comp., *The 1860 Census of Walker County, Georgia* (n.p, 1982), 38.

3. Mark Boatner, *The Civil War Dictionary*, rev. ed. (New York: David McKay, 1988), 322.

4. Proclamation of Amnesty and Reconstruction, December 8, 1863, in *The Collected Works of Abraham Lincoln*, 9 vols., ed. Roy P. Balser (New Brunswick NJ: Rutgers University Press, 1953), 7:253; Eric Foner, *Reconstruction: America's Unfinished Revolution, 1863–1877* (New York: Harper & Row, 1988), 35–36.

5. Philip S. Paludan, *A People's Contest* (New York: Harper & Row, 1988), 253.

6. Foner, *Reconstruction*, 35–76 passim; Willie Lee Rose, *Rehearsal for Reconstruction: The Port Royal Experiment* (New York: Vintage Books, 1964); James McPherson, *Abraham Lincoln and the Second American Revolution* (New York: Oxford University Press, 1991), 3–11.

7. E. D. Townsend, Special Orders No. 170, October 12, 1861, OR, 2d ser., 3:51–52.

8. C. P. Wolcott to Col. Richard Owen, June 21, 1862, and Wolcott to Col. Gustavus Loomis, June 27, 1862, OR, 2d ser., 4:48, 90.

9. Henry W. Halleck to Gen. George Thomas, July 8, 1862, OR, 2d ser., 4:150.

10. Stewart Sifakis, *Who Was Who in the Civil War* (New York: Facts on File, 1989), 312; Boatner, *The Civil War Dictionary*, 404; William Hoffman to George Thomas, July 15, 1862, OR, 2d ser., 4:223; Justin Dimick to Thomas, July 25, 1862, OR, 2d ser., 4:287.

11. Andrew Johnson, military governor of Tennessee, to President Abraham Lincoln, July 26, 1862, OR, 2d ser., 4:289.

12. Andrew Johnson, military governor of Tennessee, to P. H. Watson, assistant secretary of war, August 3, 1862, OR, 2d ser., 4:333.

13. McPherson, *Battle Cry of Freedom*, 304–5.

14. John A. Dix to Secretary of War Stanton, July 29, 1862, OR, 2d ser., 4:308.

15. Joseph H. Tucker to Adj. Gen. Lorenzo Thomas, July 30, 1862, *OR*, 2d ser., 4:313. See also Jas. A. Ekin, Asst. Quartermaster to Edwin Stanton, August 2, 1862, *OR*, 2d ser., 4:331.

16. David Tod to Edwin Stanton, August 1, 1862, *OR*, 2d ser., 4:321; C. P. Wolcott to Tod, August 2, 1862, *OR*, 2d ser., 4:328.

17. John J. Mudd to Abraham Lincoln, August 3, 1862, *OR*, 2d ser., 4:334–35.

18. For argument that the exchange system collapsed because the South improperly activated soldiers not formally exchanged and mistreated black prisoners, see McPherson, *Battle Cry of Freedom*, 792–93. For an argument that military expediency drove Grant's decision to stop the three-year exchange policy in April 1864, see Shelby Foote, *The Civil War, a Narrative*, vol. 3, *Red River to Appomattox* (New York: Vintage Books, 1986), 131.

19. Capt. H. W. Freedley to William Hoffman, August 16, 1862, *OR*, 2d ser., 4:401.

20. E. H. Sutton, 24th GA Vols., *Civil War Stories* (Demorest GA: Banner Printing, 1907), 61–63, in Miscellaneous Correspondence, GMRG 3–2741, drawer 283, box 41, GDAH. Sutton misidentified the biblical inscription as from the Old Testament. It was from the New Testament, 1 John 2:19. 19. Richard N. Current, *Lincoln's Loyalists: Union Soldiers from the Confederacy* (Boston: Northeastern University Press, 1992), 120–23.

21. P. H. Watson, asst. secretary of war, to Capt. James A. Ekin, Indianapolis, August 4, 1862, 4:336; Andrew Johnson to Gen. George Thomas, August 9, 1862, 4:362; William Hoffman to Thomas, August 9, 1862, 4:365; Thomas to Major H. S. Burton, commanding officer, Fort Delaware, August 9, 1862, 4:365, all in *OR*, 2d ser.

22. William Hoffman to Capt. H. W. Freedley, August 9, 1862, *OR*, 2d ser., 4:365; J. A. Ekin to Edwin Stanton, August 14, 1862, *OR*, 2d ser., 4:391. Indicates Hoffman's telegraph received on August 13, 1862, and the new order had stopped Johnson's commissioner, ex-governor Campbell, from continuing his assignment. War Department Adjutant General's Office: General Orders 107 Issued by E. D. Townsend at the command of Gen. H. Halleck, August 15, 1862, *OR*, 2d ser., 4:393; Ekin to Stanton, August 19, 1862, *OR*, 2d ser., 4:410.

23. William Hoffman to Major W. S. Pierson, Sandusky, Ohio, August 14, 1862, *OR*, 2d ser., 4:338. Indicates unsure whether release policy of POWs would continue, but acknowledged that many would remain north. Gen. George Thomas to Military Gov. Andrew Johnson, August 9, 1862, *OR*, 2d ser., 4:364; J. A. Ekin to Montgomery Meigs, Q.M.G., August 13, 1862, *OR*, 2d ser., 4:387. Both letters inquire as to the logistical problems of transporting released POWs who took the oath. H. W. Freedley to William Hoffman, August 12, 1862, *OR*, 2d ser., 4:380; Major Joseph Darr to Hoffman, August 14, 1862, *OR*, 2d ser., 4:392.

Freedley showed concern that other loyal Confederate prisoners threatened those who took the oath. Ekin expressed the same fear in a letter to Edwin Stanton on August 15, 1862. Ekin suggested the Tennesseans should have been discharged or at least removed from the area in which the loyalists were housed due to the bitterness of feeling expressed by the loyal prisoners; see *OR*, 2d ser., 4:396. Darr recognized that those staying north, mostly Virginians, would also need some paperwork to prevent them from being arrested again.

24. Lt. Col. William S. Pearson to Col. I. C. Bassett, January 28, 1864, with endorsements from Bassett to his commander, H. D. Terry, January 30, 1864, and from Terry to Hoffman, January 30, 1864, 6:903; Hoffman to Terry, February 15, 1864, 6:954, all in *OR*, 2d ser.

25. J. Darr to Gov. F. H. Pierpoint of Virginia, August 22, 1862, 4:422; William Hoffman to Maj. J. G. Fonda, Camp Butler, Springfield IL, September 1, 1862, 4:479; Hoffman to Col. Jesse Hildebrand, commanding officer, Alton Prison, Alton IL, September 3, 1862, 4:485, all in *OR*, 2d ser.

26. John C. Stiles (Brunswick GA), "In the Years of the War: Trying to Get Paroled," *Confederate Veteran Magazine* 26 (1918): 77.

27. Senate Resolution from 1st Confederate Cong., 2d sess., Senate, Wednesday, August 20, 1862, *SHSP*, 45 (1925): 184.

28. Capt. Stephen E. Jones, headquarters, Louisville KY, to William Hoffman, November 22, 1862, *OR*, 2d ser., 4:745. Hoffman to Maj. Peter Zinn, December 9, 1862, *OR*, 2d ser., 5:26, orders Zinn to stop releasing prisoners from Camp Chase OH.

29. Col. Henry Dent, provost marshall general, to Capt. H. W. Freedley, December 1, 1862, 5:36; Lt. Col. F. A. Dick to William Hoffman, December 3, 1862, 5:21–23; Capt. H. W. Freedley to Hoffman, December 8, 1862, 5:51, all in *OR*, 2d ser.

30. J. T. Boyle to H. G. Wright, November 30, 1862, *OR*, 2d ser., 5:28–29.

31. H. G. Wright to Gen. George Thomas, December 5, 1862, 5:27, and Henry Dent to J. T. Boyle, December 15, 1862, 5:85–86, both in *OR*, 2d ser. Dent referred to a General Order 31 issued by General Rosecrans that Dent interpreted as an invitation for Confederate soldiers to desert. Lt. Col. W. H. Ludlow, asst. inspector general, Fort Monroe, to W. Hoffman, December 27, 1862, *OR*, 2d ser., 5:127.

32. U. S. Grant to Confederate Gen. John Pemberton, December 15, 1862, *OR*, 2d ser., 5:83.

33. W. Hoffman to Capt. S. E. Jones, December 3, 1862, 5:19; W. Hoffman to P. Zinn, December 4, 1862, 5:26; H. G. Wright to W. Rosecrans, December 6, 1862, 5:32; W. Hoffman to F. A. Dick, December 12, 1862, 5:74; General Orders No. 36, issued by Acting Asst. Adj. Gen., Thomas G. Beaham on behalf of

Maj. Gen. G. Granger, December 19, 1862, 5:101; H. G. Wright to J. T. Boyle, December 22, 1862, 5:107, all in *OR*, 2d ser.

34. Maj. Gen. Gordon Granger, General Orders No. 5, January 12, 1863, headquarters, Army of Kentucky, *OR*, 2d ser., 5:173. For Rosecrans Order see note 31.

35. House Resolution, 1st Confederate Cong., 3d sess., House of Representatives, January 26, 1863, in *SHSP*, 47 (1940): 203; 1st Cong., 3d sess., H.R., February 9, 1863, Senate, March 2, 1863, *SHSP*, 48 (1941): 86, 227, 233; Senate Resolution on "Harboring Deserters," 1st Confederate Cong., 3d sess., Senate, Monday, February 16, 1863, *SHSP*, 48 (1941): 128. The death penalty received official sanction in April 1863, 1st Confederate Cong., 3d sess., Senate, Wednesday, April 1, 1863, and House, Tuesday, April 7, 1863, *SHSP*, 48 (1941): 70–71, 101.

36. For overcrowding at Elmira NY, in 1864, see Bruce Catton, *Bruce Catton's Civil War: Three Volumes in One* (New York: Fairfax Press, 1984), 621–23. For the exchange system as a deterrent to overcrowding July 1862–May 1863, see William B. Hesseltine, *Civil War Prisons: A Study in War Psychology* (Columbus OH: n.p., 1930). See also McPherson, *Battle Cry of Freedom*, 791–92. McPherson suggests overcrowding was not a problem. The letters from the Northern department and prison commanders suggest otherwise.

37. Gen. Samuel Curtis to Maj. Gen. Henry Halleck, January 24, 1863, 5:207; Halleck to Curtis, January 25, 1863, 5:214; F. A. Dick to Gen. Samuel Curtis, January 28, 1863, 5:223–24; J. Ammen, brigadier general of volunteers, to William Hoffman, January 31, 1863, February 2, 1863; Hoffman to Col. Henry Dent, February 10, 1863, 5:263; Hoffman to Stanton, March 18, 1863, 5:361; Hoffman to Dent, April 11, 1863, 5:465; Hoffman to Stephen E. Jones, May 4, 1863, 5:554; Hoffman to Gen. William Rosecrans, June 3, 1863, 5:736; Hoffman to Gen. J. H. Martindale, January 13, 1863, 5:176, all in *OR*, 2d ser.

38. William Hoffman to Edwin Stanton, March 24, 1863, 5:390–391; Hoffman to J. Mason, April 23, 1863, and May 11, 1863, 5:533, 593; memorandum (apparently to the file) George Sawin, lieutenant and quartermaster, 58th IL Reg., circa February 1863, 5:240, all in *OR*, 2d ser. Memo appears among correspondence dated February 4 and 7, 1863.

39. H. G. Wright to Brig. Gen. White, February 26, 1863, 5:299; Jno H. Winder to Secretary of War James A. Seddon, February 28, 1863, 5:841, both in *OR*, 2d ser.

40. William Hoffman to E. Stanton, June 13, 1863, endorsed by War Dept. as approved, June 18, 1863, 6:14; Hoffman to Gen. Ambrose Burnside, Comm. Dept of Ohio, June 20, 1863, 6:31; Gen. Henry W. Halleck to Col. W. H. Ludlow, Fort Monroe, July 7, 1863, 6:91; Halleck to Burnside, August 5, 1863, 6:177; Hoffman to Maj. Gen. Robert A. Schenk, July 11, 1863, 6:103; Schenk to Brig. Gen. W. W. Morris, Ft. McHenry, July 11, 1863, 6:103, all in *OR*, 2d ser.

41. William Hoffman to Brig. Gen. A. Schoepf, August 4, 1863, 6:175; Hoffman to Maj. Gen. John M. Schofield, August 5, 1863, 6:178; Hoffman to Maj. Gen. William Rosecrans, August 7, 1863, 6:186, all in OR, 2d ser.

42. General Orders No. 126, August 8, 1863, headquarters, Department of Ohio, 6:190; E. A. Hitchcock to Maj. Gen. Ambrose Burnside, August 15, 1863, 6:206; Maj. Gen. William Rosecrans to William Hoffman, August 16, 1863, 6:207, all in OR, 2d ser. For copy of General Orders No. 175 issued by Rosecrans, see *Official Records*, 1st ser., vol. 23, pt. 2, 184. For War Department's opinion on Rosecrans's suggestion, see E. A. Hitchcock, memorandum to Secretary of War, August 29, 1863, OR, 2d ser., 6:207–8; "The Advance on Washington in 1864, letter from Jubal Early to the editor of *The Republican*," in SHSP, 9 (1881): 302.

43. General Orders No. 286, August 17, 1863, War Department, Adjutant General's Office, OR, 2d ser., 6:212.

44. William Hoffman to Edwin Stanton, August 26, 1863, OR, 2d ser., 6:227–28.

45. William Hoffman to William Rosecrans, August 29, 1863, 6:239–40; Hoffman to Maj. Gen. J. G. Foster, August 30, 1863, 6:2; Hoffman to Maj. Gen. George Meade, September 3, 1863, 6:256; General Orders No. 162, headquarters, Department of Ohio, Gen. Ambrose Burnside commanding, 6:319–20, all in OR, 2d ser.

46. "Aiding Desertion from the Army," 1st Confederate Cong., 4th sess., H.R., Tuesday, December 22, 1863, and Wednesday, December 30, 1863, Senate, Tuesday, January 9, 1864, in SHSP, 50 (1953): 98, 160, 258.

47. Reputation evidence of desertion, February 10, 1865, in SHSP, 52 (1959): 326.

48. Halleck to Major General Foster, September 23, 1864, OR, 2d ser., 7:865–66; Foster to Halleck, October 24, 1864, OR, 2d ser., 7:1016.

49. Brig. Gen. G. Marston, commander, Point Lookout Prison, October 7, 1863, OR, 2d ser., 7:356–57.

50. McPherson, *Battle Cry of Freedom*, 791–92.

51. J. Holt, judge adv. gen., to Ira Harris, October 19, 1863, OR, 2d ser., 7:394–95.

52. U.S. Grant to Stanton, August 19, 1864, OR, 2d ser., 7:614–15.

53. Circular No. 31, August 31, 1864, by command of Lt. Gen. U.S. Grant and Special Orders No. 3, January 4, 1865, by command of Lt. Gen. U. S. Grant, *Official Records*, 1st ser., vol. 46, pt. 2, 828–29.

54. Address by Robert Stiles at the dedication of the monument to the Confederate dead of the University of Virginia, June 7, 1893, in SHSP, 21 (1893): 32.

55. G. W. Smith to Gov. Joe Brown, August 13, 1864, Miscellaneous Correspondence, GMRG 3–2721, drawer 283, box 22, GDAH.

56. John A. Campbell, Asst. Secretary of War, to Gen. John C. Breckenridge, March 5, 1865, in *SHSP*, 42 (1917): 53, 55–56.

57. James Longstreet to Lt. Col. W. H. Taylor, March 25, 1865, in Longstreet, *From Manassas to Appomattox*, 651.

58. Abraham Lincoln to John C. Fremont, September 2, 1861, *Collected Works of Abraham Lincoln*, 4:506; McPherson, *Battle Cry of Freedom*, 499.

59. Thaddeus Oliver, "All Quiet on the Potomac Tonight," undated, reprinted in *Atlanta Journal*, July 16, 1935, Miscellaneous Correspondence, GMRG 3–2736, drawer 283, box 36, GDAH. The "two in the low trundle bed" were Oliver's sons, Hugh and James.

3. PATTERNS OF FLIGHT

1. Court-Martial Proceedings of Pvt. Francis C. Tumlin, Co. D, 1st Georgia State Line, in *Adjutant General's Court-Martial Proceedings* (Atlanta: Georgia Department of Archives and History), GRG 3336–17, folder 1, box 1, GDAH.

2. Andrew Cain, *The History of Lumpkin County for the First 100 Years* (Spartanburg SC: Reprint, 1978), 158, 161; J. M. Brown to H. C. Wayne, October 2, 1863, Inspector General's Correspondence, GRG 57–1–3, box 16, GDAH.

3. Cain, *History of Lumpkin County*, 155, 159. See E. A. Hitchcock to Editor of *New York Times*, November 28, 1863, *OR*, 2d ser., 6:594–600; reprint of Robert Ould, October 10, 1863, notice releasing paroled prisoners in General Orders No. 59, S. S. Anderson, Asst. Adj. Gen. for Lt. Gen. E. Kirby Smith, *OR*, 2d ser., 6:601.

4. See court-martial proceedings of Francis C. Tumlin and Edward J. Tumlin, GRG 3336–17, box 1, folder 1, GDAH.

5. William Harris Bragg, *Joe Brown's Army, 1862–1865* (Macon GA: Mercer University Press, 1987), 16–21.

6. James Alfred Sartan, *History of Walker County, Georgia* (Carrollton GA: Thomasson Printing and Office Equipment Co., 1972), 1:120–21.

7. William S. Kinsland, "The Civil War Comes to Lumpkin County," *Northern Georgia Journal* 1 (summer 1984): 21–26. *New York Times* article published in the *Countryman*, published by J. A. Turner at his Turnwold, Georgia Plantation, Putnam County GA, 12–1 (#80) February 7, 1865, Emory University Microfilm #67.

8. Diary of William Sylvester Dillon, 4th Tenn. Vols., Sunday, May 1, 1864, Monday, May 2, 1864, and Tuesday, July 5, 1864, Miscellaneous Correspondence, GMRG 3–2723, drawer 283, box 24, GDAH.

9. Cain, *Lumpkin County History*, 154.

10. Diary of Thomas A. Sharp, March 29, 1864–November 17, 1864, Miscellaneous Correspondence, GMRG 3–2739, drawer 283, box 39, GDAH.

11. The raw numbers indicated 3,500 deserters, but a careful review of each de-

serter revealed 132 duplicates, men who were listed twice by the Union clerks who prepared the lists.

12. The Register of Confederate Deserters, 17–18, 26–27.

13. J. W. Adair, of the 9th GA Artillery, is one of the few Georgians shown in the register to have deserted to the enemy and secured a release before December 1863. The register shows his release date as October 18, 1863.

14. Lonn, *Desertion during the Civil War*, 27.

15. Diary of Sargent I. V. Moore, November 28, 1863, and February 23, 1864, Miscellaneous Correspondence, GMRG 3–2735, drawer 283, box 35, GDAH; "The Fight Has Begun in Dalton," *Macon Daily Telegraph*, February 25, 1864.

16. Capt. W. L. Calhoun, *Regimental History of 42d* Georgia Volunteer Infantry (Atlanta: n.p., 1900), in Miscellaneous Correspondence, GMRG 3–2719, drawer 283, box 20, GDAH.

17. Pvt. P. D. Stephenson, "Reminiscences of the Last Campaign of the Army of Tennessee, from May 1864 to January 1865," in *SHSP*, 12 (1884): 39.

18. Larry J. Daniel, *Soldiering in the Army of Tennessee: A Portrait of Life in the Confederate Army* (Chapel Hill: University of North Carolina Press, 1991), 137.

19. Henderson, *Roster of the Confederate Soldiers of Georgia*, 3:x–xi, 4:vi–vii.

20. The army affiliation of the units comes from two sources. The infantry units are identified by Henderson, ed., *Roster of the Confederate Soldiers of Georgia*. The cavalry units are identified by tracing their theater of operation within the *Official Records*. The 1st, 3d, 4th, and 6th GA Cavalry all fought in Georgia during the Atlanta campaign and were regiments in Gen. Joseph Wheeler's cavalry; see OR, 1st ser., vol. 38, pt. 3, 642, 673.

21. Longstreet, *From Manassas to Appomattox*, 435–437, 480–81, 542.

22. Henderson, *Roster of the Confederate Soldiers*, vol. 2, table of contents, vol. 6, table of contents. The 11th had three Gilmer Companies and one company each from Murray, Fannin, Catoosa, and Hall Counties. The companies from outside the Upcountry were Lee, Walton, Randolph, and Houston Counties. The 60th had five companies formed all or in part from Whitfield County. One company had Gilmer County soldiers, and one formed exclusively from Walker County. Of the counties outside the Upcountry, Chatham, Spalding, Meriwether, and Troup had one company each.

23. Maj. Jasper Whiting, asst. adj. gen., to Col. Paul J. Semmes, February 4, 1862, Miscellaneous Correspondence, GMRG 3–2739, drawer 283, box 39, GDAH.

24. A. J. Rees, Phillips Legion, to aunt, April 30, 1862, GMRG 3–2737, drawer 283, box 37; Solomon G. Harper, Co. B, 7th GA Inf., Army of Northern Virginia (ANV), to mother and father, August 9, 1862, GMRG 3–3727, drawer 283, box 27; William M. Wood, Co. F, 14th GA Inf., ANV, to sister Ella, GMRG 3–2744, drawer 283, box 44; Henry Jackson, Co. K, 3d GA Inf., ANV, to cousins Lizzie,

Beck, and Ophee, undated 1864, GMRG 3–2729, drawer 283, box 29, all in Miscellaneous Correspondence, GDAH.

25. Thomas J. Howard, Co. C., 27th GA Inf., ANV, to wife, Martha Howard, February 28, 1863, GMRG 3–2729, drawer 283, box 29; John Howard Neisler, Co. E. 5th GA Inf., Army of Tennessee (AT), to sister Jane, December 4, 1863, GMRG 3–2735, drawer 283, box 35, both in Miscellaneous Correspondence, GDAH.

26. J. W. Shank to J. B. Smith, March 19, 1864, and August 5, 1864, GMRG 3–2739, drawer 283, box 39. Capt. David H. Pope, 10th GA Inf., ANV, to wife, Martha Hodges Pope, February 10, 1864, GMRG 3–2737, drawer 283, box 37, both in Miscellaneous Correspondence, GDAH.

27. Samuel J. G. Brewer to wife, October 20, 1862, Miscellaneous Correspondence, GMRG 3–2717, drawer 283, box 18, GDAH.

28. John A. Johnson, Co. C., 19th GA Inf., to Miss Ella Arnold, Coweta County, GA, December 15, 1864, Miscellaneous Correspondence, GMRG 3–2729, drawer 283, box 29, GDAH.

29. Peter Dekle, 29th GA Inf., to wife, October 13, 1862, Miscellaneous Correspondence, GMRG 3–2722, drawer 283, box 23, GDAH. A note on the letter indicates Dekle was stationed at Caustens Bluffs below Savannah when his letter was written. For the number of Georgia infantry regiments in the Army of Northern Virginia, see Henderson, *Roster of the Confederate Soldiers of Georgia.*

30. Israel E. Linder, 27th GA Inf., to mother, A. S. Thompson, May 6, 1864, and July 18, 1864, Miscellaneous Correspondence, GMRG 3–2732, drawer 283, box 32, GDAH.

31. Cain, *Lumpkin County History*, 165; interview with Augustus H. Brantley, Co. D, 8th GA Inf., Miscellaneous Correspondence, GMRG 3–2717, drawer 283, box 18, GDAH.

32. Memoirs of Mrs. Thomas J. Lockridge, Bartow County, Miscellaneous Correspondence, GMRG 3–2731, drawer 283, box 32, GDAH.

33. William Dickey to wife, July 13, 1864, Miscellaneous Correspondence, GMRG 3–2722, drawer 283, box 16, GDAH.

34. M. B. Gray to J. Q. Farmer, July 15, 1864, Miscellaneous Correspondence, GMRG 3–2724, drawer 283, box 25, GDAH.

35. Lee Kennett, *Marching through Georgia* (New York: HarperCollins, 1995), 80.

36. W. H. Reynolds to sister Anna, September 28, 1864, Miscellaneous Correspondence, GMRG 3–2722, drawer 283, box 16, GDAH.

37. "North Georgia under the Yankee Yoke," *Southern Recorder*, May 31, 1864, 2.

38. John A. Johnson, 19th GA Inf., Co. C, to Miss Ella Arnold, June 1864, Miscellaneous Correspondence, GMRG 3–2729, drawer 283, box 29, GDAH.

39. Lucien E. Roberts, *Paulding County*, 43–44.

40. Johnson, *Toward a Patriarchal Republic*, 3; Roberts, *Paulding County*, 28, 44.

41. Johnson, *Toward a Patriarchal Republic*, 3.

42. Castel, *Decision in the West*, 336–342.

43. "Interview of Dr. J. D. Pendleton, Clerk of the Senate of Virginia with copy of a report titled, The Confederate Army: Its Numbers, Troops furnished by States, Its Losses by States and Contrasted with Grant's Forces in 1865," *Dispatch*, August 15, 1891, reprinted in SHSP, 19 (1891): 255–56.

44. Castel, *Decision in the West*, 111, 552, 558.

45. Cain, *Lumpkin County History*, 153–63.

46. Evidence from three newspapers in Georgia during the war confirms the overall pattern. The *Macon Daily Telegraph, Southern Recorder*, and *Savannah Morning News* demonstrate few desertions in 1862, more in 1863 beginning in April, and clearly increased activity in 1864. For example, the first notice of a deserter in the *Macon Daily Telegraph* appears in the March 10, 1862, edition reporting a man from Butts County who deserted in February 1862. In 1862 only six ads appear for deserters. In 1863 the frequency picks up with twelve advertisements in the first six months. One ad lists twelve men from the 61st GA, ANV. However, by 1864 the ads increase beyond the practicality of listing individual deserters.

47. Daniel, *Soldiering in the Army of Tennessee*, 130–31.

48. *Southern Recorder*, November 17, 1863.

49. *Macon Daily Telegraph*, Thursday, August 4, 1864.

50. *Macon Daily Telegraph*, Saturday, August 27, 1864.

51. *Macon Daily Telegraph*, October 1, 1864, October 4, 1864, October 11, 1864, and October 13, 1864.

52. Bragg, *Joe Brown's Army*, 102.

53. William S. Basinger, muster roll, 18th GA Inf. (n.p.) Inspector General's Correspondence, GRG, 57–1–3, box 18, GDAH.

54. Diary of William Jefferson Mosely, March 3, 1865, March 12, 1865, March 1865, Miscellaneous Correspondence, GMRG 3–2735, drawer 283, box 35, GDAH.

55. Williams, *Rich Man's War*, chaps. 4 and 5.

56. Lonn, *Desertion during the Civil War*, 231.

4. CALLS FROM HOME

1. Richard Wheeler, *Sherman's March* (New York: Harper Perennial, 1978), 58.

2. Wheeler, *Sherman's March*, 24; *Memoirs of Lousie Caroline Reese Cornwell,*

Hillsboro, Jasper County, Georgia, in Miscellaneous Correspondence, GMRG 3–2721, drawer 283, box 22, GDAH.

3. Josiah Blair Patterson, 14th GA Inf., A. P. Hill's Corps, ANV, to sister, March 28, 1862, Miscellaneous Correspondence, GMRG 3–2736, drawer 283, box 36, GDAH; OR, 1st ser., 10:656, 787. The Enlistment Records for the 1st and 2d GA Volunteer Infantry indicate both units formed in the summer of 1861: *Enlistment Records for the 1st and 2d Georgia Volunteers*, GMRG 4–376, drawer 300, box 31, GDAH. Local histories of the Upcountry counties indicate that some units formed as early as September 1861.

4. Mrs. Mahalay Hyatte to Gov. Joe Brown, January 22, 1862, Executive Department: Incoming Correspondence from Women, 1861–1865, GRG 1–1–5, 3335–04, box 35, Georgia Department of Archives and History, Atlanta.

5. Joseph F. Alexander, Co. C, 60th GA Inf., to wife Sussannah E., May 25, 1862, and June 4, 1862, Miscellaneous Correspondence, GMRG 3–2715, drawer 283, box 16, GDAH.

6. Lt. Joel Crawford Barnett to wife, Annie, March 16, 1862, Miscellaneous Correspondence, GMRG 3–2716, drawer 283, box 17, GDAH.

7. O. H. P. Chambers, Co. A, 2d Regt., Georgia State Line, to wife, July 2, 1863, Miscellaneous Correspondence, GMRG 3–2720, drawer 283, box 21, GDAH; Benjamin J. Moody to wife Martha, various dates, Miscellaneous Correspondence, GMRG 3–2734, drawer 283, box 34, GDAH.

8. Mrs. Pauline S. Wheeler to Gov. Joe Brown, October 31, 1864, Correspondence from Women, GRG 1–1–5, 3335–12, box 50, GDAH.

9. W. B. Stanley to Anna Stanley, undated, Miscellaneous Correspondence, GMRG 3–2740, drawer 283, box 40, GDAH.

10. J. B. Stanley to W. B. Stanley, February 19, 1863, Miscellaneous Correspondence, GMRG 3–2740, drawer 283, box 40, GDAH.

11. Georgia Office of the Commissary General: Families Supplied with Salt, 1862–1864, GMRG 3–2680, drawer 73, box 4, GDAH. This document will be referred to hereinafter as the Salt Census. It is a 795-page list of family names, organized by county and year. It is broken down into widows of deceased soldiers, widows with sons in the service, families solely dependent on the labor of a soldier for support, and disabled soldiers discharged. The statistics on deaths and men at risk come from the various categories listed within the census. The estimates of infantry volunteers by county are based on Henderson's *Roster of the Confederate Soldiers of Georgia*. The *Roster* lists only companies from each county. Total soldiers were estimated by multiplying the maximum number of privates per company at the start of the war times the number of companies. The maximum was eighty-two privates per company: see Mark Boatner, *The Civil War Dictionary*, rev. ed. (New York: David McKay, 1988), 612. The percentage of ca-

sualties is a number that reflects the number of widows divided by the number of men in the volunteer infantry.

12. Lucien E. Roberts, *Paulding County*, 42. The county history claims 1,000 men left the county to fight in the war between 1861 and 1865.

13. Mrs. Salina A. Cope, to Gov. Joe Brown, August 11, 1864, Correspondence from Women, GRG 1–1–5, 3335–18, box 27, GDAH.

14. J. B. Patterson to October 4, 1861, to wife and children, GMRG 3–2736, drawer 283, box 36; William Wood to wife, Ella, October 20, 1861, GMRG 3–2744, drawer 283, box 44; Wood to father, Henry Wood, November 12, 1861, and Wood to wife, Ella, February 26, 1862, both in GMRG 3–2745, drawer 283, box 45; Edwin Bass to sisters, December 3, 1861, GMRG 3–2716, drawer 283, box 17, all in Miscellaneous Correspondence, GDAH.

15. Address by Robert Stiles, dedication of monument to Confederate dead of the University of Virginia, June 7, 1893, in *SHSP*, 21 (1893): 32.

16. Ella Lonn's book on Civil War desertion cites the letter, and it appeared in one of the earliest editions of the magazine *Confederate Veteran*. Ella Lonn, *Desertion during the Civil War*, 12–13; "Deserter Pardoned by Lee," *Confederate Veteran* 3 (January 1895): 23.

17. "Deserter Pardoned by Lee," 23.

18. Lt. Staughton H. Dent to wife, December 19, 1861, in Mathis, *Land of Living*, 12. Shortly after his enlistment and transfer out, Dent wrote his wife, "I hope my love you will not feel that I have done wrong in going in [to the army]. . . . I feel it is a grave responsibility and I have tried to think of it as I ought."

19. Mary Boykin Chesnut provides two illustrative examples of the power of women's exoneration of their men. Writing on May 27, 1864, she tells of a woman who went to Mrs. Jefferson Davis begging for her husband's life. He deserted, and she claimed that she wrote him saying, "If you want to see your baby alive, come! If they won't let you, come anyhow!" In March 1865 Chesnut describes hearing a woman yelling to her husband as Confederate authorities escorted him back to his unit, "Take it easy Jake. You desert again, quick as you kin [*sic*]. Come back to your wife and children. . . . Desert Jake! Desert again Jake!" Chesnut, May 27, 1864, and March 30, 1865, in C. Vann Woodward, ed., *Mary Chesnut's Civil War* (New Haven: Yale University Press, 1981), 611, 773.

20. Peter Dekle to wife, August 16 and 21, 1862, Miscellaneous Correspondence, GMRG 3–2722, drawer 283, box 23, GDAH.

21. Peter Dekle to wife, undated, Miscellaneous Correspondence, GMRG 3–2722, drawer 283, box 23, GDAH. Based on Dekle's observations, the deserters in the register may actually reflect men deserting in September and October 1863, several months earlier than the December 1863 through December 1864 trend depicted in the register. We know that Dekle wrote his last letter to his wife some-

time between May and September 1863. His last dated letter is in May, and a letter informing her of his death comes in late September 1863.

22. Col. Tully Graybill to wife, April 14, 1862 (finished May 1, 1862), and September 26, 1862, Miscellaneous Correspondence, GMRG 3–2726, drawer 283, box 26, GDAH.

23. Tully Graybill to wife, April 8 and 10, 1863, Miscellaneous Correspondence, GMRG 3–2726, drawer 283, box 26, GDAH.

24. Tully Graybill to wife, August 24, 1863, and September 29, 1863, Miscellaneous Correspondence, GMRG 3–2726, drawer 283, box 26, GDAH.

25. Tully Graybill to wife, February 22, 1864, Miscellaneous Correspondence, GMRG 3–2726, drawer 283, box 26, GDAH.

26. Samuel J. Brewer to wife, M. E. Brewer, February 17, 1862, and June 16, 1862, Miscellaneous Correspondence, GMRG 3–2717, drawer 283, box 18, GDAH.

27. Martha J. Moody to Benjamin J. Moody, May 12, 1862, Miscellaneous Correspondence, GMRG 3–2734, drawer 283, box 34, GDAH.

28. Isaiah Hembree to Martha J. Moody, August 27, 1862, Miscellaneous Correspondence, GMRG 3–2734, drawer 283, box 34, GDAH.

29. Emaline Ammons Young to James Young, May 17, 1862, and undated, Miscellaneous Correspondence, GMRG 3–2745, drawer 283, box 45, GDAH. Gary Gallagher, *The Confederate War*, 17–59.

30. Talithra C. Fowler to George Fowler, October 19, 1863, George Fowler Certificate of Unfitness for Duty, February 13, 1864, George Fowler Discharge Papers, May 1, 1864, Miscellaneous Correspondence, GMRG 3–2724, drawer 283, box 25, GDAH.

31. Mrs. M. M. Humpheries to husband, October 4, 1864 (addressed to Darlington SC), Miscellaneous Correspondence, GMRG 3–2729, drawer 283, box 29, GDAH.

32. R. E. Lee to Mrs. Mildred Bone, April 18, 1863, headquarters, ANV, Miscellaneous Correspondence, GMRG 3–2717, drawer 283, box 18, GDAH.

33. "Governor Joseph Brown's Inaugural Address," *Southern Recorder*, November 17, 1863.

34. Kennett, *Marching through Georgia*, 33.

35. Mrs. Catherine O. Stephenson, Bartow County, to Joseph Brown, September 14, 1863, Correspondence from Women, GRG 1–1–5, 3335–10, box 47, GDAH.

36. Mary Bennett to Gov. Joe Brown, undated, Correspondence from Women, GRG 1–1–5, 3335–16, box 16, GDAH.

37. Ms. Lucinda V. Baugh to Capt. James Hudgins, or to the major of the battalion, or to the colonel of the regiment, on the grounds of necessity, May 26, 1864, Correspondence from Women, GRG 1–1–5, 3335–16, box 16, GDAH.

38. Elizabeth Kulgar to J. Brown, February 24, 1864, Correspondence from Women, GRG 3335–05, box 37, GDAH.

39. Mrs. C. M. Davis to Joe Brown, August 11, 1864, Correspondence from Women, GRG 3335–01, box 28, GDAH.

40. Mrs. Catherine McDonald to Joe Brown, October 12, 1864, Correspondence from Women, GRG 3335–06, box 39, GDAH.

41. Mrs. Catherine Miller to Gov. Joe Brown, July 11, 1864, Correspondence from Women, GRG 3335–07, box 40, GDAH.

42. Mrs. Barentha Busbee to Gov. Joe Brown, September 3, 1864, Correspondence from Women, GRG 3335–17, box 25, GDAH.

43. Petition, April 1863, Forsyth County to Gov. Joe Brown, Inspector General's Correspondence, GRG 57–1–3, box 16, GDAH; Martha P. Teasely to Gov. Joe Brown, November 8, 1864, Inspector General's Correspondence, GRG 57–1–3, box 19; Mrs. M. M. Taylor to Gov. Joe Brown, May 26, 1863, Correspondence from Women, GRG 1–1–5, 3335–10, box 47, GDAH. See also J. M. Thompson to H. Wayne, May 29, 1864. Inspector General's Correspondence, GRG 57–1–3, box 19, GDAH. Letter requested the return of John Norton, the Newton County blacksmith.

44. Mrs. Fannie Dickinson to Joe Brown, May 23, 1863, GRG 3335–01, box 29; Mrs. Margaret E. Thompson to Gov. Joe Brown, August 27, 1864, 3335–11, box 48, both in Correspondence from Women, GDAH.

45. William Turk to Jared Whitaker, September 22, 1862, W. H. Scott to Jared Whitaker, March 20, 1862, and William Dallis, Lincoln County to Jared Whitaker, April 1, 1863, all in Inspector General's Correspondence, GRG 57–1–3, box 19, GDAH; *Macon Daily Telegraph*, April 7, 1862; A. O. Bacon to James Seddon, undated, Jesse Partridge et al., Meriwether County, to Jared Whitaker, August 18, 1863, and W. C. Goddens, Jackson County to Jared Whitaker, August 10, 1863, all in Inspector General's Correspondence, GRG 57–1–3, box 13, GDAH; Sisters of Mercy Convent-Savannah to Joe Brown, January 1, 1863, Correspondence from Women, GRG 1–1–5, 3335–10, box 46, GDAH. The nuns requested salt for forty female orphans; most had fathers and brothers in the service. Brown allotted them six bushels.

46. B. J. Moody to wife, June 22, 1862, Miscellaneous Correspondence, GMRG 3–2734, drawer 283, box 34, GDAH. For a discussion of the salt problem in the Confederacy, see Ella Lonn, *Salt as a Factor in the Confederacy* (New York: n.p., 1933).

47. Mrs. Amanda Taylor to Gov. Joe Brown, September 30, 1863, Correspondence from Women, GRG 1–1–5, 3335–10, box 47, GDAH.

48. *Macon Daily Telegraph*, January 17, 1863. This notice was from H. H. Howard, the state tax collector. It gave everyone until February 1, 1863, to register or lose eligibility for relief.

49. *The Southern Recorder*, July 7, 1863. The forms came in a quire. A standard quire consisted of 24–25 sheets, far more than the average family needed.

50 James T. Harmon to Mr. Glisby, *Macon Daily Telegraph*, January 2, 1863; J.H.R., a woman to Joe Brown, June 29, 1864, Correspondence from Women, GRG 1–1–5, 3335–09, box 44, GDAH.

51. Salt Census, index; F. C. Farmer, clerk, Murray County Inferior Court, to Jared Whitaker, May 26, 1863; Inspector General's Correspondence, GRG 57–1–3, box 18, GDAH.

52. Salt Census, 115, 192; Mrs. Elizabeth Wade to Gov. Joe Brown, August 31, 1863, Correspondence from Women, GRG 1–1–5, 3335–11, box 49, GDAH.

53. Salt Census, 1, 112, 61, 78, 83, 136, 141, 146, 149, 155, 161, 170, 177, 181, 186, 254, 276, 281, 297, 307, 319, 348, 406, 418, 433, 442, 460, 466, 474, 483, 490, 494, 496, 500, 519, 546, 677, 713, 772, 779, 792.

54. Joseph Hilton to father and mother, March 23, 1863, Miscellaneous Correspondence, GMRG 3–2728, drawer 283, box 28, GDAH. Hilton wrote home asking about the salt boiling project, which indicated salt remained a scarce commodity.

55. Salt Census, 571, 592, 593, 596, 657, 658, 609, 621, 630, 636, 674, 678, 698, 703, 707, 725, 755, 757.

56. John Ethridge to brother, Booth Tarpley Hammond, April 27, 1862, GMRG 3–2726, drawer 283, box 26; William W. Head to wife Fannie, May 10, 1862, GMRG 3–2727, drawer 283, box 27; J. W. Wood to Dick Wood, June 17, 1862, GMRG 3–2744, drawer 283, box 44, all in Miscellaneous Correspondence, GDAH.

57. R. R. Hunt to Gov. Joe Brown, February 19, 1862, GRG 57–1–3, box 13; Your Friends in Pike City to Gov. Joe Brown, March 17, 1862, GRG 57–1–3, box 13, both in Inspector General's Correspondence, GDAH.

58. Hettie Oliver to Gov. Joe Brown, March 4, 1862, Correspondence from Women, GRG 1–1–5, 3335–08, box 42, GDAH.

59. William H. Lopper to mother and father, August 14, 1862, Miscellaneous Correspondence, GMRG 3–2732, drawer 283, box 32, GDAH.

60. Margaret Hudlow to Gov. Joe Brown, September 186-, Correspondence from Women, GRG 1–1–5, 3335–04, box 35, GDAH.

61. Bell Irvin Wiley, *Confederate Women* (Westport CT: Greenwood Press, 1975) 197. For contentions that women's pleas to return caused men to desert in 1865, see Faust, *Mothers of Invention*, 283; Miss M. Black to Pvt. Henry R. Johnson, July 29, 1864, Miscellaneous Correspondence, GMRG 3–2729, drawer 283, box 29, GDAH.

62. Mrs. Dr. Wellborn to Gov. Joe Brown, November 16, 1862, Correspondence from Women, GRG, 1–1–5, 3335–11, box 49, GDAH.

63. *Macon Daily Telegraph*, March 23, 1863; E. Yulee to Joe Brown, April 19, 1864, Inspector General's Correspondence, GRG 57–1–3, box 19, GDAH.

64. *Macon Daily Telegraph*, September 17, 1863, copied from a story out of Jonesboro, dated September 12, 1863, in the *Atlanta Intelligencer*.

65. *The Southern Recorder*, November 24, 1863, February 16, 1864. The distribution was as follows: Catoosa, Dade, and Gilmer Counties, 8,000 bushels each. Murray received 7,000 bushels, Chattooga, 6,000, Towns and Habersham 4,000 each, Dawson, White, Rabun, Lumpkin, Pickens and Walker all received 3,000 bushels.

66. Kennett, *Marching through Georgia*, 31–32. For discussion of relief efforts in southwest Georgia, see Williams, *Rich Man's War*, 107–13.

67. Minister of Gospel, Whitfield County, December 2, 1862, box 18; J. Bryan to Joe Brown, December 20, 1862, box 13; Jas. Wilson to H. C. Wayne, October 15, 1863, box 15, all in Inspector General's Correspondence, GRG 57–1–3, GDAH. "Tories in White County," *Columbus Daily Enquirer*, November 18, 1863; Williams, *Rich Man's War*, 141–50.

68. Simon B. Buckner to Gov. Joe Brown, June 9, 1863, Inspector General's Correspondence, 1–1–5, 3335–17, box 25, GDAH; Boatner, *The Civil War Dictionary*, 258; *OR*, 4th ser., 1:1176.

69. Thomas R. Trammell to Joseph Brown, June 23, 1863, Inspector General's Correspondence, GRG 57–1–3, box 19, GDAH.

70. J. F. Walker, Co. B, Cobb's Legion to Mr. J. C. Huff, September 19, 1861, Miscellaneous Correspondence, GMRG 3–2743, drawer 283, box 43, GDAH.

71. Richard E. Berenger, Herman Hattaway, Archer Jones, and William Still Jr., *Why the South Lost the War* (Athens: University of Georgia Press, 1986), 198, 20, 333, 350.

72. McPherson, *Drawn with the Sword*, 129.

73. Gary Gallagher, *A Confederate War*, chap. 3.

74. Stephen Hahn, *Roots of Southern Populism* (New York: Oxford University Press, 1983), 86–87.

5. FACES OF DESERTION

1. Unsigned letter, Catoosa County to Gov. Joe Brown, undated, Inspector General's Correspondence, GRG 57–1–3, box 18, GDAH.

2. Unsigned letter, "A Woman: A Friend to Her Country," to Gen. H. C. Wayne, September 1862, Inspector General's Correspondence, GRG 57–1–3, box 13, GDAH.

3. Mark Boatner, *The Civil War Dictionary*, rev. ed. (New York: David McKay, 1988), 542; Gen. Hugh W. Mercer, General Orders No. 66, March 7, 1863, Inspector General's Correspondence, GRG 57–1–3, box 12, GDAH.

4. Sarah S. Wright to J. Brown, May 27, 1861, Correspondence from Women, GRG 1–1–5, 3335–12, box 51, GDAH.

5. Stephen Hahn, *The Roots of Southern Populism* (New York: Oxford University Press, 1983), 86–87.

6. Boatner, *Civil War Dictionary*, 172. The Confederate Congress instituted the draft in April 1862, and in September 1862 broadened the age categories to include all able-bodied white males ages eighteen to thirty-five. In February 1864, the Confederate Congress passed a new conscription act to include all men seventeen to fifty. For the Georgia Militia Law, see "An Act to Re-organize the Militia of the State of Georgia and for Other Purposes, December 14, 1863" (microfilm), drawer 245, box 4, GDAH.

7. Sec. 10, pt. 4, An Act to Organize Forces to Serve during the War, February 17, 1864, *OR*, 4th ser., 3:178–81.

8. "Persons Exempt in the State of Georgia under Part IV, Section X from Conscription under the Confederate Act of 1864 and Persons Detailed," GRG 193–12–14, 5173–14, GDAH. The ledger lists the names of each person exempted under the act. Each entry occupies two facing pages. In addition to name, the ledger lists the exempted party's county of residence, the name of his principle, his surety (s), the financial penalty for failure to provide his meat allotment, the number of slaves between the ages of sixteen and fifty, the size of his meat allotment broken down by bacon and beef, and any remarks by the official. There are nineteen names per double page. The first 180 pages list those exempted under the act. The numbering picks up thereafter on page 250 with those men who received work details and therefore were not subject to the act and runs to page 346. Regretfully, the first seventy-three pages are missing; however, there is nothing from the surviving pages to indicate that the conclusions drawn from the surviving portion would be significantly altered. Nineteen men appear on each double page. By multiplying the number of men by the number of pages, $90 \times 19 = 9,810$ and $58 \times 19 = 1,102$, one can arrive at a figure for able-bodied men who complied with the law and thus evaded the Confederate conscription law in 1864. A total of at least 10,912 from Georgia secured exemptions from the draft or detailed jobs that otherwise enabled them to avoid service.

9. For the Upcountry and upper Piedmont men exempted or detailed, see "Persons Exempt in the State of Georgia under Part IV, Section X," 112–13, 252–54, 256, 258, 260, 290, 292, 294, 304, 306, 316, 338. The counties of those exempted were Twiggs, Liberty, Macon, Coweta, Jefferson, Harris, Clay, Putnam, Jackson, Burke, Clarke, Jasper, Dooley, Laurens, Randolph, Baldwin, Morgan, Dougherty, Decatur, Richmond, Upson, Calhoun, Greene, Meriwether, Newton, Heard, Walton, Early, Mitchell, Taliaferro, Tattnall, Baker, Schley, Screven, Lee, Wayne, Pulaski, Thomas, Chatham, Monroe, Wilkinson, Chattahoochee, Houston, Stewart, Columbia, Emanuel, Troup, and Washington. In the Upcountry, only Gordon County with four men, Hall County with eight, Forsyth County with one man, and Floyd County with one man listed detailed citizens.

10. Georgia Militia Act, secs. 1, 2, 11, 24, microfilm, drawer 245, box 4, GDAH.

11. Georgia Militia Act, secs. 16 and 24, microfilm, drawer 245, box 4, GDAH.

12. *State of Georgia—Office of Adjutant and Inspector General: Militia Enrollment Lists*, microfilm, drawer 245, boxes 4,5,6, 7, 8, and 9, GDAH. A perusal of the enrollment lists reveals the ages and occupations of the men eligible for militia duty. They were either very young or very old. The most common occupation was farmer. Exemption requests varied from county to county, but since the exemption is that which was claimed, there is no way to determine whether the exemption was actually granted.

13. William Dickey to wife, Anna, October 26, 1864, October 28, 1864, and November 12, 1864, Miscellaneous Correspondence, GMRG 3–2722, drawer 283, box 23, GDAH.

14. Mrs. Polley Tillery, Lincoln County, to Gov. Joe Brown, July 27, 1864, GRG 1–1–5, 3335–11, box 48; Mrs. M. J. Porter, Effingham County, to Gov. Joe Brown, July 22, 1864, GRG 3335–08, box 43; Mary A. Hilsman, Madison County, to Gov. Joe Brown, August 25, 1864, GRG 3335–04, box 34, all in Correspondence from Women, GDAH.

15. McPherson, *Battle Cry of Freedom*, 607–8; Robertson, *Soldiers Blue and Gray*, 37–38.

16. James McPherson, *Ordeal by Fire* (New York: McGraw-Hill, 1992), 8–9, 29, 33.

17. William C. Davis, *Jefferson Davis: The Man and His Hour*, 452–53, 486.

18. For recent coverage of slave resistance and its effects including historiography of slave resistance, see David Williams, "The 'Faithful Slave' Is About Played Out," *Alabama Review* 52 (April 1999): 85–104.

19. Shelby Foote, *The Civil War, a Narrative*, vol. 1, *Fort Sumter to Perryville* (New York: First Vintage Books, 1986), 394–95.

20. Grover Calvin Alexander, comp. and ed., *1860 U.S. Manuscript Census for Floyd County, Georgia* (n.p), 33, GDAH. Each deserter listed hereafter was matched from the register to the 1860 Manuscript Census.

21. Alexander, *Floyd County*, 110.

22. Alexander, *Floyd County*, 206.

23. Griffin, *1860 Manuscript Census of Walker County, Georgia* (n.p., 1982), 103, GDAH.

24. Griffin, *1860 Manuscript Census*, 122.

25. Griffin, *1860 Manuscript Census*, 40.

26. Griffin, *1860 Manuscript Census*, 91.

27. Griffin, *1860 Manuscript Census*, 15.

28. Griffin, *1860 Manuscript Census*, 65.

29. Reid Mitchell, "The Northern Soldier and His Community," in Vinovskis, *Toward a Social History of the Civil War*, 78–92.

30. These examples are not isolated; manuscript census data exist for many of

the deserters listed in the register. The examples provided here came from census compilations for Floyd, Walker, and Rabun Counties. In addition, men from Towns County were also identified. Examples from two upper Piedmont counties, Campbell and Carroll, also had been compiled from the 1860 U.S. Census Records. The compilations alphabetized the last names of heads of households and made tracing these men much easier. However, many of these deserters were not heads of their households but rather sons in their father's home. In addition, if the deserter or his family was not in the county he claimed as his residence upon taking the oath, there would be no information on that man's family. Still, those deserters who could be located allowed for a specific analysis of their particular family situation and provided valuable insight into their decision to desert. A total of eighty-seven men from the four Upcountry counties and twenty-four from the two upper Piedmont counties were identified in the census records.

31. Alexander, *Floyd County 1860 Census*, 31; John T. Coleman, comp., *The 1860 Census Rabun County, Georgia* (Marietta GA: Heritage Center, n.d.), household numbers 343 and 310.

32. *Carroll County, Georgia, Census 1860* (Carroll County Genealogical Society, 1982), 121, GDAH.

33. Vernon Robertson Mitchem, comp., *1860 Census of Old Campbell County, Georgia* (Atlanta: n.p., 1971–72), 224 (Argo Lewis), 198 (James Blair), 23 (Abraham Brown), 156 (Chas Deadwiley), 275 (Dudley Duggs), 159 (William L. Dorsett), 8 (Andrew and William Forsyth), 187 (William P. Mitchel), 188 (William F. Mosely), 174 (William Newburn), 128 (James O. Pennington), 278 (William Sewell), 193 (James M. Smith).

34. *The 1860 Census of Chatham County, Georgia*, Genealogical Committee of the Georgia Historical Society, comp. (Southern Historical Press, 1980), 11, 17, 26, 30–31, 35, 46, 72–73, 89, 111, 134–35, 177, 166, 181, 194, 201, 228, 235, 249, 250, 271, 277, 281, 287, 303. 360–61.

35. McPherson, *Battle Cry of Freedom*, 7, 32–33, 134, 493–94.

36. Melvin Dwinell to brother Albert, September 30, 1865, Miscellaneous Correspondence, GMRG 3–2723, drawer 283, box 24, GDAH.

37. Robert David Carlson, "Wiregrass Runner: Conscription, Desertion, and the Origins of Discontent in Civil War South Georgia," M.A. thesis, Valdosta State University, 1999, 72, 86–106.

38. Henderson, *Roster of the Confederate Soldiers of Georgia*.

39. Williams, *Rich Man's War*, chap. 4.

6. UNANSWERED CALLS

1. Henderson, *Roster of the Confederate Soldiers of Georgia*, 5:ix.

2. Resolution, by 57th GA Inf., March 7, 1864, Savannah, Georgia, Miscellaneous Correspondence, GMRG 3–2719, drawer 283, box 20, GDAH.

3. Printed Message Delivered on the Night of February 1, 1865, to 57th GA Reg., Cleburne's (Old) Division by Miss B, Columbus, Georgia, Miscellaneous Correspondence, GMRG 3–2721, drawer 283, box 22, GDAH.

4. Mrs. J. C. C. Blackburn to Gov. Joe Brown, May 24, 1861, Correspondence from Women, GRG 1–1–5, 3335–17, box 24, GDAH; Wyatt-Brown, *Southern Honor*, 39–40, 52–54, 172.

5. Edwin Salsbury Bass to sister, April 22, 1861, Miscellaneous Correspondence, GMRG 3–2716, drawer 283, box 17, GDAH.

6. Bass to sister, December 3, 1861, Miscellaneous Correspondence, GMRG 3–2716, drawer 283, box 17, GDAH.

7. Reminiscences of Martha Virginia Stevens, fifth daughter of James Stevens and Jersusha Barnes, wife of L. R. Cason, Co. A, 28th GA Vols., Miscellaneous Correspondence, GMRG 3–2719, drawer 283, box 20, GDAH; Henderson, *Roster of the Confederate Soldiers of Georgia*, 3:vii. Only five men from that county deserted: one from the 57th GA, one of only six to desert from that unit, one from a Georgia militia unit, and three from non-Georgia units: the 63d VA Infantry, the 1st TX Cavalry, and the 1st TN Infantry. The register listed no deserters to the enemy from Company A. of the 28th.

8. Anonymous Woman to Ivy W. Duggan, 49th GA Inf., December 31, 1863, Miscellaneous Correspondence, GMRG 3–2723, drawer 283, box 24, GDAH.

9. Mary E. Gross to Pvt. William M. Jones, March 4 and April 20, 1863, Miscellaneous Correspondence, GMRG 3–2726, drawer 283, box 26, GDAH.

10. Capt. David H. Pope, 10th GA Inf., to wife, Martha Hodges Pope, February 10, 1864, Miscellaneous Correspondence, GMRG 3–2737, drawer 283, box 37, GDAH.

11. Pope to wife, March 13, 1864, Miscellaneous Correspondence, GMRG 3–2737, drawer 283, box 37, GDAH.

12. Two came from Gordon County; the remaining nine came from Campbell, Cobb, Gilmer, and Milton Counties. These nine men listed as members of the 4th GA Inf. is an unlikely possibility given the counties that contributed soldiers to the unit. There are two likely alternative explanations. One is that rather than 4th Infantry, these men were 4th Cavalry, a unit with a large Upcountry enlistment, or they were in the 40th, 41st, 42d, or 43d GA Infantry, all units with strong Upcountry/upper Piedmont enlistments. Since we are dealing with a source prepared by hand, clerical errors of this nature could account for the affiliation of men with the unit from counties other than where the unit formed. The other possibility, perhaps the strongest, is that these men were part of the one company formed in Gordon County, thus making all desertion from the 4th GA essentially upper Piedmont or Upcountry soldiers. See Henderson, *Roster of the Confederate Soldiers of Georgia*, 1:vi, viii.

13. Lucias Todd Cicero Lovelace to father, March 31, 1862, Miscellaneous Correspondence, GMRG 3–2732, drawer 283, box 32, GDAH.

14. J. W. Shank, Irvin Artillery, to Col. J. B. Smith, August 27, 1863, Miscellaneous Correspondence, GMRG 3–2739, drawer 283, box 39, GDAH.

15. J. W. Shank to J. B. Smith, March 19, 1864, and August 9, 1864, , Miscellaneous Correspondence, GMRG 3–2739, drawer 283, box 39, GDAH.

16. Joseph Bogle, *Some Recollections of the Civil War* (n.p.: September 26, 1901), 12–13, Miscellaneous Correspondence, GMRG 3–2717, drawer 283, box 18, GDAH. See also diary of William Sylvester Dillon, 4th TN Vols., October 15, 1864, Miscellaneous Correspondence, GMRG 3–2723, drawer 283, box 24, GDAH. Dillon wrote that the Union prison officials reduced the prisoners to half rations in an effort to get eight hundred men to take the oath of allegiance. He believed that Lincoln stopped the prisoner exchange for "the diabolical purpose of starving as many as possible into the ranks of the (Union) army and in this manner deplete the ranks of the Confederate armies and defeat them in this way."

17. Henderson, *Roster of the Confederate Soldiers of Georgia*, 4:vii. The entire 40th GA came from Upcountry or upper Piedmont counties.

18. Virgil M. White to Mollie, June 30, 1864, Miscellaneous Correspondence, GMRG 3–2728, drawer 283, box 28, GDAH.

19. Virgil White to wife, Mollie, August 5, 1864, and August (undated) 1864, Miscellaneous Correspondence, GMRG 3–2728, drawer 283, box 28, GDAH.

20. Blanton Fortson to mother, June 3, 1864, Miscellaneous Correspondence, GMRG 3–2724, drawer 283, box 24, GDAH.

21. Lt. Col. L. P. Thomas to Capt. J. M. Mitchell, January 28, 1895, Miscellaneous Correspondence, GMRG 3–2742, drawer 283, box 42, GDAH.

22. Henderson, *Roster of the Confederate Soldiers of Georgia*, 2:vi–vii. Of the ten companies in the 14th, only three came from the Upcountry: one from Cherokee County, one from Bartow County, and one from Forsyth County. The remaining companies came from Monroe, Wilkinson, Jasper, Johnson, Worth, Laurens, and Butts Counties.

23. Josiah Blair Patterson to wife and children, August 5, 1862, Miscellaneous Correspondence, GMRG 3–2736, drawer 283, box 36, GDAH. For mention of his son, see Patterson to wife and children, October 4, 1861, Miscellaneous Correspondence, GMRG 3–2736, drawer 283, box 36, GDAH.

24. J. B. Patterson to wife and children, August 21, 1861, October 4, 1861, and December 4, 1861, Miscellaneous Correspondence, GMRG 3–2736, drawer 283, box 36, GDAH.

25. J. B. Patterson to wife and children, February 15, 1862, Miscellaneous Correspondence, GMRG 3–2736, drawer 283, box 36, GDAH.

26. J. B. Patterson to family, February 27, 1862, and J. B. Patterson to daugh-

ter, March 28, 1862, Miscellaneous Correspondence, GMRG 3–2736, drawer 283, box 36, GDAH.

27. J. B. Patterson to daughter, August 18, 1863, Miscellaneous Correspondence, GMRG 3–2736, drawer 283, box 36, GDAH.

28. Wyatt-Brown, *Southern Honor*, 51–53.

29. J. B. Patterson to niece Lizzie, March 17, 1864, Miscellaneous Correspondence, GMRG 3–2736, drawer 283, box 36, GDAH.

30. Bureau of the Census, *Manuscript Census of the United States, 1870*, RG M593, roll 150/361, National Archives, Washington DC.

31. Lt. Col. J. C. Mounger, 9th GA Reg., ANV, to Brig. Gen. G. T. Anderson, May 30, 1863, Miscellaneous Correspondence, GMRG 3–2735, drawer 283, box 35, GDAH.

32. Wyatt-Brown, *Southern Honor*, 44. Men with a large kinship network both benefited from and suffered under its weight. Members of a large family were assumed to possess equal moral strength. However, this required them to live up to familial values. As the patriarch of the family, Mounger had little choice but to lead his family into the conflict.

33. Boatner, *Civil War Dictionary*, 13. Lt. Col. Mounger died on the second day of Gettysburg while leading the 9th GA of G. T. Anderson's Brigade, John Bell Hood's Division of Longstreet's Corps. A shell fragment struck him as he led his regiment through an open field east of the Emmitsburg Road in the opening moments of Longstreet's assault on the Union left. John and Tom Mounger to mother, July 18, 1863, GMRG 3–2735, drawer 283, box 35, GDAH; Harry W. Pfanz, *Gettysburg: The Second Day* (Chapel Hill: University of North Carolina Press, 1987), 175–76, 459.

34. Lucie H. Mounger to Edwin John Mounger, September 1, 1864, Miscellaneous Correspondence, GMRG 3–2735, drawer 283, roll 35, GDAH.

35. Mrs. Mary Jones to Col. Charles C. Jones, May 29, 1863, June 1, 1863, in Myers, *Children of Pride*, 1066–67.

36. Richard Wheeler, *Sherman's March* (New York: Harper Perennial, 1978), 70–71.

37. Wheeler, *Sherman's March*, 131.

38. Mrs. John G. Green to Gov. Joe Brown, December 11, 1863, Correspondence from Women, GRG 1–1–5, 3335–03, box 32, GDAH.

39. Peter Kolchin, *American Slavery* (New York: Hill & Wang, 1993), 156.

40. Kolchin, *American Slavery*, 203–4; Kennett, *Marching through Georgia*, 34–36; Mark Grimsley, *The Hard Hand of War* (Cambridge: Cambridge University Press, 1995), 20, 33, 52, 92, 122, 134–35; Clarence L. Mohr, *On the Threshold of Freedom: Masters and Slaves in Civil War Georgia* (Athens: University of Georgia Press, 1986), 4–8.

41. Mrs. Mitchell Jones to Gov. Joe Brown, August 23, 1864, Correspondence from Women, GRG 1–1–5, 3335–05, box 36, GDAH.

42. Mrs. Francis B. Tillery to Gov. Joe Brown, July 26, 1864, Correspondence from Women, GRG 1–1–5, 3335–11, box 48, GDAH.

43. Farmer to Gov. Joe Brown, February 22, 2862, Inspector General's Correspondence, GRG 57–1–3, box 18, GDAH.

44. J. William Harris, *Plain Folk and Gentry in a Slave Society* (Middletown CT: Wesleyan University Press, 1985), 170–74.

45. For more subtle examples of slave resistance, see Williams, *Rich Man's War*, chap. 6.

46. Mrs. Elizabeth Clark to Gov. Joe Brown, Jan 11, 1863, Mrs. Nancy Colbert to Gov. Joe Brown, 1863, Correspondence from Women, GRG 1–1–5, 3335–18, box 27, GDAH.

47. The absentee master, although not the rule in the South, prevailed throughout Georgia's plantation belt. In the coastal low country, or rice belt, owner absenteeism had existed since the American Revolution and fostered a system whereby slaves and masters existed virtually isolated from one another. Desertion to the enemy from the riceland coast was almost nonexistent. Cries from women that they were having problems managing slaves in the absence of their husbands or masters would have meant almost nothing to a class of men who had grown up in an atmosphere of absentee ownership. Kolchin, *American Slavery*, 35, 75.

48. Kolchin, *American Slavery*, 203–5.

49. Lucinda Culbreth to Gov. Joe Brown, March 9, 1863, GRG 1–1–5, 3335–01, box 28; Mrs. E. M. Douglas to Joe Brown, August 13, 1864, and Mrs. Ophelia Dozier to Joe Brown, August 25, 1864, GRG 1–1–5, 3335–01, box 29, Mrs. S. B. Hadwick to J. Brown, February 25, 1862, GRG 1–1–5, 3335–03, box 33; Mrs. Sarah E. Leeves to Gov. Joe Brown, March 6, 1862, GRG 1–1–5, 3335–06, box 38, all in Correspondence from Women, GDAH.

50. Anne Firor Scott, *The Southern Lady: From Pedestal to Politics, 1830–1930* (Chicago: University of Chicago Press, 1970), 28–32.

51. Wiley, *Confederate Women*, 148; Joan Cashin, "Since the War Broke Out: The Marriage of Kate and William McClure," in Clinton and Sibler, *Divided Houses*, 200–212.

52. Faust, *Mothers of Invention*, 74–79, 251.

53. Madison Kilpatrick to wife, August 12, 1864, October 17, 1864, and October 23, 1864, Miscellaneous Correspondence, GMRG 3–2720, drawer 283, box 30, GDAH.

54. Julie Pope Stanley to Marcellus Stanley, August 1, 1864, Miscellaneous Correspondence, GMRG 3–2740, drawer 283, box 40, GDAH.

55. Robert Fogel and Stanley Engermann, *Time on the Cross: The Economics of*

American Negro Slavery (Boston: Little, Brown, 1974), 109–26; Clinton, *Plantation Mistress*, 29, 30, 191.

56. John T. Swan to wife, Bettie, December 28, 1863, Miscellaneous Correspondence, GMRG 3–2741, drawer 283, box 41, GDAH.

57. John T. Swan to wife, Bettie, August 6, 1863, December 10, 1863, December 28, 1863, February 24, 1864, March 27, 1864, John W. McCollum to Mrs. Swan, March 3, 1864, Miscellaneous Correspondence, GMRG 3–2741, drawer 283, box 41, GDAH.

58. The figures for Carroll County's slaveholders are from James C. Bonner, *Georgia's Last Frontier,* 204–12. Of the 325 slaveholders, 18 had names that clearly identified them as women and they were subtracted from the total eligible for service. The 68 deserters were those listed in the register. Indicative of the upper Piedmont, Carroll County had only a handful of planters in 1860. Only 3 men owned more than 30 slaves, and none owned more than 50.

59. Faust, *Mothers of Invention*, 246.

60. Grimsley, *The Hard Hand of War*, 190–200; Kennett, *Marching through Georgia*, 93–96; Emma LeConte, January 1, 1865, in *When the World Ended: The Diary of Emma LeConte*, ed. Earl Schenck Miers (Lincoln: University of Nebraska Press, 1987), 6. LeConte indicated her father had written from Thomasville, Georgia, and reported the Union movement through Liberty County.

61. Diary entries, Mrs. Mary S. Mallard, December 13–16, 1864, Mrs. Mary Jones, December 22, 1864, January 3, 1865, in Myers, *Children of Pride*, 1220–27, 1233, 1239.

62. Memoirs of Mrs. Louise Caroline Reese Cornwell, Miscellaneous Correspondence, GMRG 3–2721, drawer 283, box 22, GDAH.

63. John H. Boyce to mother, August 4, 1864, Miscellaneous Correspondence, GMRG 3–2717, drawer 283, box 18, GDAH.

64. The register indicates six men deserted from Troup County. One left in February 1864, and one deserted February 1865. The other four all deserted in July or August 1864. The ability to desert clearly existed. Boyce just seemed to have no reason that would compel him to forsake his military duty. Anne J. Bailey and Walter J. Fraser Jr., *Portraits of Conflict: A Photographic History of Georgia in the Civil War* (Fayetteville: University of Arkansas Press, 1996), 297.

65. H. T. Howard to wife, August 11, 1864, Miscellaneous Correspondence, GMRG 3–2728, drawer 283, box 28, GDAH.

66. Victoria Kottman Stark to John Stark, January 10 and 12, 1865, Miscellaneous Correspondence, GMRG 3–2740, drawer 283, box 40, GDAH.

67. Victoria Stark to John Stark, February 5 and 9, 1865, Miscellaneous Correspondence, GMRG 3–2740, drawer 283, box 40, GDAH.

68. Burke Davis, *The Civil War: Strange and Fascinating Facts* (New York: Wings Books, 1982), 142.

CONCLUSION

1. Larry Daniel, *Soldiering in the Army of Tennessee*, 129–30.

2. Alfred Hough claimed that men from Louisiana came across into the lines in August 1863. Gen. John Beatty and Maj. James Connally reported the same thing in late August and September 1863. Daniel, *Soldiering in the Army of Tennessee*, 130–31.

3. Gary Gallagher, *The Confederate War*, 31–32.

4. Fred Anderson, *A People's Army*, 28–29.

5. Martin, *Desertion of Alabama Troops*, 130.

6. McPherson, *Drawn with the Sword*, 119–20.

Bibliographical Essay

The following is an abbreviated discussion of the sources that I used to write this book. Far from an inclusive bibliography, it reflects those sources most important to the construction of the story and argument.

The primary source for this study is the Register of Confederate Deserters, 1863–1865. Now a part of the National Archives, the register was compiled by the Union commissary general of prisoners and was indispensable to the identification of Georgia's deserters. When combined with U.S. census data, the study of Georgian desertion took on a human form never before possible. Equally vital to this project were the materials housed in the Georgia Department of Archives and History (GDAH) in Atlanta. The Adjutant and Inspector General of Georgia's Incoming Correspondence, 1861–1865, Incoming Correspondence from Women to Governor Joseph Brown, 1861–1865, and Civil War Miscellaneous Correspondence contained hundreds of letters, interviews, and diaries that established a home front and battlefield context for Georgia's desertion pattern. In addition to the personal letter collections, the GDAH records provided information on court-martial proceedings, militia and regimental enrollments, exemptions from the Confederate draft, and data on the distribution of salt rations throughout the state, cited herein as the Salt Census. The GDAH also provided easy access to Georgia newspapers and periodicals from Atlanta, Macon, Milledgeville, Savannah, and Columbus.

In addition to these unpublished sources, several published primary sources contributed to this work. *The Official Records of the Rebellion of the Union and Confederate Armies*, 70 vols., 128 bks. (Washington DC: Government Printing Office, 1880–1909) proved essential to identifying the Union desertion policy that ultimately generated the register. I am also indebted to the *Southern Historical Society Papers*, 52 vols. (Millswood NY: Krause Reprint, 1977), which provided personal accounts and served as an invaluable source of Confederate congressional acts.

Published manuscript census for several Georgia counties made it possible to bring life to some of the many names that appeared in the register. The *1860 Manuscript Census for Floyd County, Georgia* (n.p.), *Carroll County, Georgia Census 1860* (Carroll County Genealogical Society, 1982), the *1860 Census of Rabun*

County, Georgia (Marietta GA: Heritage Club, n.d.), the *1860 Census of Chatham County, Georgia* (Southern Historical Press, 1980), the *1860 Census of Walker County, Georgia* (n.p., 1982), and the *1860 Census of Old Campbell County, Georgia* (n.p., 1971–72) all proved invaluable to locating data on the lives and families of many of the deserters.

No desertion study can escape the work of its predecessors, and both Ella Lonn's *Desertion during the Civil War* (1928; reprint, Gloucester MA: Peter Smith, 1966), and Bessie Martin's *Desertion among Alabama Troops* (1932; reprint, New York: AMS, 1966), provided essential background for this work.

Published primary works and secondary sources provided the material for developing antebellum and wartime Georgia. The most important were James C. Bonner, *A History of Georgia Agriculture, 1732–1860* (Athens: University of Georgia Press, 1964), and *Georgia's Last Frontier: A History of Carroll County* (Athens: University of Georgia Press, 1971); Frederick A. Bode, *Farm Tenancy and the Census in Antebellum Georgia* (Athens: University of Georgia Press, 1986); William Harris Bragg, *Joe Brown's Army, 1862–1865* (Macon GA: Mercer University Press, 1987); William W. Freehling and Craig M. Simpson, eds., *Secession Debated: Georgia's Showdown in 1860* (New York: Oxford University Press, 1992); Gary W. Gallagher, *The Confederate War* (Cambridge: Harvard University Press, 1997); J. William Harris, *Plain Folk and Gentry in a Slave Society* (Middletown CT: Wesleyan University Press, 1985); Stephen Hahn, *The Roots of Southern Populism* (New York: Oxford University Press, 1983); Michael P. Johnson, *Toward a Patriarchal Republic: The Secession of Georgia* (Baton Rouge: Louisiana State University Press, 1977); Spencer B. King Jr., comp., *Georgia Voices: A Documentary History to 1872* (Athens: University of Georgia Press, 1966); Robert Mason Myers, ed., *The Children of Pride: A True Story of Georgia and the Civil War* (New Haven: Yale University Press, 1972); Julia Floyd Smith, *Slavery and Rice Culture in Low Country Georgia, 1750–1860* (Knoxville: University of Tennessee Press, 1985); and David Williams, *The Georgia Gold Rush: Twenty-niners, Cherokees, and Gold Fever* (Columbia: University of South Carolina Press, 1993), and *A Rich Man's War: Class, Caste, and Confederate Defeat in the Lower Chattahoochee Valley* (Athens: University of Georgia Press, 1998). In addition, the histories of Fayette, Gilmer, Gordon, Lumpkin, Murray, Paulding, Walker, and Union Counties helped construct an image of the Upcountry before and during the war.

For insight into gender, women in society, honor, and Southern culture, I relied on Catherine Clinton, *The Plantation Mistress: Women's World in the Old South* (New York: Pantheon Books, 1982); Dickson D. Bruce Jr., *Violence and Culture in the Antebellum South* (Austin: University of Texas Press, 1979); Drew Gilpin Faust, *Mothers of Invention: Women of the Slaveholding South in the American Civil War* (Chapel Hill: University of North Carolina Press, 1996); John

Hope Franklin, *The Militant South, 1800–1861* (Cambridge: Harvard University Press, 1956); Elizabeth Fox-Genovese, *Within the Plantation Household: Black and White Women of the Old South* (Chapel Hill: University of North Carolina Press, 1988); Anne Firor Scott, *The Southern Lady: From Pedestal to Politics, 1830–1930* (Chicago: University of Chicago Press, 1971); LeeAnn Whites, *The Civil War as a Crisis in Gender: Augusta, Georgia, 1860–1890* (Athens: University of Georgia Press, 1995); and Bertram Wyatt-Brown, *Southern Honor: Ethics and Behavior in the Old South* (New York: Oxford University Press, 1982).

To describe the effects of Sherman's March to the Sea and the overall Union occupation of Georgia, I looked to Mark Grimsley, *The Hard Hand of War* (Cambridge: Cambridge University Press, 1995); Lee Kennett, *Marching through Georgia* (New York: HarperCollins, 1995); and Richard Wheeler, *Sherman's March* (New York: Harper Perennial, 1978).

In addition to the works already cited, for insight into slavery and its role in Georgia's wartime experiences, I relied on Ira Berlin et al., *Free at Last: A Documentary History of Slavery, Freedom, and the Civil War* (Edison NJ: Blue and Grey Press, 1997); Clarence L. Mohr, *On the Threshold of Freedom: Masters and Slaves in Civil War Georgia* (Athens: University of Georgia Press, 1986); Booker T. Washington, *Up from Slavery* (1900; reprint, New York: New York Limited Editions Club, 1970); Robert Fogel and Stanley Engermann, *Time on the Cross: The Economics of American Negro Slavery* (Boston: Little, Brown, 1974); and Peter Kolchin, *American Slavery* (New York: Hill & Wang, 1993).

Lillian Henderson, ed., *Roster of the Confederate Soldiers of Georgia, 1861–1865*, 6 vols. (Hapeville GA: Longino & Porter, 1955–62), and Stewart Sifakis, *Compendium of the Confederate Armies: South Carolina and Georgia* (New York: Facts on File, 1995), proved invaluable in determining the county makeup of Georgia units and the numerical size of each geographic region's contribution to the war effort.

Finally, because the story takes place in the context of war, several works proved crucial to the military argument. On the nature of American armies, I relied on Fred Anderson, *A People's Army: Massachusetts Soldiers and Society in the Seven Years' War* (Chapel Hill: University of North Carolina Press, 1984); Robert Gross, *The Minutemen and Their World* (New York: Hill & Wang, 1976); and Donald Higginbotham, *War and Society in Revolutionary America: The Wider Dimensions of Conflict* (Columbia: University of South Carolina Press, 1988). For the details of Sherman's Atlanta campaign, I found no better source than Albert Castel, *Decision in the West: The Atlanta Campaign of 1864* (Lawrence: University Press of Kansas, 1992). The works of Stephen E. Ambrose, ed., *A Wisconsin Boy in Dixie* (Madison: University of Wisconsin Press, 1961); William C. Davis, *The Orphan Brigade: The Kentucky Confederates Who Couldn't Go Home* (Garden City NY: Doubleday, 1980); Roy Mathis, ed., *In the Land of the Living: War Time Let-*

ters by Confederate Soldiers from the Chattahoochee Valley of Alabama and Georgia (Troy AL: Troy State University Press, 1981); Reid Mitchell, *The Vacant Chair: The Northern Soldier Leaves Home* (New York: Oxford University Press, 1993); James I. Robertson, *Soldiers Blue and Gray* (Columbia: University of South Carolina Press, 1988); and Maris Vinovskis, ed., *Toward a Social History of the Civil War* (Columbia: University of South Carolina Press, 1990), gave insight into the lives of the common soldier and provided a sound framework for the unpublished primary material.

Index

Abrams, Lewis D., 130
absent without leave. *See* AWOL
Alabama, 2, 65, 84; studies of desertion
    in, 2–3, 67, 171–74; troops, 3, 8, 69,
    76, 97
Alexander, Joseph F., 92
Allison, Albert, 131
American Revolution, 24, 31–32, 37, 157
Anderson, G. T., 154
Antietam, 154
Appalachia, 19, 187
Appling County, *13*, 29
Arkansas, 12, 178
Army of Northern Virginia, 29–30, 59,
    69, 71, 74–75, 81, 88, 92, 96, 99, 108,
    118–19, 132, 145, 154, 162
Army of Tennessee, 29–30, 46, 58, 68,
    69, 72, 74–76 , 78, 81–82, 85, 95–96,
    115, 117, 130, 132–33, 136, 139–40,
    149, 166, 172
Atlanta, battle of, 70, 80, 126, 133, 136
Atlanta campaign, 3, 9, 30, 65, 68, 79–
    80, 82, 85, 125, 147–48; in contrast to
    March to the Sea, 9, 156, 164–65, 172;
    destruction of, 79, 88, 136; effect on
    Southern morale of, 21, 75, 77, 81,
    118, 148; and the elimination of Con-
    federate authority, 9, 61, 65, 75, 77–
    79, 85, 88, 126, 130

Atlanta GA, 20, 75–77, 79, 84–85, 90,
    125, 134, 148–49, 155, 163, 166, 172
Augusta GA, 81, 82
AWOL (absent without leave), 5, 46–47,
    63–64, 85, 87, 173

Bacon, A. O., 108
Baker County, *13*, 29, 160
Baldwin County, *13*, 108, 140
Banks County, *13*, 107
Bankston, William and James, 131–32
Barnett, Joel Crawford, 92–93
Bartow County, *13*, 18, 19, 70, 71–72,
    75, 77, 79, 84, 104, 147
Basinger, William S., 87–88
Bass, Edwin, 96, 142
Baugh, Lucinda, 104
Bennett, Mary, 104
Bentonville SC, 68
Berrien County, *13*
Bibb County, *13*, 70, 81–82, 87, 109
Bigbie, Thomas, 8
Bird, Samuel, 35
Blackburn, Mrs. J. C. C., 141, 145
Blackstock, William Jasper, 106
Blackwell, James, 66
Blair, B., 109
Bobcock, Thomas S., 81
Bogle, Joseph, 147
Bone, Mildred, 201